Spiritual Doctrine of St. Augustine

Cross and Crown Series of Spirituality

LITERARY EDITOR

Reverend Jordan Aumann, O.P., S.T.D.

NUMBER 25

Spiritual Doctrine of St. Augustine

IGNATIUS M. BARRACHINA, O.C.D.

translated by

EDWARD JAMES SCHUSTER, *Ph.D.*

B. HERDER BOOK CO.

15 & 17 South Broadway, St. Louis 2, Mo.
2/3 Doughty Mews, London, W.C.1

A translation of *Hombre, Mundo, Redención,* by Ignacio María de la Eucaristía, O.C.D., published by Ediciones Mediterraneo, Valencia, 1954.

Censor: J. S. Considine, O.P.

Imprimatur: Rt. Rev. Msgr. George J. Casey, V.G.
June 20, 1963

Manufactured in the United States of America
Library of Congress Catalog Card Number: 63-19829

Prologue

THE CATECHISM WARNS US AGAINST three enemies with whom our soul necessarily must fight if it does not wish to be their slave: the world, the devil and the flesh. In works of piety and edification there appear abundant instructions concerning the methods of combat employed by these enemies, as well as the means we can use to defend ourselves against them, and they abound in inverse proportion to the order in which these menaces are listed in the catechism.

Concerning the flesh, the most immediate and persistent of these enemies, there is a very abundant literature. Moral theology, indeed, has clearly defined the sinful aspects of this instinct. Exhortations to caution and vigilance, to open opposition, are always essential and timely; these, moreover, are plentiful and of demonstrated effectiveness. An occasional book which treats of these matters may not be as discreet as it ought to be, but the majority are replete with delicacy and a Christian spirit.

When the flesh is considered not as the inclination which each person possesses, but as the scandal which sinners give, either deliberately or otherwise, that is, the social influence which they exercise for evil, then this is attributable to the world rather than to the flesh itself. Any worldly scandal that arouses lust is always sinful. The instinct itself is something natural, capable of being controlled, but it is also capable of overflowing in a sinful manner.

The devil, too, has his literature, though not as plentiful as the flesh. There are theological studies which consider the fall of the rebel angel, his punishment, and the limits which the Lord imposes on the devil's mysterious actions. Only recently he was the subject of a wretched book, a sad and senile work by Papini, which gives this topic a certain ephemeral, morbid popularity.

Exhortations against the wiles of the devil are more frequent in patristic and medieval literature. Today there seems to be some hesitancy in speaking of this subject, but instructions and exhortations are not wanting.

The devil also has his involvements with the world. He exercises, as Holy Scripture informs us, a baneful and mysterious leadership; he is the prince of this world.

In spite of quite characteristic involvements of these two, the flesh and the devil, and despite their special perversity, the first enemy which the catechism names, the world, has a notably smaller repertory of writings which warn against its wiles and deceptions. To be sure, the Fathers of the Church do not fail to mention it; the shameful avoidance of this subject is more recent, nor is it universal. In what has been written more recently concerning the world, there appear certain admirable observations regarding its manner of operation. The most dangerous is that of subtly insinuating its maxims among people who are insufficiently warned against them: those terse and cynical formulations are accepted as well-tested norms of "adult living." The world is a master in imposing these; but their acceptance remains as infamous as it is extensive. To describe this action there is no other way except to resort to those phrases which the world imposes on us: the slogans of the world.

Another astute observation is that we must wound the world with the weapon which can inflict a mortal blow upon it: contempt. In the final test it disguises itself as the general opinion of sensible people, in order to be recognized by all as both prudent and acceptable.

But it is appropriate to recall the meaning of this word, contempt, which the worldly know how to turn to their advantage, making it signify something of little value. They make it seem inelegant to adopt an excessively dramatic attitude toward the world; they maintain that co-existence is possible, that compromise is sometimes desirable.

Flight from the world is a kind of contempt; all that the world offers is nothing when compared to serving God. Flight can reflect a fear of the world's dangers, but one does not reject the world merely by an attitude of flight; one also approaches God. If we do not flee from the world physically, we must combat it by disdaining it, demonstrating by word and deed that nothing that the world is or says or promises is worthy of even a moment's consideration, for we know that it is all deception and wickedness.

Yet it is necessary to know well what the world is, for another trick of the worldly is to classify certain things as secular which are not intrinsically or totally of this world, but to deny the classification of worldly to other things which are indeed sinful, yet for which the world—and this is its function—finds numerous and subtle excuses. It invents euphemisms for the flesh and paints the devil as a poor, harmless creature.

Father Ignatius has immersed himself profoundly in the study of this subject and has sought an exceptional guide, St. Augustine. The result of his reflection and original labor is this splendid book for which, with singular kindness, he has asked me to write these lines. My words should, therefore, fulfill a duty, which is to remark that the reading of this book is not only useful but even necessary for some. We should indeed consider many things in this world of ours as the "world" which Christ anathematized. It will certainly be necessary to bring about not a few corrections in contemporary thought; indeed, this is precisely what is needed. To achieve it there is nothing better than this serious and profound theology, ever old and ever new, at once so stimulating and so serene, so beautifully expressed by Father Ignatius, that it is actually a reward for well-intentioned readers, who wish to become acquainted with such transcendental truths, to be able to enjoy this simple, lively prose.

I find in this book another merit of no small value: by a methodical re-examination of all or practically all the passages from Augustine which relate to this subject, it clarifies the terrible dilemma of these two cities. Above all there appears in full light, sinister but splendidly instructive, what is really meant by the "city of selfishness." He makes abundantly clear that this was the city whose foundation was laid by the rebel angels, whose walls were constructed by Cain, whose ruler is Satan; this city is the world, enemy of souls, enemy of God, and especially of Christ and His work.

The ancient disputes as to whether St. Augustine considered the State (specifically the Roman State) to be the "city of sin," lose their significance, or receive it, from the anti-Christian behavior of this or that State.

Those who asserted that they saw in *The City of God* a final echo of Augustine's Manichean period, and who cite the name of Tyconius, will find in this present work that the essential inspiration of St. Augustine was the Gospel of St. John. This they seem to have forgotten.

The most recent and authorized interpretations which discern in the Church of Christ the actual, contemporary "city of God" are confirmed and substantiated when they observe how truly the world, that tortured city of unsatisfied selfishness, turns its implacable hostility against the Church.

We live committed to a severe struggle, and we would deceive ourselves if we thought that the age in which we live finds an explanation in its immediate surroundings. We have a brilliant if painful assurance of a triumphant conclusion, an unfailing hope. Christ has revealed this to us. He overcame the world, and with Him we also move forward victorious, incorporated in the city of God, pilgrims here on earth, but one day splendid and triumphant, when the glory of God is revealed in all its fullness.

José López Ortiz
Bishop of Tuy

Author's Preface

IT IS READILY OBSERVABLE that whereas the Gospel and ascetical theology make frequent references to the world, the writers of dogmatic theology scarcely ever speak of it. Thus, the *Dictionnaire de Théologie Catholique* does not even list the word. We may therefore rightly ask whether the notion of the world is too simple a concept for theology or whether it is a concept which we have lost along the way.

I decided to study this question and, in looking for the best possible theological source, I decided to study it in St. Augustine. The result is this book.

The book treats of man, of man as a citizen of the world, the kingdom of the devil, and of man as a citizen of the Church, the kingdom of God. In other words, it treats of the concept of man and of human life brought to us by the Church when at last history revealed what man is and what is the meaning of his life.

St. Augustine studies man in relation to the two possible societies which are pointed out by the Gospel: the world and the Church. The world is the society of evil, for which Christ refused to pray (John 17:9). The Church is the society of goodness, the society of all those who believe. The Augustinian doctrine on man is therefore the history of man under the sign of Adam or under the sign of Christ. It is an adequate evaluation of man outside Redemption or under Redemption, taking into account all the potentialities of human nature in the two situations.

This theme is eminently relevant to the contemporary world because what is put forth today as a challenge against Christianity is its conception of man. The interpretation of this or that text of the Bible or the truth of this or that theological conclusion continue to be disputed, but these are inherited arguments. What is denied of the Church today is her humanism.

Man has been under discussion for many centuries and since the time of Socrates there has been a humanism to suit every taste. Many types of humanism are already dead, and no one regrets it, Catholics less than anyone else. Like Christ, Catholicism knows what man really is. The basic disagreement between Christian humanism and all the others lies in the very roots of man. For them, for the best of them, man is supported by the four cardinal virtues: prudence, justice, fortitude and temperance; for Christianity, man is supported by the three theological virtues: faith, hope and charity. Man's evil, as St. Augustine will say throughout this book, is not a lack of temperance, but a lack of faith.

After Christ, it is St. Augustine who has been most preoccupied with man. Possessing a profound humanistic and philosophical preparation and gifted with the clairvoyance of a true genius, he discovered the enigma of man. He himself admits that he could not discover it until he had learned the fundamental truth (given to him perhaps by his master Plato) concerning the existence of a personal God.[1]

St. Augustine poses the question which all thinkers have seen since the birth of philosophy and politics, namely, whether we can be men or can continue to be men without God. In our days, for example, Communism says yes. St. Augustine says no, because man's relationship with God flows from his very essence.

He proves it in this book, showing that man is necessarily a citizen in one of two "Cities" which include all humanity: the "City of God" or the "City of the World," within Redemption or outside Redemption. To put it in the language of the Gospel, man will belong either to the world or the Church. Proceeding from these two exhaustive and mutually exclusive citizenships, St. Augustine reaches gratifying depths in the human soul and in plumbing the mysteries of God and of evil. One of the most amazing is the mystery of the Church. The Church is the masterpiece of Christ, the summit of creation and the new and mysterious creature, because the Church and Christ are one.[2]

I believe that no one has insisted as much as St. Augustine on this key truth, and I also believe that it will be necessary to study the works of St. Augustine more profoundly in order to clarify certain questions about which so many obscure statements have been made. For example, the Church and the Holy Ghost are theological questions which have been so variously explained that the concept of obedience to the Church has likewise been subjected to a variety of interpretations. Another question which has again come to the fore in our day is whether we should believe *in* the Church. Many new aspects and applications of such questions would be revealed if more theologians would begin their investigations with St. Augustine's fundamental statement that Christ and the Church are one person. They would also arrive at the logical and necessary conclusion that to break with the Church, in spite of all personal reservations and distinctions, is to break with Christ.

However, I beg the reader not to seek here a complete treatise on the theology of the Church. Many questions are outside the scope of this book. Nevertheless, it contains what is basic in Augustinian thought and especially that which, apart from all controversy, will serve to give knowledge and greater love of the Church. In a word, this book is a guide-book on the "City of Evil" and the "City of God" and it is directed to all those who want to leave the former and find the Church. It was written basically by St. Augustine, who knew both cities well and who, by reason of the talent that God gave him, is the best guide that modern man could choose.

I wish to express publicly my sincere gratitude to the two men who have made it possible for this book to appear in English. The Very Reverend John Ferrando, O.C.D., Provincial of the Discalced Carmelite Fathers of the Province of St. Therese in the United States, judged this book worthy of translation and worked energetically to find a willing publisher. Reverend Jordan Aumann, O.P., literary editor of the *Cross and Crown Series of Spirituality* and a well-known translator in his own right, made all arrangements for translation and edited the entire manuscript for publication. I wish, finally, to express my thanks to the people of the United States, among whom it was my pleasure to live and work for several years. I hold their religious spirit in high esteem and consider them to be a magnificent example for the rest of the Christian world.

Ignatius Barrachina, O.C.D.

Valencia, Spain

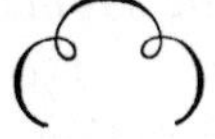

Contents

PART TWO

ONE

And the world knew Him not

JOHN 1:10

1

Man as a Problem

PHILOSOPHY HAD THOUGHT ABOUT MAN for only a short time when it found that the subject became a problem. Attempting, now, to evaluate the solutions that have been offered, we can assert that this problem has been the greatest enigma proposed to men. Almost all philosophies agreed in stating that the problem was clinical, that it was a question of operating upon a sick man, and that everything depended on the diagnosis in order to determine which was the healthy tissue and which was diseased. Yet, during the last century there have appeared some humanists who claim that the sick man is not really sick. If perchance he has some weakness, this will be completely cured by humanism.

When Christianity gave its answer to the problem, it was received as an emancipation. It was a liberation not only from cosmic forces and cosmic terrors which so fatally shackled it, but also from those things which voluntarily fettered it, and a liberation from itself. All are grateful that Christianity has freed man from cosmic terrors, but in seeking to free him from himself and from those things which he loves of his own volition, it receives less thanks. Thus, for a century Christianity has been accused of reducing man's stature because it has linked him with God. It is necessary "to abolish God," they say, in order that man may exist in a pure, integral, "supernatural" intellectualism, re-assessing and re-evaluating whatever is human, introducing a new concept of life and of the world.

St. Augustine is one of the best qualified exponents of Catholic thought concerning these issues. Not only was it he who deduced the most far-reaching consequences from the principles of revelation, but his ideas have also transcended all the world's crises, so that most of them have reached our own time with undiminished validity. From the time he first began to think, the problem of man and life disturbed him. He understood it when faith illuminated his way and his own inner life.

Philosophy was stupefied the day that it came to realize that man was a microcosm. It had discovered a serious truth, the congruent harmony of creation. Yet, what attracted St. Augustine's intellect is precisely the discord which exists in created things. Fully admitting creation's harmony, he finds that the greatness of man is not derived from this, but rather from attributes which differentiate him from the rest of creation. Man has a body, senses, physical health; but the animals possess these also. What truly distinguishes man is the mind by which he can know the truth, know the Author of all things, and cling to Him.[1] The brilliance and vitality of his intellect, the precious gift of freedom, and his destiny according to the divine plan, place him above all earthly things.[2] He himself informs us in the *Confessions* that his knowledge of man had two stages, separated as with a boundary by the discovery that we are the "image of God." [3] When he discerned this, he did not hesitate to assert that the soul of man is worth more than the whole world, and that only God is above man.[4]

When he had refuted ideas which would subordinate man to the inexorable laws of the universe, from whose "ontological slavery" only a few initiated ones escaped,[5] and when he had acknowledged man's greatness, his freedom, and even the "hallowing" of man through the mystery of God dwelling within him, then both reason and revelation taught St. Augustine as well as all mankind that man's greatness was also a tragedy, since there still remained other forces of evil to overcome. The shining prerogative of his intelligence aggravated man's tragedy, the tragedy of seeing himself divided in the presence of good and evil, the tragedy of his obscurity, of his decisions and of his needs.[6] Man's greatness as "God's image" makes him the best mirror in which to see God,[7] for his human nature already possesses a certain fellowship with God,[8] while it is only man who feels an abiding thirst for God.[9] Yet this is a frustrated greatness, because man observes his helplessness, his nothingness, his scars and his internal wounds.

St. Augustine, following St. Paul, reduces the entire diversity of human beings, with their respective interpretations of life, to two types: the Adam-type[10] and the Christ-type.[11] Moreover, after this analysis no one has excelled him in evaluating the component parts which he has examined; no one has so profoundly gauged the value of what is natural, under the sign of Adam, and perhaps none has better understood the supernatural man, under the sign of Christ. It is he who derived the most radical consequences from the Pauline principle that it is not the Law which justifies, but grace and faith. And the Christian religion finds in the works of St. Augustine its most impressive differentiation from an essentially Pelagian Judaism.

2

The Problem of Evil

FOR ST. AUGUSTINE the problem of evil was a veritable nightmare. He found the solution on the day that he comprehended the Pauline idea of original sin. When Pelagius formulated his optimistic theories, he re-opened the question; then St. Augustine drew all the consequences which the Pauline principles contained.

Before sin, man possessed in a perfect way "the image of God" in his soul. His was a nature endowed and provided in superabundant measure with all those gifts which bring happiness. Man's being maintained the perfect balance of things, and he experienced a true, vital contentment. His soul moved under the guidance of that truth which was impressed upon it, while his body, possessing absolute nobility of feelings and absence of evil, was obedient to the soul. Soul and body "were vested with light divine,"[1] that grace of God which elevated and transfigured them.

But St. Augustine says tersely, "They sought to usurp divinity, and lost happiness."[2] Men had sought to violate that subordination which they owed to God, in order to be, like Him, independent; and God punished them, depriving them of His righteousness, disrupting that inner subordination of forces which constituted the balance of man's being. Dark, lower forces undertook to wage war against the spirit,[3] beginning those invasions of darkness and bestiality which were to reduce his value. What had been sound and healthy became diseased; what had been united burst asunder;[4] what was alive, died. Forces which are even lower now came to harass his body, and after continually mistreating it, ended by corrupting it.

This is not the despairing pessimism of Protestantism; man's fall is not his total destruction.[5] It is an eclipse of his being, a paralysis which has become progressive. "Man did not fall in such a manner that he became nothing; but rather, being turned entirely in upon himself, he was less than he had been before but still united to Him who is the greatest of all."[6]

The door remained open, so that He who was to restore this ruined palace might enter in. There remained, moreover, an interior force which struggled to return to God: "the image of God," which man bears impressed upon his nature and does not entirely lose, no matter how degraded he becomes.[7] It is certain that sins can deform that nature, but God can always reshape and reform it. There always remains some bond with God; and although sinners, by reason of their blindness, do not recognize this image of God which they bear within themselves, yet God is merciful, and in a moment can enlighten the most profound darkness. We are like a coin which bears impressed upon it an emperor's image; we can circulate among all the world's filth, but never will this image be rubbed out, for God will always recognize it, no matter how stained it may be.[8] So that man may never forget this, even when he abides in the shadow of some trifling material pleasure, he was given the goad or spur of hunger and thirst after God, which, though not always conscious, is insatiable in its longing for the infinite.[9] Finally, since Adam we are a fallen race; [10] we roam about in nomadic fashion in our state of nobility and of misery, but we are not incurable. No matter how badly crushed we may be, we ought never to despair, for God did not despair of us.[11]

St. Augustine distinguishes two states along the road of the decline and fall: selfishness and bestiality. "He who was slipping and sliding . . . , beginning with his culpable ambition to be like God, descends even to the likeness of brutes. . . . If he yields to the desire of experiencing his own power, *he falls back upon himself*, as an intermediate stage. And thus, seeking to be like Him who is subject to no power whatsoever, he is ejected from his intermediate position, that is, he is thrown into the arena of those things which are the pleasures of beasts. And although his greatest honor is his resemblance to God, now his deepest disgrace resides in his likeness to brutes. How can he fall from such heights to such depths without passing through himself, that is, encountering his own position? [12]

It is interesting to note this thought of St. Augustine, for he places it ahead of all the clever systems of humanism, before all forms of human degradation. Gladly we observe a re-evaluation of the human element, which the fatalism of some Protestants has so despised. We recognize the nobility which is to be sought in man, but St. Augustine cautions us that sterile humanism is a half-way station in the fall. Those who are nauseated by the sub-human, let them know that it is impossible for us to remain satisfied with the human element if we aspire to rise higher. Once more, either God or bestiality.[13] Even beforehand St. Augustine warns that the purely human element cannot survive. Perhaps this arouses questions in many who sincerely wished for a humanity unmixed with brutality. St. Augustine, who knows that it is impossible to remain in a state of suspension when one is falling, explains why it is impossible to halt at a human stage: *in punishment for his pride,* man was reduced from his intermediate position to the very lowest. As the problem of man is expressed in concrete historical terms, there is no "pure" humanism which is not a proud and arrogant *selfishness.* It is the same whether it be simply idealist in the manner of Feuerbach, blasphemous like Nietzsche, or despairing like Sartre; this is undiluted pride, and nothing more. It is an old story in the world, a tale which always has the same ending, with the penalty of terminating in *bestiality.*

We should add, moreover, that this is only half of Augustinian thought. In parallel and reverse direction man's redemption from bestiality will also have its intermediary stage in man himself. For man's redemption will have to include man's return to himself, to his own "interior." We can say more: man's redemption will have to be through the man, except that this time, in order to cure the last vestiges of pride, it is not just any man, it is Christ.[14]

3

Egoism and the World

ST. AUGUSTINE'S THOUGHT must be grasped in its synthesis in order subsequently to comprehend its entire scope. It is a supreme synthesis: God is the source of being, of truth, of goodness.

1) *Source of being.* God is being and the source of all being. For St. Augustine this is as solid and certain as a rock. The immutability of God's being and the mutability of all other beings will be one of the keys to the Augustinian argument. In the order of being, God alone possesses fullness. We achieve our relative plentitude as we approach God.

2) *Source of truth.* God is the source of truth. He is the truth. And He is the light of minds. Not only are we bound to God in a static sense with respect to being; we are bound in a dynamic manner through the intellect. Knowledge is an act which we share with God, who thus penetrates our knowledge and our consciousness.

3) *Source of goodness.* God is goodness, and outside of

Him there exists no source of goodness. Morever, as the supreme good, the source of goodness, He is man's final end.

These are the metaphysical foundations of man's reintegration with God. On the supernatural level, in a parallel manner, God is the beginning of our supernatural existence, conferring grace upon us. He is the very source of our supernatural truth, by means of revelation and faith—the means of knowing it subjectively—and He is the principle of our supernatural good because He loves us. In the natural as well as the supernatural order, knowledge of truth reveals to us our dependence in the order of being and opens to us the knowledge of other truths. But in the supernatural order, to unite ourselves with God, we also possess the virtues of charity and hope.

If now we introduce man, seeking to disengage himself from God in any of the ways that St. Augustine presents him as metaphysically and supernaturally bound to God, we will immediately understand that the Saint sees profound cleavages, foolish because impossible, heretical, sacrilegious, diabolical, and no description seems adequate to him. Pride, he says, was a draught which the devil gave Adam from his own cup.[1] This pride, "the head and source of all wickedness and all evil,"[2] lay in Adam's desiring to live according to his own will.[3] Thus, it is stated without metaphysical or rhetorical embellishment, "because he wished to live according to his own pleasure." This is what cast him "out" from God; this is what exiles everyone: acting according to one's own will.[4] In the same passage the Saint contrasts this with the attitude of Christ, who came not to do His own will; and Christ "will not cast out" one who renounces his own pride in order to do God's will. This banishment, this casting out, makes us shiver. It is as it were a storm of God and of Christ—a black sort of storm, because the darkness also banishes him from the truth. "By this vice of pride, which is the head and source of all vices, since all vices arise immediately from it, apostasy toward God was consummated, with the soul moving toward darkness." [5]

This rebellion occurs in the area of *life*. Therefore, it is the most basic and widespread of rebellions, because it is given to few persons to *think*, to wield *power*, to *possess;* but life is common to all men; it is the fundamental attribute of all. If there is a universal pride, it must necessarily be a pride based on life. And since man cannot separate himself from God metaphysically in order to establish elsewhere the source of his life, then his rebellion must necessarily consist in his ways of life: "to live according to one's own will." This means to arrogate to one's self the kind of existence which is appropriate to divinity, that is, absolute independence, and to become a law unto one's self.[6]

Actually this diabolical potion has infected all men. Today's disease is the same as that which Adam contracted, because it has the same symptoms, the same fever: "Even if we succeeded in demonstrating mathematically that God exists, I would not desire that He exist, because He would limit my own greatness." [7] It is no longer by scientific conclusions that men struggle against God, but by an act of consummate pride: "because He would limit my own greatness." It is the same as with Adam. As Nietzsche said, it is our own inclination which decides against Christianity, not the arguments.

When it became old-fashioned to proclaim freedom of thought (which evidently was only partial pride, or a partial manifestation of the basic problem), a generation appeared which came to the heart of the matter, and began philosophically to justify total rebellion, a rebellion of life itself, which can have far-reaching significance. In the name of complete intellectual humanism, a "pure, healthy" humanism, they proclaimed the death of God, because He minimizes and reduces the greatness which "belongs" to man alone. It was a humanism which reversed the terms of St. Augustine's humanism. For St. Augustine, man is the clearest mirror of God, since man is "the image of God." Now it is exactly the reverse: God is "the image of man," because man, in an unconscious act of mental weakness, has attributed to God the grandeur of his own being. By this "alienation" he has created a false, fantastic being which is pure nothingness. This figment of his mind, nevertheless, enables us to see the qualities of man, because this God is the mirror of man. Religion is nothing more than mental alienation. It is the same now as in Adam's time, but with philosophical arguments. This is an old story which St. Augustine already analyzed in part. After examining it, he told us in all sincerity that what he found was not God.[8] Nor are men gods merely because they exist, no matter what superabundance of things they may possess. There is indeed a deification of man, but it is not exactly because he exists.[9] St. Augustine attempts to bring man to reason, and says to him kindly: "You are commanded to be humble; and in directing you to conduct yourself thus, the Commandments do not tell you to be an animal. Now if God (who was not a man) became man, you also should recognize that you are a man; all humility resides in your knowing yourself." [10]

What Adam and the devil accomplished on that day when they looked for a human dimension in life, was to establish "the world." Adam's act laid the cornerstone of the kingdom of man. St. Augustine says, explaining Christ's words, "You are not of the world": "If you consider how the apostles were born and from whom they descended, since all came from Adam, all were of the world. . . . Let no one say, my brothers, 'I am not of this world.' Whoever is a man is of this world. . . . We all were born in sin; during our lives we all have added more sins to that which we possessed when we were born, and we have become the world even more than when we were born of our parents." [11]

The assertion that the "world" began with Adam's sin, is constant in the works of St. Augustine. And since we shall continually encounter it, I do not think it is necessary here to provide quotations. In general, let us observe what is already known: that this concept is the plot of his work, *The City of God*, and that it is constantly repeated in his *Commentaries on the Psalms*. In the *Commentaries on St. John* it is the central idea around which revolves his whole analysis and exposition of the world, and he proceeds from this to explain the complete meaning of that response which is Christ's work.

4

The Human Dimension of Life

IT IS EASY TO IMAGINE what would happen to a man seated in a magnificent office, brightly illuminated and comfortable, who on a certain night, insisting that he is independent of the electric company, cuts off the light. What happened to Adam was also a "cutting off." He declared himself independent of God, and presumed that everything would remain as bright and happy as before. Let us explain this.

Adam's attitude toward God was not a hostile act in a belligerent sense. At the beginning of the world Adam did not in any sense resemble the heroes of political revolutions seeking independence. All this latter is stained with blood; and bloodshed begins with Cain. Neither was this a diabolical act in the sense that it arose from hatred. Those who hate God cannot claim Adam as a precursor. Adam's conduct was an act of "pure humanism," an affirmation of self. Perhaps he even thought that after some explanations to God, things would be right again.[1]

This is the foreunner of all the humanisms which are separated from God, before they acquire their accidental variety. St. Augustine takes special pains to point out the humanistic aspect of Adam's sin. Perhaps in following this road we may proceed more directly to the essence of original sin as modern theologians understand it. Today we face the need of formulating humanistic problems, and in our study I believe that we have confronted the previous question of determining the origins of these problems. We said that Adam's act is the affirmation of the human. Here there is no mention of bestiality, hatreds, wars, or satanic power; Adam did not aspire to any of these. All this came afterward, during the second phase. Adam wished "to live as a man," [2] he wished to live according to his own will,[3] he wished to rely upon himself,[4] enjoying his own power and independence.[5] And when St. Augustine summarizes the characteristics of the two cities which Adam's sin occasioned here on earth, he does not tell us that one will be the city of God and the other the city of the devil (because the demons also enter the city of Babylon, as citizens and not as a "fifth column"); [6] he tells us that Babylon will be the *city of man,*[7] because it will be the city where he will live "as a man." [8] We have stated previously that through Adam's sin there arose two cities which differed from one another, and were even in opposition, since some men lived according to the flesh and others according to the spirit; some lived according to man and others according to God.[9] From these and other passages which will be quoted it appears that for St. Augustine, Adam's sin was the first act of an independent humanism. It was the act by which "pure humanism" originated; and all the rest are related to this basic act or are its consequences. It is fitting to add likewise that the punishment which God meted out for this sin consisted in condemning men to that very humanism to which they had aspired.

Today almost all are in agreement that Adam's deed was an

act of pride. St. Augustine will repeat this almost to the point of tiring us, and he will not be satisfied until he has constantly emphasized, by way of response, Christ's humility and our own. It was an act of pride inspired by his perverse will. This latter originated in man's freedom, and not from any necessity.[10] It is essential to stress that the evil begins in the perverse will, which is entirely free.[11] This wicked intent will consist simply in separating one's self from the Supreme Good [12] and in finding satisfaction in one's self, in leaning toward self.

St. Thomas distinguishes three kinds of pride: 1) deviation from God's commandments (since it is pride which forms part of every sin, St. Augustine terms this pride of a general type); 2) inordinate desire for one's own excellence, which is the particular sin of pride; 3) a certain inclination toward sin or certain restless tendencies, and this is attributed to the corruption of human nature.[13] It appears that Adam was guilty of the first two types of sin.[14] St. Augustine insists strongly that he was guilty of the second type of pride.[15]

Adam still retained an intellect unclouded by sin, nor did his passions speak to him in a confused clamor. Hence, he knew too much metaphysics and had too much common sense to yield to a temptation which offered him complete identification with God. Adam could commit the sin of learned men, but not the sin of fools. Neither could he presume to a likeness to God which he already possessed, since he was indeed "the image of God." How, then, did he seek to resemble God? He wished to be judge and arbiter of good and evil; he refused to acknowledge a master.[16] This is what St. Augustine explains fully in his *Commentary on Genesis:* "It was a sin of pride, because men wished to be autonomous and not subjected to God's might, so as not to keep His law, as if they were resentful of not ruling themselves, thinking, moreover, that they did not need the 'inner light,' but rather that they could now distinguish good and evil by their own judgment. . . . They were persuaded that they should abandon the intermediate position which they were occupying in creation, and become like God. . . . However, human nature has not received the power to rule itself rather than to be ruled by God; and with this it may be happy, for there is only One who is happy while free of all subjugation to any other power—God." [17]

But let us not forget that here the supernatural order comes into play, that we must evaluate all these statements in terms of this order, in order to see the contrast that exists between such selfishness and the supernatural order. "A prohibition was imposed upon him for the purpose of demonstrating to him that it is not the nature of the rational soul to be an independent being, but rather to be subject to God's might, and thus through obedience to observe the order and regimen of salvation." [18] Salvation entered into this consideration, and Adam knew it. That freedom which he craved would of necessity impose a harsh and miserable state of slavery; desiring the death of his soul, and forsaking life eternal, he was disobedient even unto death.[19] That is, the alternatives which Adam confronted were an independent humanism and the supernatural order.

Bearing in mind the distinctions which St. Thomas notes between the sin of the angels and Adam's sin,[20] I believe we can apply to this humanism the explanation which St. Thomas gives concerning the naturalism of the angels, as stated in the *Summa:* "They sinned either because they sought this perfect happiness in what their own nature could achieve, abandoning the desire for supernatural happiness which is attained by the grace of God, or because they sought to achieve by their own natural powers that resemblance to God which grace confers." [21]

We believe that this is the thought of St. Augustine, who frequently draws a parallel between the angel's sin and that of

Adam.[22] It is interesting to know the details of this humanism, because we are exploring the characteristics of a basic act, and these attributes, as marks essential to the world's constitution and preceding every sin which was to follow, will exist as a constant in the world; moreover, it will suffice that they exist, without any other kind of sin, for the world or the worldly to exist. Rather than man's deprivation of grace, rather than man's disintegration, pervading all creatures, world means *naturalism* —if we are to classify it in terms of the bad angels—and *humanism*—if we include only members of the human race. It is a humanism cut off from God, separated, disconnected from the supernatural by man's own will.

Between the human order and the divine there was something like a drawbridge. The first section of the bridge was raised from the human side; the second, from the divine. God charged Adam's free will to keep his side of the bridge down, and He promised to keep His own side down. But Adam, swollen with pride in his own excellence, in his happiness, and desiring to be independent in his kingdom, raised the bridge which joined him with the supernatural. God lifted His section of the bridge also, abandoning Adam to his own humanism. Since then, men have never been able with their own section of the bridge to reach the margin of the supernatural. Man has remained isolated within the confines of human life.

Formidable indeed was the flood of misfortunes which rained down on Adam. He had sought the annihilation of the supernatural, but God further punished him by denying to him those things he had possessed before he rebelled. "Inclined toward self, he became less than he had been. . . . Therefore, having abandoned God, he experienced that to exist unto himself, that is, to bring pleasure to one's self, is not to annihilate self, but to move toward annihilation." [23]

Separatist humanism is in itself a reduction in man's status and worth, not because it turns him toward external things, though it does this. Aside from that debasement which comes to man from this direction, from the exterior, pure humanism is in itself a vital depreciation of man, a grievous reduction of man's being. We say this as we think of those humanistic movements which act in good faith, which take up arms against the degradation of a bestial humanism, but we caution them that they possess only half the truth in their program, because "it is good to lift up the heart," but not to self, which is pride, but to God, which is obedience. And truly this is a great distinction which differentiates the one city from the other.[24]

Man's immediate punishment for separating himself from God was to be cast upon himself; [25] to be handed over to self.[26] After they had sinned "they hid themselves" (Gen. 3:8), which means they hid in the tree which was in the midst of the Garden of Paradise, for they occupied an intermediate position between God and created things. Therefore they hid *in themselves,* to be tortured by miserable errors, having abandoned the light of truth, which was not theirs. The soul can participate in truth, but incommunicable truth is of God, is above the soul. Whoever separates himself from that truth, relying on self, rejoicing in his independence and not in God, will bring darkness upon himself by his lie, because whoever talks about what he possesses is lying.[27] And upon encountering themselves, finding themselves naked, since they had absolutely nothing which was their own, they began to grow dissatisfied with themselves,[28] to experience misery.[29] What they did not know is that "when man lives according to his own nature and not according to God, he resembles the devil." [30] A moral resemblance, to be sure, resides in the fact that the demon also desired to live according to self and not according to God. But this implies a servitude toward self, so that man had to count on this unwelcome guest in what he believed was his own kingdom.

From Adam's basic act were born two cities of opposing character. The city of man, which begins in the region of self-love and extends to contempt of God, comprising all the areas of pride, bestiality and foolishness, and the city of God, which begins in love of God and reaches to contempt of self.[31] The first citizen of humanism was Cain, who was the material builder of the city.[32]

When Christ came into the world, He found in men the full enjoyment of the feast of pride, which deprived them of their human glory and inflamed the flesh. Diseased with a frenzied narcism, they caressed themselves with all the affectation of self-worshipping over-indulgence.[33] His very relatives urged Christ to show Himself and to share in the festivities as quickly as possible. "They advised Him to seek His own glory, and because of their love of the world, they did not want Him to hide His face or to remain unknown." [34]

But Christ came to redeem us, and He used the method of response in order to readjust that which is human, that which was out of joint. St. Augustine feels a shiver of emotion when he meditates how the Word was made flesh, not only to save all men, but also to save each and every man,[35] thus giving definitively the norm of a healthy, balanced humanism.

5

Constitution of the City of Man

IN ORDER NOT TO WEAKEN the assertions of the Saint, we should note that here he refers specifically to Rome and to Roman laws. But that Rome is not merely the political state of two thousand years ago; it is also the moral reality of today. It is that city of man which successively has its head, indeed its several heads, in various cities that are leaders in distinct types of worldly civilization.[1]

Much has been said of St. Augustine's pessimism, and this page is full of evidence of it. However, what distinguishes St. Augustine from the school of pessimists in the style of Socrates and Tacitus, what places him in a separate category, is the root of his pessimism, as well as its universality. I mean that the "humanistic" pessimists are desperate because in their disillusionment they discern the absurd trajectory of human conduct, the incomprehensible corruption of the purest ideals. Moreover, they are pessimists only with respect to a particular moment of history, a particular nation or people. St. Augustine's pessimism is more universal, it includes all nations; its conclusions are equally applicable to ancient Rome and to modern Paris because, in simple terms, they are the characteristics of the city of man. The universality of this pessimism arises from his knowledge of the root of evil in men. In the first chapters of his *Confessions* he described impressively how wickedness awoke early in his youthful heart and perverted his ways. In the instructions which he will give later to his flock, and in his denunciations of the Manicheans and Pelagians, he will show the nature of this evil which distorts the human race. Basically this consists solely in man's having separated himself from God in order to attempt to live a completely "human" life.

Neither Socrates nor Tacitus nor many of those who today oppose a return to St. Augustine share this pessimism of his. Yet none of them is able to explain from the standpoint of his pure humanism, optimistic after the manner of Rousseau, the perversion of human conduct. No one advocated human degradation. Nor did anyone deliberately promote the corruption of humanistic movements which began as pure ideals. Why did these so readily degenerate into bestiality? Where is the inoculation which thus changed human history? Where is the origin of such unexpected perversion? What is it that men do not recognize, yet which defrauds them? St. Augustine had stated it previously: "He who falls . . . , beginning with the guilty desire to be like God, ends by becoming like the beasts. . . . If he yields to the temptation to experience his own power, he falls back upon himself, as an intermediate stage. Hence, in seeking to live without being subject to anyone, he reverts to self as a punishment, declines to the lowest possible position, that is, he descends even to those things that are the delight and diversion of beasts. Whereas his greatest glory formerly consisted in his resemblance to God, now his greatest shame is his likeness to brutes."[2] Then, in another passage: "Abandoning God in order to live unto one's self, I mean, to please one's self, means nothing but to approach more closely to nothingness." [3]

The page which follows is the short history of this last stage of the fall. It is the story of the city of man approaching annihilation, under the sign of the beast. This is not the account of an evil minority, but the history of men in general. This is not the description of an isolated group; it is the history of the city of man.

He accuses the Romans of having made for themselves false gods who led them into vice. "Read to us any precepts which the gods promulgated against luxury, ambition, lust." Youth became corrupted. The Republic became obscene in its preoccupations, given over to licentious, extravagant living, dissolute, corrupt and cruel.[4] The rulers of the Republic who are, moreover, followers of the gods in wickedness and crime, are not concerned if the State is wicked and dissolute, but only (provided there is an abundance of everything) that the State enjoy glorious victories and, what is even better, the tranquillity of uninterrupted peace. If the Republic has these, it can tolerate all the rest without anxiety. Finally, what interests each person most is that all should continue to prosper, increasing their wealth, in order to take care of their day-to-day expenses and to control those who are beneath them. They desire only that the poor should respect the rich, in order to be able to eat and take care of their minimum needs, so that in the shadow of the wealthy they may enjoy peace and protection. The rulers wish only that the rich should use the poor for their service, for their own pleasure and ostentatious display; that people should applaud those who provide entertainment for them; that rulers should not require difficult tasks or prohibit obscene conduct; that kings should not be concerned as to whether their subjects are good and virtuous, but rather whether they obey them, if only outwardly and not sincerely; that they thank their rulers for entertaining them; that the laws should effectively protect property, and to this end inflict more severe penalties on him who robs a vineyard than on one who harms himself. And they advocate not disturbing anyone whose conduct does not harm others (provided only that his habits are not too profligate), so that he may do what he wants with his own, with what belongs to him, and with those he loves; the rulers believe that houses of ill fame should be readily available for whoever cares to visit them, especially for those who cannot afford the luxury of their own special mistress or lover; that elegant and sumptuous houses be constructed where parties are given, with frequent banquets, where day and night, according to his whims, one may play, drink, vomit, give one's self over to all manner of vicious pleasures, throw money away, and "triumph." The worldly are concerned that there be many dances and balls, that theaters should echo with thunderous applause and laughter, that audiences be stirred up by bold and lascivious shows. Moreover, they advocate that anyone who disapproves of this kind of joy be considered a public enemy.[5] In order that no doubt should remain as to whether this State, which is concretely equated with the Roman Empire, is actually the city of the world, he begins to make express reference to the vices of the earthly city, which are, in summary form, those that are here enumerated.[6]

Let no one make a pharisaical gesture of denial! That religion has become the guardian of vices, that the remainder of its power has been used in defense of the mighty, is not a characteristic of ancient Rome only. That politics should be a deception in the service of those who have, rather than a sacrifice on the altar of the general welfare, is a universal sin. That the law gives preferential treatment and protection to money interests is a present-day fact rather than ancient history. If youth prefers the joys of leisure to austere observance of tradition and of religion itself, and if this was the gate through which fifth century barbarians entered, through this same gate twentieth century barbarians can enter. The mob's worship of gladiators was no greater than the adoration of today's athletic heroes. Moreover, violations of marital fidelity, scandalous display of vices in elegant salons, as well as the saying: "Command nothing difficult, forbid no form of filth or lewdness," which places men on the level of carniverous animals, these are also prevalent today.

In the following pages the same Saint will continue to comment upon and elaborate these thoughts which we state here as basic. But first of all let us attempt to define the world, gathering elements which are dispersed throughout the works of St. Augustine.

From here onward let us take note of the judgment which Christians merit in the eyes of the world, not the only condemnation, to be sure, but perhaps the one which explains most: We are "joy killers," pouring cold water on their pleasures. "Let whoever is disgusted with this kind of entertainment be considered a public enemy."

6

Definition of the World

ST. AUGUSTINE DOES NOT GIVE one, but many, definitions of the world;[1] it is a subject to which he continually returns. He provides definitions in which we do not always find the same elements, because he does not always have the same end in view when he is formulating the definition. Let us follow his pattern. We will arrange the definitions into four groups, and will attempt to find a definition which includes all the elements.

DEFINITION BY METONYMY

The simplest definition, which comes to his pen most frequently, is *amatores mundi, mundus,* "lovers of the world [are] the world." Those who love the things which exist here on earth are the world in a moral sense. It is a citizenship which love confers. Because they love the world, they are called the world. Where love is, there our hearts dwell. Because of their loving, they deserve to be called by the name of the place where they dwell. Therefore, we give the same name to both the world and those who love it; both are called "the world." [2]

This is a citizenship which we acquire voluntarily, and it is born of love. Nothing so separates men as love; if loves are opposed to one another, then as a consequence men become enemies. "Where your treasure is, there are your thoughts. If you amass treasures in the earth, you are earthly, you do not detach yourself from the earth. If you store up treasures in heaven, then your heart will not descend from thence." [3] (Cf. Matt. 6:21). It follows that the fundamental division among men resides in the different things that they love. Some have centered their love in the earth, and others have centered their love in heaven. This division is so radical that no matter how hard they have tried, men have not found a way to put their heart simultaneously in both places.

DEFINITION IN RELATION TO GOD

This love of earthly things is so opposed to the love of God that it makes men sinners. There are two loves, he says, love of the world and love of God. God is like a gardener who wishes to plant love in our hearts. Yet this is impossible if we do not first of all root out the rough weeds of love of the world. These are the words which will destroy the rank growth: "Do not love the world, or that which is in the world. If anyone loves the world, the love of the Father is not in him." Summarily expressed, the world is nothing but desire of the flesh, desire of the eye (all kinds of curiosity, whether in diversions, in knowing vain things, occult subjects, etc.), and pride of life (ambition, vainglory, desire for power, etc.)

And the Saint raises a difficulty: Can we not love those things which God made? This is precisely what Satan says: "You are supposed to rejoice in God's creatures. Why did He make them, if not that you should enjoy them?" And they become intoxicated, they lose themselves, *they forget their Creator.* "When men use created things, not with temperance but with wanton licentiousness, they despise the Creator. . . . He does not forbid you to love them, but He commands you to love them without expecting to find your happiness in them." And here another difficulty arises: "Are we to grow bored, without being able to use anything—without being able to eat, drink, or marry?" He says that none of these things is stated: "What you are commanded is that you observe order and moderation for the sake of your Creator, for love of your Creature." And this moderation he at once defines precisely, clarifying it: "Do not love for the sake of pleasure that which was given to you simply for your use." [4]

Let us observe that there are three points in this comment: 1) As regards God, forgetfulness and disdain for His commandments and His ways in using created things. 2) With respect to creatures, improper love and improper use. He does not deny that the world has its norms, but he affirms that these norms should be those laid down by the Creator, and no one else. (Here he includes all possible sins, which in St. John's summary are the three forms of concupiscence previously recalled.) 3) With respect to the devil, the assertion that he is the crafty promotor of whatever is characteristically human: "Rejoice in God's creatures!" At the foundation of all this, as the formal element: "You shall love unto happiness." Love the created, seeking happiness in it; not any happiness but happiness unto beatitude—complete happiness, the happiness which satisfies and causes us to renounce all other joy.

In another place the Saint remarks: The world as creation was made by God. The world in an evil sense—that world which the devil rules—so far as it consists of men, was also made by God. But to the extent that men are lovers of the world they are not made by God, because it is sin to love the world, and God is not the author of sin.[5]

This sinful world receives the blackest colors and most terrible descriptions in St. Augustine's works. It consists of adulterers, thieves, misers, the impious and in general all kinds of sinners. All sins belong to the world. "The prince of this world hath no part in Me." "The prince, not of creatures, but of sinners, who are here called the world." [6] In his continual repetition of this concept, St. Augustine weaves a list of all possible sins; and while he names only certain ones, it is because he is concerned only with those at the moment. Yet when he wishes to reduce all sins to one comprehensive, synthetical expression, when he seeks to express the synthesis of all sinners, he calls them all THE WORLD.

DEFINITION IN RELATION TO THE REDEEMER

While St. Augustine studies the disorientation of love in relation to God as Creator, when he discusses the world in relation to the Redeemer, he concentrates upon the disorientation of the intellect. It is a disorientation which contradicts the supernatural order established by the Redemption, and it assumes concrete form in its opposition to faith—faith both in its formal sense and in its fullest meaning—but always opposition to faith.

It is unnecessary to remark that the study of the world in this new relationship epitomizes all that has been stated previously and adds to it this new aspect. In an antithesis which he presents to us in his *Commentary on the Gospel of St. John,* we find the definition which we seek: (a) all men, as descendants of Adam, constitute the world, and because of their own personal sins they are even more the world; (b) since they are sinners, they dwell in darkness; (c) because they dwell in darkness, they are impious and unbelieving. All this stands in opposition to the corresponding supernatural values: the world is from here *below;* Christ is from *above.* The world comes from Adam; Christ comes from the Father. They are of the earth; Christ is from heaven. (To be of the earth by reason of the citizenship which love confers, is the basis of the first definition which we studied.) They are sinners who will die in their sins. Their criterion is concupiscence, which is directly opposed to charity. (This is the second of the definitions studied.) And since they are sinners, they are darkness. That darkness is opposed to the Light, which is Christ. It is opposed to that faith which is the principle of regeneration and of justification. All this opposition has a single trajectory which, coming from Adam, assumes concrete form in sin, and in that same state of sin it reaches despair, which is death. Christ summarizes it in two assertions: "You (the Jews who opposed Him) are of the world; I am not of the world." The darkness did not comprehend Christ; it was antagonistic and hostile to Him. The other statement was made to the apostles: "I have chosen you out of the world." What was the difference between the apostles and the other Jews? The Saint answers: The difference which exists between light and darkness, between faith and unbelief, between hope and despair, between love and concupiscence.[7] St. John understood this antagonism; it runs through his entire Gospel,[8] but it remained for St. Augustine to comprehend and to expound this tirelessly, until it becomes the thread which runs through all his thought on the redemption of men, their salvation or damnation.

Now calling upon all the elements which he had combined in the preceding definitions and those which we analyzed earlier when we studied the world established through Adam's sin, let us try to group them together in one definition. Considering the humanistic elements which entered as causes into Adam's sin, converting them into a focal point, then considering the consequences of all this with respect to man and with respect to God, we can say that the world is:

a) *objectively*, a name by which *every moral evil* is designated,

b) *subjectively*, a naturalistic way of life, seeking happiness independently of God, the Author of nature, and apart from Christ the Redeemer.

In presenting these definitions we have borne in mind that St. Augustine includes demons among the citizens of this world. Yet since we are not here concerned with the world so far as its citizens are demons, but rather with the world in its human aspect, we can synthesize the subjective definition by saying with St. Augustine, that the world means "to live according to man." [9] We understand this definition in the sense that man becomes a rule unto himself, independent of the supernatural. We can extend the definition to include two "mental images": with regard to *state* and with regard to *action*. As regards *state*, all men, at birth, belong to the world, for they are in a state of sin even before sinning personally. From the point of view of *action*, the world is a concept anterior to the personal sinful act, and consists simply in man's becoming separated from the supernatural. Then there will be an actual sin, either very serious or so light as scarcely to have any external importance. But the root will reside in the fact that man lived in an exclusively human manner, without referring this act, this intention, to the supernatural. This is prior to hate, prior to diabolical intent, prior to any sin. Moreover, it is antecedent to any sin because it is the ingredient of each and every imperfection. If there were one single aspect of evil which the world did not include, then St. Augustine's idea would be false, and if we do not place the world in this momentary or continual break with the supernatural, then it cannot include all evil.

Hence it follows that acts which are not generally classified as sinful and have no place in codes of morality that consider only pathologically serious sins, are nevertheless evil because they are worldly. They are so because St. Augustine is not so much concerned as to whether the acts are serious or trivial, but whether or not they are worldly. Who considers it a sin to rejoice because he is getting married? Who can think it a sin to enjoy buying and selling? Indeed, these are not sins, but they are worldly acts if they are done with joy. Explaining the counsels which St. Paul gives us for using the world in a Christian manner, St. Augustine says: "And if because of his own weakness the Christian marries, he rather weeps because he cannot live without a woman than rejoices because he is marrying. Neither does he who sells rejoice, for he knows that even if he possessed a thing forever, it would not make him happy. Nor does he who buys rejoice, for he knows that all things pass away." [10] It will not surprise us, then, if later the Saint informs us that the love of the world is an obstacle to perfection. Nor will it confuse us when, in the full Augustinian tradition, St. John of the Cross begins his *Cautions* against the world by putting us on our guard against a love of our own kinfolk which is based on a purely natural motive.[11]

A FURTHER MEANING OF THE WORLD

Still another and unusual meaning is the one which St. Augustine believes that Jesus uses at times in the Gospel: the world as related to the Church of Christ. "If you were of the world, the world would love its own." This he says of the Church Universal, which he occasionally includes under the term "world," as when St. Paul says: "For God was truly in Christ, reconciling the world to Himself" (II Cor. 5:19). And again: "For God did not send His Son into the world in order to judge the world, but that the world might be saved through Him" (John 3:17). And in St. John's epistle it is written: "We have an advocate with the Father, Jesus Christ the just, and He is a propitiation for our sins; not for ours only, but also for those of the whole world" (I John 2:1–2). According to these quotations, the whole world is the Church.[12] I do not believe that this exegesis of the Saint has been widely accepted, yet we must take it into account in order to understand his thought.

And here the Saint draws conclusions from this thought, on comparing the two worlds which he finds in the Gospels. The Church is the world as reconciled, saved, predestined, and elect. The other, which takes its lineage from Adam, is the world as hostile, damned, stained, a mass of corruption, belonging to the dominion of wrath, vessels prepared for damnation.[13] All who are to be saved, even though at a particular moment they may not belong to the Church, are not the world as condemned, hostile, etc. All who belong to the Church but who are going to damn themselves, are with us for a time only, yet in reality they belong to the world as "a condemned mass [of corruption]."

If we stated earlier that "world" is a word used to designate every moral evil, now we should add that this word refers to all who are evil, those who in God's judgment are definitely evil.

This radical separation of the two "worlds,"—one the celestial city of good and the other the city of evil—polarizes all history. But this is not something which St. Augustine invented nor is it a Manichean remnant in his thoughts, because the Gospel itself speaks of no other principle of evil than the world, and it describes the devil as "the prince of this world."

These two worlds polarize history in an antithetical manner, with antagonisms that arise from their essence and their way of acting. It is an antagonism which signifies the capture of the one by the other, the invasion and conquest of every possible area. They are enemies, although the word "enemy" here possesses a distinct meaning in the relations of one to the other. For example, while the world in the sense of nucleus of wickedness (and it is in this sense that we shall use it from now on, unless otherwise noted) is the enemy of Christ and of the Church, even to the point of having shed Christ's blood together with that of many Christians, the Church responds to this hatred with love of its enemies. Moreover, this is not only an affective but an effective love, which is translated into prayers and the preaching of the Gospel, so that this enemy may be enlightened by faith and justified.

The pages which follow contain something of this history. We shall consider only what is useful to us in order to understand the world's mode of action, its spirit, its intentions, its rule; and we shall include even a few words as to its end. We shall analyze the intimate life of the world, from the theological point of view, beginning with an examination of the function of what we consider to be the basis of all that is worldly, the historical "constant" of the world: pure humanism. We shall see its results in all humanity, as a consequence of Adam's sin, and its aggravation in those who personally have persisted in this tendency to rebellion. It is the first of the two stages which St. Augustine discerns in the fall of the human race. We shall see whether it is true that man's having acquired perfect solitude (because he has been deprived of God) has really been "an immense good" and the possibility of his achieving greatness.[14]

Then we shall descend to less idealistic manifestations of the world, to observe its evaluation of those goods which are common to men and animals, to the good and the evil. We shall see man's selfishness extend even to those things where animals ruminate in pleasure and we shall note his new appearance, "the mark of the beast," which he has acquired after so much freedom.[15] We shall study its relations to the Redemption, in particular under two aspects, which are stated in the Gospel: that of rejecting Christ and His work and that of hating Him.

Then there will follow another comment on the spirit of the world, its dependence on the devil, a dependence which indeed explains the meaning of many acts that seem purposeless. It is a dependence which is the greatest humiliation of citizens of this world; a dependence which, through the cunning of the prince of this world, is denied by the worldly themselves, because they are not actually conscious of it; yet it cannot be denied, since it is clearly stated in the sources of revelation.

And to complete the analysis of all that the world signifies, in a second part of this study we shall see its antithesis, the main lines of the elect world, the city of God, yet only so far as it bears relation to the other, whether this be in order better to observe its judgment, to understand its malice more fully, or better to understand its spirit and its essence.

7

Pathless and in Anxiety

CHRISTIANITY IS A TOTAL CONCEPT of life. It is based upon belief in a personal and transcendent God, who is present everywhere, who rules over all. It is a total concept of real life, of life become personal. Therefore the discussions concerning man do not come unexpectedly. And because the Church is aware that she possesses the solution, that she is the mother of mankind, she has never hesitated to discuss all those aspects which are obscure to man. Accordingly, those same subjects which philosophy presents for study, the Church studied long ago in order to cure them. Significantly, these subjects of transcendency, of restlessness, of anxiety, she has known for a long time, because life has long been burdensome and painful to man.

Existentialists have noted that they possess a good precedent in St. Augustine. Atheistic existentialists, however, often use St. Augustine's terminology without the Augustinian meaning. A world of ideas separates them. More things separate them than unite them. Nevertheless the precedent of St. Augustine is well chosen, for Augustine, as few others, felt the painful burden of existence. He went through the phase of confusion of soul and boredom with life. As a consequence, his chapters on anxiety are no mere romanticism, no rhetorical pose. Finally he reached the happy stage of faith, and from that day forward his anxiety was changed to patience, his problem became an experience. What fundamentally divides St. Augustine from godless existentialists is that Augustine is a convert, and specifically, a convert from Manicheism to Christianity, whereas the existentialists of whom I speak are frequently apostates from our Christian civilization who embraced another Manicheism. After taking another look at the enigma of sin, these existentialists have discovered the new idea that sin is existence itself. To exist in the world, that is the true fall of man.[1] Yet it was precisely the distinction between sin and existence which unlocked for Augustine the doors of the mystery of human life. Afterwards, guided by faith, he completed his idea of man with the knowledge of Christ and His teachings. St. Augustine not only records the psychological fact of human anxiety, but also, transcending a childish attitude which could regard his own case as a novelty, he gives us the theology of anxiety together with the problems of man as an anxious pilgrim.

Life is not a world closed on all sides, asphyxiating man; nor is it a world closed on every side except one, namely, death, so that man must despair of it. Life has its transcendence, its openings, which permit man to see the direction of his path, to orientate himself. Correcting, therefore, a false concept of life, rather than one of Sartre's works, we can say that for Augustine, life begins with faith and achieves its fullness beyond hope itself. " 'He who hears My word,' said Jesus, 'and believes Him who sent Me, has life everlasting, and does not come to judgment, but has passed from death to life.' . . . In this life, which still is not life, he shall pass from death to life. . . . Why did I say that it is not yet life? If this were life, the Lord would not say: 'If thou wilt enter into life, keep the commandments' (Matt. 19:17). . . . And He did not say 'life eternal' but simply 'life.' Therefore this life does not deserve the name of life, because it is not true life." [2]

This life, which is not life, is life as a human element, before being transformed by faith into something supernatural. "I shall bless Thee in my life . . . ; in the life which Thou hast given men, not in that which I have chosen with others *according to the world,* among the many kinds of life, but in that which in Thy mercy Thou hast given me. . . . For Thy mercy is better than many lives. What lives? Those which men choose for themselves. Some choose a business career, some a life of farming, some philosophy, some the military life; some choose this, some that. . . . But Thou givest one that is better than all of ours, whatever be the life we have chosen in the world." [3] "Now then, make the transition to life. What is your life? The faith; 'the just man lives by faith.' And those who do not believe? They are dead. . . . The hour is now come and is even at hand when the dead shall hear the voice of the Son of God, and those that hear it shall live. Whence shall they live? Through life. By what life? The life of Christ." [4] Suffocation occurs when life is imprisoned in selfishness, with worldly standards, and when it is not allowed to have that supernatural transcendence which God bestows on it.

And who has ever suffered such a tortured and unbearable life as St. Augustine suffered? He came to hate everything; and when they asked him why he was sad, he fell into a very labyrinth of doubt. He also failed to have recourse to God so that his sadness might be healed, for it seemed to him that God was a pure phantasm (*Confessions,* IV, 4, 9). He wept bitterly, and found solace in his bitterness. He came to love his miserable life because it *was* miserable. He experienced a tremendous boredom with life and, at the same time, an overpowering fear of death (*Confessions*, IV, 6, 11). "I carried a broken spirit," he says, "and in living flesh, restless at bearing it, and I found nowhere to lay my burden. . . . Everything horrified me, even the light. . . . To Thee, Lord, I should have lifted up my heart to be healed. I knew it; but I did not wish to, nor could I. All the more because what I thought of Thee was neither consistent nor certain, but I thought that Thou wert a phantasm. Mine was the error, my God. If I wished to place my soul in Thy hands to see whether it would find rest, I slipped and fell once again into myself; I was a wretched dwelling place for myself, whence I could neither abide nor flee. To what refuge could my heart escape when it was fleeing from itself? Whence could I flee from myself? Where would I not be following myself?" (*Confessions*, IV, 7, 12).

And that sudden feeling of "having lost one's self," which so many experience who have lost the faith completely, St. Augustine was to feel like a sharp knife, because when years later he describes life to us, it is precisely in the likeness of an anguished pilgrim who, hungry and thirsty, wanders through a pathless, unending desert. Our life wanders like a pilgrim through a desert. "Indeed it is an understatement to speak of a place where no one lives as a desert!" Moreover, it is a land without a path, without water. If only this desert had some end, some way out! At least the wayfarer would know where this exit is! But nothing; he does not even have the consolation of seeing the trace of the road. He wanders through it, pathless and lost. If only he had water as refreshment, since he cannot escape! What an evil desert, how horrible, how frightful! . . . If man is concerned in this desert to demand a cure for his troubles from the desert itself, he will not find the remedy. He will discover no path, he will find no water to assuage him on his journey. He will die of thirst.[5]

But let no one be so naïve as to suppose that this is all

Adam's fault. Personal sins, too, are a source of this tragedy: "In the days of my misery I said: 'O Lord, deliver me . . . !' I can call these the days of my misery and dying, *according to Adam,* days filled with labor and sweat, days which are according to the old age of my corruption. . . . I call them *my* days, because in abandoning Him, I myself made them. And as He rules everywhere, is everywhere omnipotent, He lifted up His hand and cast me into prison, that prison which was my own darkness, and into the clutches of death." [6]

It is perfectly clear. Life according to Adam, the life which men choose *for themselves,* life lived according to worldly standards, this is no life. It has no transcendence. Life which is not illuminated by the faith and does not attain supernatural stature becomes diseased, filled with perplexity and anguish. A frightful experience that is realized in living flesh, in what is truly "living according to human nature." St. Augustine is a witness who had personal experience, who testifies sorrowfully to the profound disaster of that "city" which revolted against God in order to live "according to man." Nor is he the only one; in our own days there are others who say the same; some already are enlightened by the faith, others are still without the faith, without hope.

But St. Augustine did not describe the illness of life for the pleasure of reopening his wounds. He wrote all this in the capacity of a physician, in order to heal wretchedness of humanity, so far as it can be cured here on earth. Therefore he had to search out the root of the evil. On this account he went beyond anxiety. He reached the very bottom of the malady. He listened attentively to the cry, and knew how to distinguish the cries of pain. He heard the groans of creation and the moaning of man, lamentation of hearts and bodies. And in this symphony of suffering he recognized the mysterious voice of Christ, who also suffered life's burden and the horror of death, for us and with us. Yet all this is no longer existentialism, or if so, it is a vaster, more profound existentialism.

Adam's sin changed man into a vain being. And since man, although he had lost his intermediate position in the rule of the world, still holds the central position in the microcosm, the creatures which enter into the composition of man groan within him, awaiting their liberation, because they also were subjected to vanity. And they obstinately complain, because their punishment was imposed upon them, rather than voluntarily chosen, as sin had been chosen by man. This personification of cosmic suffering is not found in the ancient notions which make man a victim of cosmic terror rather than an instrument of cosmic suffering. Nor is it found in the existentialist ideas, which do not achieve such a mighty synthesis. Neither is it Manichean, for St. Paul was not a Manichean, and Augustine, in giving us this doctrine, is presenting it to us in the literal sense of the Epistle to the Romans, as he understood it. On the other hand, the Saint begins his commentary by denouncing the Manichean heresy. These are Christian concepts which comprehend the very roots of evil as well as the overwhelming consequences of sin.

All creation groans, awaiting the revelation which manifests the hidden mystery of the children of God, because punishment was not imposed on us in order that we should despair, but rather was given together with hope. In every man is hidden a new life which, moreover, is a divine filiation. There is always the possibility that this life will eventually exist in those who do not now possess it. And the creatures which moan are looking forward to the manifestation of this mystery. It is the lament of those who were made to serve their Creator, when they see themselves subjected to purely human norms. They groan in expectation of the true life. But among those who groan, there is a fundamental division: those who already possess in their souls the first fruits of Redemption, through faith, even if they do not yet possess them in their body, and those who do not possess even that. These latter cry out as mere creatures; we could even say that they are not really in the category of men, since they lack the life and liberty of God's children. But some of them do attain faith, and on this account their groaning is prophetic, since their soul will reach the light through the rough road of painful error.[7]

Let us carefully observe these ideas: groaning, worry, and anxiety are universal, but among those who groan, there are categories which are fundamentally different. Faith will establish the definitive classification; faith to which God calls some at the first hour of their existence, and others along the painful road of torturing errors. But all are groaning, both those of us who possess the faith and those who will not possess it.

We Christians also know what it means to pay the price of sin by the sweat of our body, the sorrows of our heart, and the anguish which we do not understand. Our life is conscious that we are debtors who are forever paying, little by little, with coins of suffering which are among the few possessions that have remained to us after the fall.[8] And we Christians not only groan, but in a sense we shall complain yet more, because we know what is wanting in us.[9] Yet our sorrow is not devoid of hope. Our life groans in the same desert where all living persons wander. Our soul murmurs, for it thirsts after wisdom, and knows that it will not slake its thirst for truth as long as it does not see God. Our flesh groans, for it thirsts after God, and is anxious for the resurrection. Here within us is a gnawing hunger for some other happiness besides that which thieves and wicked men possess. Our flesh, our spirit, our life are thirsting, continually beseeching God for water, refreshment, help, support, joy, happiness. But not for that alleviation which terminates with this world; on the contrary, we seek the happiness which is beyond this life—that water, refreshment, help, support, joy and happiness which is God Himself.[10]

There is more. Our weariness is more profound because we realize that we are pilgrims. We are wandering through this world toward our homeland. This transcendent aspect of our life makes the desert still more lonely.[11] The evil treatment that we receive from the inhabitants of this world, from those who despise our supernatural aspirations, increases our suffering.[12] Nevertheless we have some compensations. In this sense we are not solitary hermits filled with boredom, on the verge of despair and madness. We are an expeditionary force, we are a corps of the elect, famished but hopeful. We are the Church. We are those who were called, who have heard a mysterious voice in the very center of our soul. From the deepest core of our being we cried out; and God heard us. We are traveling through the desert, but we have a path. We are traveling through the desert, but we have a fountain of water. And here within we have a great light, together with occasional consolations.[13] We have our road, our way, and our way is Christ. It is He who has prepared a place for those who thirst, for those who are weary.

Nor would Augustine's thought be completely stated unless we added that it is Christ Himself who accompanies us on this journey, who suffers and agonizes along with us. Yet this idea also includes that of the world persecuting Christ and His followers. When we discuss that subject we shall develop it more fully.[14] Let us leave the topic unfinished here, in order to discuss it more fully later. It need only be added that those who do not believe, those who will not believe, cannot in all fairness be called pilgrims, for they have no other home except that in which they now reside; hence they are not conscious of this pilgrimage. Their burden is what they inflict on themselves.

Their anguish is that of having relied on themselves. The cause of their restlessness is that they are burdened, for although all men are called to enduring happiness, they have a dark feeling that they are not worthy of it.[15]

8

Like Beasts

ARTICLE 1. *The relative existence of creatures and their relative natural goodness*

Man is created in such a way that when he approaches God he is enlightened, and when he separates himself from God, he is in darkness.[1] So that there may be no doubt as to the intensity of that darkness, Augustine himself informs us that "as one departs from God, one plunges progressively into darkness." [2] On this point history is no more than a commentary on theology.

Let us recall that Augustine has said that man's fall was in itself a punishment,[3] and let us also remember that this is only one step in his descent. At the final stage he halts where the brutes find their pleasure.[4] He says this in another way: "I saw all things which are beneath Thee, and I saw that they do not possess either full *existence* or complete *non-existence*. They exist, indeed, because they come from Thee; but they are non-existent because they are not as Thou art. What truly exists is changeless. As for me, my good consists in clinging to my God, for if I abide not in Him, then I myself cannot continue to exist." [5] When man abandons God, he falls back upon himself and encounters an intolerable dwelling-place. And as a person who lives in a house where everything is badly arranged, dark and puzzling, goes out into the street, so also man flees from himself to the suburbs of materialism and to the fields where beasts find their delights.[6] Augustine has a very human simile for expressing this: A man who abandons God, who turns his back on Him in this second stage of his flight, is turning his back upon himself.[7]

Then man remains in the fatal shadow: "I had my back turned to the light, with my face turned toward things that were illuminated, for which reason my face, which beheld the things that were illumined, was not itself illuminated." [8] If we add to this the fact that material things, in their turn, are mockeries, that they merely offer their dose of pleasure,[9] then it is not surprising that man throws overboard the little judgment which remains to him and abandons himself to exterior things.[10] St. Augustine calls this "fornication" because the love which man owes to God is given to created things, and the happiness which should be sought in God is sought in that which but remotely imitates the excellencies and goodness of the Creator.[11] If morally speaking this flight is fornication, metaphysically it is an absurdity: "Man must find his happiness in Him from whom he received his being." [12]

But we are in the trajectory of a fall and hence we should find ourselves in the same line of descent which was traced initially. Indeed, Adam's fall consisted in searching for happiness apart from God, or at least outside the order which God had established. And here it is the same; driven onward by the force of the original impulse as well as by his own interior indigence, man continues to fall in the same direction, along the road of creatures. If besides this we apply the law of velocity in falling bodies, is it surprising that man becomes continually worse?

Therefore too it has transpired that material things, all God's creatures, which are but gifts of His goodness and marks of His greatness and power, become impediments to our return to God, inasmuch as man's intention as he uses these gifts is that they should replace God and the gifts which He wishes to confer on him. Therefore it may well be asserted that man adopts an attitude of fornication toward them, whereby he prostitutes things and brutalizes himself. "I burned with desire to satiate myself in the most depraved, most despicable and repugnant things, I vegetated in the darkest loves, my youth faded away, while I grew corrupt in Thy sight in order to please myself." [13] It is a stupid idolatry which bows low before created things, begging an alms of happiness, of truth, of life. "Those who wish to find joy in external things readily grow vain and dissipate themselves in visible, temporal things; with their ravenous thoughts they go licking the shadow of material things." [14] To be sure, this madness of man as well as the wretchedness of the creature is known only when one knows God. It is from love's heights that created things seem small, even as it is within the heart illumined by faith that we sense the feeble pulse of creatures. Only from the supernatural standpoint can we perceive when it is that the love of earthly things terminates in adultery.

At the time when St. Augustine was studying the problem of good and evil in things, the world of thinkers was divided into optimists and pessimists. Within Christendom it appeared in two extreme tendencies: the pessimism of the Manicheans and the optimism of the Pelagians. It was the Platonists who set St. Augustine on the road of optimism, showing him that things are good in themselves, in their innate being.[15] But he owes to Catholicism the balancing of this optimism, together with his profound insight into the natural goodness of things. All creatures are good in their being, their origin, and their end. Moreover, they are good in a universal sense, because they are gifts of God, mirrors of His majesty, marks which God has sent upon His own creation, to make man's return to God easier through love.[16] These creatures are graduated in their being and, proportionately, in their goodness, so that the lower are supported by those still lower, while each procures happiness for the other. But at the very summit of being and of goodness is God, who has reserved to Himself "personally" the function of making man happy. "Thus, for example, the sheep finds its happiness in filling its belly, in being always satiated, in sleeping, frolicking about, living, enjoying health, breeding. For you, O soul, no lesser good is your good, but the Supreme Good is your good. You who are joint-heir with Christ, why do you rejoice to be companion of sheep?" [17]

St. Augustine distinguishes three criteria for evaluating the relationships which exist between man and his possessions. 1) *The pagan concept:* the pagans were so attached to the goods of this world that they not only loved them, but even begged the demons for them if they were wanting. 2) *The Jewish concept:* the Jews had become materialistic and served God for the material rewards which He had promised them; it was not these promises which aroused the traditional materialism of the Jewish race, but rather God accommodated Himself to their worldly heart in the Old Testament.[18] This led the Jews to apostasy, for when they saw that God was giving to pagans gifts which they themselves did not possess (in spite of all His promises to favor them and His threats against the pagans), they abandoned God and set out in search of what God did not give them. 3) *The Christian concept:* we Christians know that earthly goods are common to the good and the bad. They are even common to the beasts. Moreover, we know that according to His providence, He takes worldly possession from the righteous as well as from evil-doers. We also know that there is one thing which He does not take away from the righteous, which He gives only to them, and this is Himself.[19]

Here we have an example of the progressive lesson which God teaches in the Bible. The goodness of things as well as their place in man's life was already made clear in the Old Testament; but only in Christianity does this revelation achieve its fullness. Thus, for example, the goodness of creation appears already in Genesis and is generously lauded in the Psalms; but if we compare this concept of goodness with that of the New Testament, we will observe a profound difference. The book of Ecclesiasticus is a hymn about the goodness of created things, because God made them. But if they are God's creation, why not use them? Yet this criterion was definitely transcended by Christianity. St. Paul terms the desire for material things "prudence of the flesh," [20] and St. Augustine prays, saying: "Permit not, O Lord, that we should still love what is earthly and of the Old Testament, after the New Covenant has been proclaimed. Let the serpent devour me if I still enjoy what is earthly, if I am still proud, after the New Testament has been promulgated." [21]

Christianity will concentrate on a transcendental relationship which abides in the goodness of created things. In a certain manner they reproduce the goodness of the divine beauty, and they are mirrors, no matter how imperfect, but mirrors which reflect God's goodness. Sin alone does not possess this attribute of representative reflection. God avails Himself of that reflected goodness in order to reveal to us in a certain manner the truth of what He is, and to hold out to us a constant invitation to love.

This doctrine is in the Gospel itself, and in St. Paul. Jesus speaks to us of the goodness of the Father, which is demonstrated in the opulence of creation. St. Paul will speak to us of the probative value of creation in recognizing God's existence. Therefore the Alexandrine school will find allegories of God in creatures, and St. Augustine will develop the concept, applying it to the knowledge of the one God, the triune God, and the Incarnate Word.[22]

But the creature is not the end; it is the means to the end. If man loves things for their own sake, he is guilty of fornication. If he separates himself from God in order to love the creature without reference to God, "You depart from the immortal fire [of God's love]; you grow cold, you become corrupt. Do not depart, for that will be your corruption, your adultery." [23] It is not the creature which is evil, but rather the will of man. None of the [physical] components of sin is wicked—neither gold, nor beautiful bodies, nothing—but the will [or intention] with which they are used. "Therefore whoever loves inordinately any of nature's goods, even though he obtains it, he is evil and miserable in that good, because he deprives himself of something which is better." [24]

It is the transcendence of things united to the transcendence of human life, which should be directed toward God. "Let none of these things be your end, for they all pass away. Some there are who seek money; in order that this be not your end, convince yourself that you are a pilgrim, that you cannot rest in things. If you seek health of body, do not look for it in such a way that you are satisfied with a diseased kind of good health which prevents you from accomplishing good works. If you seek honors, see that you are not praised for any of these as truly your own, but rather strive that everything that is yours be praised in God, and thus your honor will not perish. We use all these things in passing, as one uses the rooms of an inn, and we again take up our journey when we have enjoyed the necessary repose. No matter where you may arrive, do not halt there.

The object of all this [traveling and activity] is to love God. And where there is love there is no anxiety, because love broadens our life.[25]

It is necessary to carry this principle to its ultimate consequences: The love of men cannot be pure and balanced unless it comes from God. Men rely on many things, he informs us: "There are those who rely on their friends, those who rely on their power, still others on their riches. These are boastings of the human race which does not rely on God. Let man trust in Him who died for his sake, in order that man might not die forever; let man rely on Him who humbled Himself, that man might be exalted. . . . If He does not save you, will man save you? Will a man redeem you, if the Son of Man redeem you not? If Christ has not redeemed you, will Adam accomplish this?" [26] Love that depends on another human being, that lacks supernatural support, does not liberate man. A redemption of man by man will always be a deception: "If Christ did not redeem you, will Adam redeem you?" This is the question which we should ask of the humanists, and among these, of Communism, which Pius XI denounced as the redemption of man by man.[27]

St. Augustine reproves himself for not having known how to love his fellow men until he had turned to God. If that love becomes a substitute for love of God, then it is only a consoling fable, a false relationship.[28] If it is a friendship with purely human standards, without being directed toward God, it is not enduring, because it does not rest on a secure foundation,[29] and in addition, it tortures the soul.[30]

Stated in another way, if earlier we saw that life has a transcendence with respect to itself, by virtue of which transcendence it is directed toward God, now we see that it also possesses a transcendence with respect to creatures. If the inner transcendence was needed so that life might not suffocate at being shut off within itself, without the expanding horizons of transcendental solutions which it receives from God, now it is necessary that it should not become shipwrecked on any created thing nor in any human activity, because life has the urgency and the transcendency of love. All who have reflected a little concerning the consequences of pure humanism, even without accepting Catholic principles, have felt the difficulty implied in confining human life within itself, or confining it to things. All this is very small; and life is like water which putrefies when it stagnates. Some persons have attempted to solve this serious difficulty by advocating that man should cultivate a humanism which is not selfish or egocentric, but concentrated on a community, which would undertake to achieve humanistic ideals suitable to man. Communism is one of those systems. In this way they intend to put a stop to the selfishness which has caused so many barbarities and injustices throughout history. Christianity reaches different conclusions because it begins with the principle that only God and nothing else is man's center. The goal or center of man is outside of man, but it is not beyond him. The center is outside of man, it transcends all limitations which life sets for it, all human situations, all history, everything. Man's center is in God.

Therefore, to divert man from himself as his own center is not to dehumanize him, but to "divinize" him. The demand that he should not eat dirt or drink shadows on the journey of his pilgrimage is only so that he will not sit down and fall asleep in the cursed shadow of the fruit trees in the desert. Christianity teaches that our whole heart, our whole life, all our faculties of thinking and acting are for God. It knows that selfishness takes two roads: that of enclosing self in self, and that of scattering one's self, dissipating one's self among riches—the riches of *knowledge,* of *possessions,* and of *power*—where man has the illusion that he is multiplying himself in them.[31] This is the egotism which seeks to destroy, because it is manifestly the prolongation of Adam's pride. But even in its grammatical or etymological sense, egotism has two parts: the fundamental meaning, expressed by the ego, and the "diseased" portion, which is the inflation of the ego. What Christianity is seeking to extirpate (let it be carefully noted) is the swelling and the disease, leaving the human personality unimpaired. What Communism has done, and with it all "humanisms," is either to devaluate the ego or to destroy it.

At this point all Christian asceticism is in agreement. The extensive works of St. Augustine will have this ascetical pivot, to convince man that he must make his life revolve around God and not around himself. To this purpose he will repeat the fundamental principle hundreds of times: "Thou shalt love the Lord thy God with thy *whole* heart, with *all* thy strength and *all* thy might" (Deut. 6:5); and he will repeat the consequences: Do not place thy *happiness* in creatures, nor thy *hope* in things created, do not *mourn* that which perchance should be thy joy, *nor fear* where there is no cause to be afraid.[32]

ARTICLE 2. *Hope as the sin of the world*

A) PRUDENCE OF THE FLESH

We have said that one of the things on which men base their presumption is riches. Wealth involves a temptation to self-assurance; it constitutes a refuge from the feeling of deprivation which we experience both naturally and supernaturally. In some manner riches seek to be a kind of redemption for man. And this folly reaches its zenith when man believes that wealth actually possesses some supernatural quality or value. St. Augustine opposed various sects, among them the Pelagians, who considered riches to be wicked and evil. Riches are not evil. To be rich is not bad; it is good; like being poor. The evil consists in being proud. Let them know, he warns, that their hope ought not to be placed in gold, in silver or in any other transitory thing. I am satisfied if it does not harm them; it cannot profit them. What is of profit to them is works of mercy—the rich man, by saying and doing, the poor man, since he is unable to do anything, at least through good intentions. When man rejects all that makes him proud, God inclines His ear and will graciously hear his prayer, whereas formerly God did not hear him since he was proud.[33] The rich, indeed, are quick to consider themselves happy because they have an abundance of all those temporal possessions which are necessary in this life. Wherefore, too, their heart is hardened against receiving grace; it freezes in God's presence. Thus they bring forth no fruit. Besides this, they give themselves more airs than necessary, believing that they are superior to the rest of mankind, while actually they are much inferior by reason of their evil deeds. They come to believe at times that the goods which they hold are rewards from God because they have served Him well. But if on some occasion they are deprived of worldly possessions, or do not receive them, they think they have been serving Him in vain.[34]

The fact is that it becomes very difficult to find an inoculation against the infections of wealth. And more precisely, "man necessarily tends to become proud of things which he possesses for himself." [35] Since pride is the mother of all sins, when fear of God is lost, men readily fall into all manner of iniquity. The Saint must have known persons of all classes who were thus infected, since he gives us examples from every walk of life. Some are still with us, such as the sin of not having children so that we may better provide for those that we have.[36] Pride makes others so rebellious that if they sin, they think they have excuses for their transgressions, if they even trouble to make excuses.[37] At times he is so disgusted with them that he upbraids them publicly, promising them the most shocking surprise. The haughty, insolent rich, who are sleeping off their intoxication of wealth without sensing the wrath of God, "now swagger and boast against God, demanding, 'Who are these Christians? Who is Christ? Is anyone more stupid than these Christians, who believe in something they do not see? And for love of that invisible something they give up the pleasures of here and now?' Sleep and bray; say anything you like against God. . . . How long, how long will sinners boast? When will those who are gnawing at us consume themselves? . . . You are sound asleep! But when you awake you will find nothing at all in your hands, and then you will see how full of glory are the hands of the poor whom you have despised!" [38]

The reason for this contempt lies very deep, reaching even to the roots of the world itself. The fact is that the Christian has his life directed toward God, whereas the world can conceive of no life except for itself. On this account it considers Christian self-denial and renunciation as stupid and insane. St. Augustine summarizes these two concepts of life by saying: "My soul lives for God. And my soul, which in despising the world has died, according to man's opinion, does not live to itself alone, but for God." [39]

Explaining St. Paul, he informs us that this desire to possess is born of the spirit of this world and is called carnal prudence. This prudence of the flesh implies a special "sense" for the things of this world, a fear of losing them, because here things which will not endure as long as man himself are considered of great value. Such prudence cannot be combined with observance of God's law. For obedience to God's commandments appears when carnal prudence is suppressed and spiritual prudence appears, that prudence of the spirit by virtue of which we neither place our hope in the goods of this world nor fear to lose them.[40] And in another passage: "Love of this world is revealed by two things especially—desire for one's own glory and desire for wealth." [41]

So long as we do not understand the opposition to the truth of Christ, which is implied in the vanity of this world, so long as we do not understand how to free ourselves of this conflict by means of hope, in that measure we fail to understand that there is no way of reconciling the tranquillity of an interior life hidden in Christ (in whom we repose our hope) with a life thrown off balance by its inclination toward external things, toward riches, thus creating an illusion of security which conceals the basic destitution of mankind. While this situation prevails, we will not understand why Christ and the world cannot be reconciled, why we cannot serve two masters.[42]

B) TWO CONCEPTS OF LIFE AND WEALTH

St. Augustine lashes out at the world's stupidity, that ignorance which loves the things that bring it pleasure. It would like to perpetuate itself in them: "There is a type of individual who would like to be happy and immortal in those things which he loves: in earthly desires for pleasure [what is here termed earthly desires is not a collection of mortal sins or capital sins; he does not tell us what these are], and perhaps he prays and adores to this end, so that he may be left for a long time in the [enjoyment of] his delights, [praying] that nothing which he is enjoying may vanish—neither gold nor silver nor possessions—that his wife, his children, his friends may not perish. He would like to live forever in such happiness. But because he cannot, because he knows already that he is mortal, then perhaps it is on this account that he adores God, that he groans and prays that these things may be left to him until the end, until old age. And if God should say to him, 'Good; I will make you immortal in order that you may possess these forever,' this would give him such joy that he could not contain himself." [43]

St. Augustine differentiates three kinds of men: those who have Christ as the foundation of their life; those who have the world as their foundation and standard (that is, any worldly thing); and those that have Christ as their foundation, yet place some worldly thing above Him. The first, because they have built solidly, are saved. The second, because their foundation is of straw, will be burned with the straw. The third, since they have built on a secure foundation, will also be saved, but first they will have to burn the straw that they have laid down.[44] St. Augustine is consistent with his own principles; he does not say that the rich will be damned. It will depend on what they have laid down as the foundation of their life. It is certain that when the young man asked Jesus what he should do in order to obtain life everlasting and when in the face of his answer to Jesus' requirement that he keep the Commandments ("All these have I kept from my childhood"), Jesus told him to sell all his goods and give the proceeds to the poor if he wished to have treasures in the eternal life, it is certain, I say, that the apostles considered him in a very black light and stated: If things are thus, who shall be saved? But what is impossible for men is easy for God. "The rich also," our Saint teaches, "have received of God their mode and manner of salvation, their way of singing in exile the hymn of their fatherland (the Saint is expounding the Psalm *Super Flumina* and states that *Sion* means fatherland, *Babylon* is the world, the rivers are the ephemeral things of this earth which flow into the bitter sea of damnation).

"The Apostle previously had said: 'Command the rich of this world that they not become conceited nor place their hope in the insecurity of wealth, but rather to hope in the living God who will give us abundantly that which is necessary for our happiness.' . . . This is the song of the rich. First of all, that they be not proud and boastful . . . , for this is what wealth occasions, and this is what they should especially avoid. . . . It is not that gold is evil, for God made it. It is man who is wicked when he becomes avaricious and deserts his Maker, permitting himself to be thrown off balance by his devotion to created things." This is what St. Augustine cautions him: be not proud! Second, he advises that he put not his trust in transitory riches. "If he does this, he will be seated above the waters of Babylon. But if someone should say to him: 'What are you doing, squandering your wealth in almsgiving? You should invest your money for the sake of your children,' do not exhaust yourself in attempting to explain to him, for he will not understand you." And the Saint ends with this forceful argument, which is an appeal for supernatural hope: "You entrust something to a servant, and he does not lose it; will Christ lose things entrusted to Him?" [45]

Evidently we are here confronted by two antagonistic ideas of life and its purpose: the mundane and the Christian ideas. The mundane idea represents a "full, rich" life; the Christian idea signifies a lofty life. Christianity also wants a rich life, but it has a broader notion of what constitutes wealth and value. Christianity has the greatest range of values and the most extensive catalogue of riches, since it classifies and judges them from the eternal and supernatural point of view. The apex of prosperity, the climax of the desires of this world's children is that of Psalm 143:11–15: "Deliver me and rescue me out of the hand of strange children, whose mouth hath spoken vanity, and their right hand is the right hand of iniquity: whose sons are as new plants in their youth; their daughters decked out, adorned round about after the similitude of a temple; their storehouses full, flowing out of this into that; their sheep fruitful in young, abounding in their goings forth; their oxen fat. There is no breach of wall, nor passage, nor crying out in their streets. They have called the people happy, that hath these things; but happy is that people whose God is the Lord."

God is more just than man; He has traced a more comprehensive ideal of riches, which excludes no one. The wealth of this world begets pride in him that possesses it and resentment in the man that does not possess it. God's wealth divides the earth in a more humane and righteous manner. Given the fact of our patrimony of poverty, God became man. He became poor, as all of us men are poor, in order to enrich us. But with this exception, that the riches which He confers upon us do not conform to worldly standards of wealth.

St. Augustine understood the transcendence of the restoration of the supernatural order through the Incarnation and applies this innovation to the scale of values, thus giving us an ample compendium of riches. Let us observe that here he anticipates modern sociology, carrying the notion of wealth beyond that which sociology itself ventures to do: "Why are men rich? I think it is because they have gold, silver, noble ancestry, extensive lands. But God conferred all this. Who is wealthier than He who created all these treasures, even though they are not true wealth? He also created the treasures of talents, good memory, customs, life, health, the senses, the symmetry and beauty of our bodily members. With these, even impoverished persons are rich. God also created other, loftier possessions: faith, piety, righteousness, charity, chastity, good habits. We hold these only as gifts of Him who justifies the wicked. You now understand that He is rich!" And this God, in whom all men are rich, became poor: "The Word was made flesh and dwelt among us. . . . He became Thy servant, the son of Thy handmaid. He attends to that chaste handmaiden, that virgin and mother, from whom He received our poverty, in whom He clothed Himself, so that His opulence might not blind you and you not dare approach Him because of your lowly condition. There He took the form of a servant, there He clothed Himself in our poverty, there He became destitute, there He enriched us." [46] Thus, within Christianity the concept of possession is ample and broad, as is our hope. And from this aspect we evaluate the limited conception of worldly wealth.

C) THE VALUE OF CREATED GOODS IN CHRISTIAN TEACHING

St. Paul's advice to Timothy, "Charge the rich of this world not to be proud, or to trust in the uncertainty of riches, but in God, who provides all things in abundance for our enjoyment" (I Tim. 6:17), goes to the root of the problem. Nobody wishes to be rich except to exalt himself among those with whom he dwells, in order that they will consider him superior. When the Apostle exhorts them not to be proud, he makes them equal to those that have nothing.[47] And it is the New Testament which, in giving man a complete notion of his purpose and end, of his value and his exact situation in the supernatural cosmography, taught him what to ask for when he prays.[48] It taught him that he should never ask for material goods unconditionally, for they are not absolute goods.[49] They are not the proper object either of worship or of prayer.[50] Moreover, it is the Spirit of Christ who has taught men the transcendent relationship which exists between created things and the God who gave them to us; He has taught us even the precise measure of those goods.[51]

Their measure is indeed precise and exact; wealth is in itself more of a dream than a reality. The rich man is like one who is dreaming that all goes well with him; and when he awakens, he finds himself poor, since he placed nothing in Christ's hands.[52] "Wealth is like a swelling, a tumor. What does the rich man possess? Gold. What does he *not* possess? Life everlasting. Let him give what he has, and buy what he does not have." [53] Those who look for riches are like men who look for bandages to bind up feet which pain them.[54] And so also coins are made round in shape, to indicate their instability.[55] Do not think that God gives magnificent gifts to the wicked, because if evil persons receive them, they cannot be great.[56]

Yet such things are not contemptible in themselves, for we already stated that the evil resides in man's bad will. They are like drops of rain which God sends to His wheat while it is planted in the fields of this world. What we should ask is that He gather it soon into his granary. "If we were keenly aware of our misery as pilgrims, we would not love this world, but would march directly toward that to which He has called us; we would cry out to Him from our hearts. . . . We shall obtain this if we open our hearts and desires as much as we are able. . . . Love as I do. Whoever loves God will not love money inordinately. Because I have suffered from this disease, I do not dare to say simply 'he does not love money,' but rather, 'he does not love money inordinately.' It is as if one should love money, but not too much. If we really love God as He deserves, we will not love money at all! Let money be your pilgrim's staff, not an itching desire. You should use it for your needs instead of for your pleasures. Love God; and if aught be lacking, then let it be lacking, and give praise to Him. Use the world, but do not let the world enslave you. . . . You are on a journey and the world is merely an inn." [57]

One of the marks of the Christian is to be convinced that he should undergo privations. A hunger supported by God, who does not abandon us. Now is the time for hunger; the time for feasting will come later. "That which does not now satisfy us in the hunger of our corruption, how shall it fill us to satiety when we become immortal? . . . Let us indeed look for things of beauty, but let us await them from Him who is everlasting beauty." And the God who helps us on this pilgrimage of hunger will also aid us in the fight and will protect us against the burning sun. "He will not forsake you. Bear the heavy burdens, for 'he who perseveres unto the end shall be saved.' "[58] This hunger comes from our being destined for another life, for everlasting happiness. It is a hunger that arises from love, and is not content with crumbs. Indeed, such crumbs merely arouse the appetite still more. For one who loves, the very creature things of earth lead him to love of the Creator; and he cannot rest in any one of them, since none is his Beloved.[59]

Therefore Augustine, from his expectant, restless, hopeful vigil of love, thinks that if God were to grant us all the happiness which created things can give us, on condition that we see Him not, this would be a grievous misfortune. Whoever does not feel this way has not yet begun to love God, nor is he convinced that he is a pilgrim.[60] Therefore, Christianity reached a different conclusion than did Judaism. The Christian is not scandalized when God grants His gifts to the wicked but denies them to him. Nor is he scandalized even by the situation of one who could have acquired wealth by sinning but nevertheless continued in his poverty, while another has become rich through wicked acts . . . and nothing happens. He knows that what is going to happen has not yet occurred and that God promises His peace, not in this world, but in the next.[61]

It is appropriate to add that our hope, transferred to the next world, where God will give us the gifts that we do not have here, is not merely a subterfuge which postpones the triumph we cannot here achieve. This is an unworthy way of thinking and hoping. "You wish to possess in heaven the very thing you were forced to leave here on earth. *Mutare vis voluptatem carnalem, non amputare.* Is it possible that you shall find anything better than God's countenance to look upon? Wretched indeed is this love of yours." [62]

Viewed with the eye of the Christian, the goods of this world are far more inadequate than when they are viewed with the eyes of the economist. Wealth not only is inadequate in an acquisitive sense, but what is more important, it is unsatisfactory in providing satisfaction. In their ultimate essence, things retain the flavor of clay and nothingness. In heaven God will become our treasure, our all-sufficient treasure.[63] At present wealth is a good scattered among a multitude of things, so that life requires a diversity of goods in order continually to receive the support which is essential to its sustenance. We have to beg alms among many material things and knock at many doors before we obtain what we need, because even in this, material goods are trying to tell us that we are pilgrims: "Bread is not water, shelter is not light; but God is at once our fountain and our light. He is a fountain if you are thirsty, a light if you are blind. Open your eyes that they may see the light, open your heart that it may drink at this fount. And that which you drink is the same as what you see and hear. All this becomes God for you, because what you love in all created things, all this was made for you. If you concentrate on external appearances, bread is not God, water is not God, this light is not God, clothing is not God, your house is not God. All this is visible and singular, limited. . . . Yet God is all these things for you. If you are hungry, He is bread; if you are thirsty, He is water for you; if you are in darkness, He is your light, who remains incorruptible; if you are naked, He clothes you with immortality. . . . We can predicate all things of God; and all are inadequate when we attribute them to Him. There is no greater insufficiency than this. You seek a name which is adequate, and you do not find it. You look for the precise word to express this fullness, and you do not find it." [64]

D) OUR COMMON HOPE, THE CHRISTIAN USE OF CREATED GOODS

Christianity, which has come to put order among things, not from the standpoint of human, carnal prudence but according to divine norms, cannot overlook monetary wealth or any other form of wealth. For the present it has been a great mercy of God to divert man's hope from temporal things. This has been the true emancipation of mankind. There were and still are many who have no hope, who are without God (Eph. 2:12), and Christian teaching has opened their souls to the most consoling hope. Man's first duty with respect to things, however trivial they may be, is to love the God who has given them to us, to love Him by means of them and because of them, finding in all things a love tryst. If all created things are lovable and beautiful, how vast is He who excels them all? "Whatever thing you love, He is that thing for you. Learn to love the Creator in the creature, the Maker in His deeds. Do not be enslaved by that which He has made and thus lose Him for whose sake you and that thing were made." [65]

We should realize that we are Christians only to the extent that we have hope of glory, and not because we hope in the goods of the earth. And let no one here promise himself the happiness of this world because he is a Christian. Let this present happiness be used if it can be used, as it can be used, when it can be used, and to the extent that it can be used. But if this happiness be lacking, thanks be to God. Let the Christian everywhere be thankful, let him never be ungrateful.[66] Furthermore, the Christian who does not observe this order of things is a perfect hypocrite, though it be only in his heart that he does not acknowledge contempt for the goods of this world.[67]

However, the Christian attitude not only reaches the heart, but also touches the use of worldly goods. Riches have a Christian use. What is called in modern times the social function of wealth has long since been surpassed by Christianity when it assigned to wealth a supernatural function beyond that which it can have in society. "Let us suppose," says the Saint, "that you have wheat in your granary which is moist. A friend comes and tells you to take it out because in a few days it will germinate and go to waste. He advises you to place it in a dry section of the building where it will be exposed to the air. But if you pay attention to your friend who knows about wheat, why do you not listen to Christ, who tells you to put your treasures in a higher place? Make yourself Christ's creditor, giving Him some of your earthly possessions so that He may give you heaven." [68] In St. Augustine this notion of giving to the poor as one of the obligations of wealth is tirelessly repeated. It becomes the touchstone for recognizing the worldly individual in his use of wealth. "He who does not wish to give to the poor seeks riches." [69] Therefore Augustine feels that Christianity has reached perfection when they sell what they possess and lay the proceeds at the feet of the apostles (Acts 2:45).[70]

E) A MAN CANNOT SERVE TWO MASTERS

Finally, let us observe two relationships which the rich have with God and with their fellow Christians. (We call those persons rich who are such in their heart and their desires, though they may not be such in fact.) Those who abound in wealth and place their confidence in riches, believe that they have no need for God. According to them, God is a consolation for those who are dissatisfied or face economic problems. It is unnecessary to add that such persons are merely stupid.[71]

Another well-known story is that of persons who are afraid to turn to God because they do not wish to abandon their unethical business practices. "If you rebuke them," says the Saint, "they answer: 'And how am I going to eat? There is no trade without its trick, no business without theft. . . . Don't you see that plutocrat? He is quite shameless. Well then, while I lived in the fear of God I remained poor. And that in spite of kneeling and praying all day in church!' " St. Augustine insists that we fear God, and he asks: "When God fills you with spiritual treasures, will you really be poor?" [72] He says the same thing in another way in another passage: that ill-gotten riches cause the loss of faith.

With respect to Christians, if worldly men were logical they would leave them in peace, since the former, if they are not hypocrites, do not intend to compete for worldly goods. But no; "for the same reason that Christians place their trust in God, these wicked men abandon Him." [73] Not only do they abandon Him, they revile Him. Even the needy of this world despise us Christians, because we do not place our hope in the things of this earth. St. Augustine says: "Let the rich of this world be puffed up now, let the impious insult the devout, the faithless revile believers as they say to them: 'What advantage do you derive from your faith? What have you gained when you have won Christ?' . . . It is night. As long as the night lasts we do not see things clearly. While it is winter the grass is wet, the tree is without leaves. The dawn will come, and we shall see everything. The warm sun will return and dry the grass, and the tree will appear in all its beauty." [74]

Fundamentally, this is the problem that arose in Paradise; man believes that he himself can discern good and evil. He is unwilling to acknowledge that the goods of this world come marked by some outside authority and, according to their relationship with the other life or with spiritual values, these things are only good in a relative sense, and at times they may even be evil. Further, because the worldling believes that his norms are correct, he despises those who disagree with him, and at times will even persecute them.

ARTICLE 3. *Happiness as a problem which cannot be resolved in this world*

A) IN WHAT HAPPINESS CONSISTS

St. Augustine has stated, following St. Paul, that one of the characteristics of carnal prudence is that it finds its joy in the pleasures of this world. Speaking as we would today, we can say that this is equivalent to placing our happiness in the things of this world.

The problem of happiness has given St. Augustine great concern. It is a basic preoccupation in life, and any philosophy or theology which does not neglect the whole man cannot disregard it. Every life has a natural tendency to happiness. Such being the case, there are only three directions to which it may turn in order to find this source: toward ourselves; toward the outer world, to seek what is there; toward God, to find our happiness in Him. St. Augustine has examined all three possibilities at length. The crisis of happiness which is sought in created things is constant in Augustine's pastoral and theological writings, addressed to the people. This is the fundamental problem in the *Confessions*, where he proceeds by degrees to find that happiness is in God, but by means of turning back upon self, to find that God is within us. Happiness as a problem is resolved in St. Augustine's works within the synthesis of his thought, as we already have outlined it: God is the source of being, the source of truth, the source of goodness. Thus, happiness is an equation: happiness is equal to wisdom; wisdom is equal to God; therefore God is happiness. For us, in a concrete sense, it will be the enjoyment of truth which we apprehend or possess.[75]

St. Augustine differentiates two classes of happiness, natural and supernatural. Natural happiness is always imperfect; supernatural happiness can be perfect or imperfect, according to whether we possess the good—God—only by faith or whether we possess Him perfectly in glory. It follows from this that our earth does not belong to the cosmography of happiness.

The road of happiness which St. Augustine has chosen differs from the route which schools of philosophy follow, and differs from that followed by persons who disassociate themselves from philosophies and seek their happiness in things. However, in opposition to the position which the Platonists defend, neither does happiness consist in the subjective contemplation of eternal ideas. This last position, with the necessary corrections, will be true only in the other life, when we contemplate God.[76]

B) HAPPINESS AS A REALITY AND A HOPE HERE ON EARTH

Yet Augustine's notion of happiness is not on this account a dehumanized thought which transfers man's bliss to the next life, leaving him in an embittered hope that no one could support. St. Augustine knows that earthly things have their drop of pleasure placed in them by God as aids along life's highway. Nowhere does he deny that content of happiness; what he reproves is worldly anxiety and concern, of which this drop is the source; and he reproves the false notion that the drop is a fountain and that this fanciful fountain could satisfy. Augustine is decisive: "If the joys of the wicked appear to you as happiness, it is because you have no faith." [77] This goes to the root of the problem. The individual who is dissociated from the supernatural cannot be happy. Moreover he says: "Let men know that God never will permit the wicked to be happy; and if we think they are, it is because we ourselves do not know what happiness is." [78]

All the wickedness of the worldly consists in their drinking this drop of joy which things gladly offer, drinking it as if it were unto everlasting blessedness (*ad beatitudinem*), seeking ultimate happiness therein, being content with that and renouncing what God promised them in the next life if they observe the order of love which He has stipulated in this life. This does not mean that men expect *complete* happiness in each created thing—they think it would be better if it were thus—but rather, believing that they will receive it neither in this life nor the next, they proceed to amass more and more material possessions, to see whether by gathering together the drops they can quench their thirst. This is the problem of inner restlessness; it is the false cure for their perplexity, their bewilderment and confusion, which are manifested in the hoarding of things, in exchanging them for other things when they tire of them. This is a constantly accelerated exchange which is motivated by man's inner insatiability and the insufficiency of created things.

God utilizes this natural desire for happiness in order to call man through every created thing; and frequently He awaits him in the days of great thirst. He waits for man's unsatisfied thirst even as He waited for Augustine, to inform him convincingly that He is the water that Augustine needed. The Saint adds this: "All men desire to be happy, for happiness is a great good. But this is the extraordinary fact: that the good, in order to be happy, becomes better, while the evil, in order to be happy, becomes more evil. Hence it transpires that one who finds his joy in lust, in rape, in rebellion, feels unhappy if he does not carry out his desires; but is also unhappy and dissatisfied if he does. The same happens with the avaricious individual, with the vengeful, the domineering, the cruel individual. . . . The divine voice cries out to these misguided persons who are looking for false happiness in genuine misery; it calls them back to the right way, saying to them: 'Blessed are the clean.' Depart from the ways of wickedness, since you cannot give up your desire for happiness. Vainly do you seek it where you defile yourself. He did not say, 'Blessed are they who are steeped in wickedness and error, who follow the mistaken paths of this world,' but rather, 'Blessed are the undefiled in the way, who walk in the law of the Lord.' "[79]

We Christians know that here on earth happiness remains a hope rather than a reality. Happiness is the result of completing the redemption of our body and soul. By faith we have begun the redemption of our soul, but the body has not yet been included. When this also has put on immortality, then shall we possess full happiness, whereas now we have it only as a pledge and a hope.[80] In this world, therefore, our happiness properly resides in our being redeemed, since this gives us hope of attaining the heavenly fatherland. This confers true joy upon us. If we rejoice in this, we have our joy from God. But so long as we rejoice in worldly pleasures, we become only an impudent clamor.[81] Looking at the matter reasonably, no man can promise himself more happiness in this life than Christ Himself. Now if this is true for every man, for whom Christ should be the example, then it is much more for those who in reality are already members of Christ. If He will not glorify His own body, but rather subject it to the tortures and penalties of life, neither should we expect to walk along some other road.[82] This notion runs through St. Augustine's whole work: the imitation of Christ gives us our greatest happiness in this life and in the next. Man's true joy is found in serving

God, and in knowing Him according to the revelation which He has given us through His Son and His messengers, the apostles. Beyond this, man finds no peace or rest, no true happiness.[83]

Consequently, all excessive happiness which we derive from earthly things is deficient so far as it is not an imitation of Christ and so far as we do not know whether it be for God's greater service; therefore we should look upon such joy with suspicion. All happiness should beget fear rather than assurance within us. David's example frequently comes to Augustine's mind. While David was being persecuted he was neither adulterer nor murderer. When fortune smiled on him, he fell into wickedness: "Brothers, we should be more sharply on the alert against happiness." [84] Happiness has at times something of the mystery of predestination. "God is merciful to us when He denies us something we love inordinately, even when we beg Him for it. If He is angry with someone, He grants him his request for what he loves inordinately. True happiness consists in loving what we should love, and loving it as God wishes us to. And then it is that God grants us what we ask for." [85] Therefore a man should distrust the joys of this world. He should consider himself a pilgrim, and not rejoice in his captivity. "If you enjoy your pilgrimage, this is because you do not love your fatherland." [86] An objection is raised: If a man does not find happiness, he is condemned to the most wretched misery. But Augustine answers inexorably: "What is called happiness among human things is more to be feared than misery, because often man derives good fruit from tribulation, while happiness corrupts the soul with a false security and perpares the way for the diabolical tempter to enter." [87]

Here again we find two distinct interpretations of life, dividing men into two fundamental groups: those who seek everlasting happiness and those who look for earthly happiness.

The former are the children of God; their great joy resides in feeling that they are redeemed by Jesus Christ at the cost of His blood. The others are children of the world, of Satan, or simply that *other* group which is not of God. The latter place their happiness in the vigor of their children, the beauty of their wives, the fullness of their warehouses, etc.; they are not looking for everlasting happiness, because they already have enough with this life.[88] Here we are confronted by another example of the radical separation which exists among men and was occasioned by original sin: those who seek happiness apart from God and the order imposed by God, because they expect to have enough with what they can acquire for themselves, without having recourse to God (at least not to the God of the supernatural order); and those who, founding their lives on God, know that their happiness is the result of their trial and election. Those who know that their happiness is in God and that they have not yet reached the hour of possessing Him, make their pilgrimage through life on the highway to their fatherland, happy in the sure hope which God has given them and in the helps He confers on them along the way. These latter possess a secret: they know that bygone times were never good, for the days of this world have always been evil; but those evil days were good for God. The solution is to have patience and hope. Finally, Christ did not have one good day on earth.[89]

It is not only the tense expectation of the day that gives meaning to all that now lies hidden and perhaps disdained, but the transcendence of life which is not destroyed by things and is not brought to its knees before the things of this earth, asking for impossible satisfactions. Morever, it is the secret of being happy even though the trials may be most distressing. This is so, not because Chistianity is merely a consoling doctrine in view of the fact that happiness is impossible in this world, but because the hope which we have is of a concrete, certain reality, and of this reality we have an advance pledge here within us. . . . Yet one who does not possess this, must necessarily think that Christianity is no more than a consoling influence. Whoever does not have it and can imagine no happiness, save that which is expressed in created things, is unable to understand the conduct of Christians. "Why am I an enigma to many? Because I believe what I do not see. They are happy in what they see; they rejoice in lust, in drinking, in obscenity, in greed, in wealth, in theft, in this world's honors, in whitewashing their walls. They take pleasure in all this. On the other hand, I walk another road, contemptuous of what is present, distrusting the happiness of the world, sure of nothing except God's promises. The others, reflecting that life is short and that tomorrow we must die, say: 'Let us eat and drink,' but we who understand that life is short, say precisely the opposite: 'Let us not eat or drink, but let us fast and fear.' . . . O Lord, draw nigh and say to me: 'Falter not in the narrow way. I went before you. I am carrying you, I bear you within Myself, I am bringing you toward Me!' Therefore, although I am an enigma to many, I fear not, for Thou, O mighty One, dost help me." [90]

We start out from concepts of life which are poles apart, and therefore we react differently to the impact of the same concrete phenomena. But we understand each other, not because we have an unthinking indifference toward things which bring happiness—whatever it be and in whatever quantity—but because we know that this is not satisfaction. Moreover, since we are not so perfect or so dehumanized that only the spirit vibrates within us, we inevitably place our hope in God, not in our own strength; and He will not allow us to faint on our pilgrimage. Here it becomes apparent that we are two different plants—the worldly and the Christian—for they flourish in life's winter but we await the splendor of the Sun.[91]

But the worldly person not only does not understand the Christian (the Church has always been unknown by its enemies), but precisely on this account he hates the Christian. We shall study this at greater length subsequently, but here we wish to suggest the idea. The worldling is convinced that life is a collection of calamities; "but they should allow us to enjoy ourselves," he says; "let them not deprive us of entertainment, the theater, the sporting events, parties, singing, sexual indulgence. It seems that Christianity undertakes to make the happy person unhappy, fostering in him the psychosis of suffering, by promises of eternal blessings and love everlasting." Such a person adds, with the pagans of old: "Christianity has not brought us any benefit which we did not already possess; it has deprived us of the goods we had and left us with the evils we had." St. Augustine replies that if you explain that Christianity has caused men to renounce their possessions and give them to the needy, they laugh because they consider such persons fools. They emphatically prefer the age of freedom when, without restraint from anyone, they enjoyed unrestricted liberty, were as free as an olive on its branch, swayed by the wind.[92] It is interesting to point out this lack of comprehension on the part of the worldly, for there arises from this a hatred which, if it is not initially diabolical, frequently becomes so. It is also necessary to point out that this observation of St. Augustine is still timely. A heart resolved to accept externals as the source of its happiness is a heart which reacts like a dog deprived of its food; the least it does is to respond by barking, a reaction which not only appears in those who lead an uncultured existence, but also in persons of greater social prominence who blame Christianity for promoting unhappiness among mankind.

C) INABILITY OF CREATED THINGS TO SATISFY; SIN AS AN ELEMENT OF UNHAPPINESS

But let us analyze this thing called happiness more carefully. There is no disadvantage in repeating once again that created things contain a dose of sugar for this life.[93] Yet we should also draw attention to its judgments in order to appreciate its value in providing satisfaction. For the present we all agree in asserting that created things quickly pass. St. Augustine constantly reiterates this. He likens these things to the river which flowed through Babylon, which, in its fluid inconstancy, quickly flowed away and disappeared. He presents a worldly person who feels satisfied; everything in the world smiles at him; no one close to him dies, on his vineyard nothing has dried up or fallen off the vine, his sheep do not perish, he is not deprived of any position, his friends are alive, his customers do not desert him, his children bring him no unpleasantness, his servants are trustworthy, his wife is not cantankerous. To sum up, he has what is called a happy home. Such a contented individual realizes this and, "filled with a kind of bloated joy, he exclaims, 'I am happy.'" But he should be alert and assure himself that this happiness is not enduring. If what rejoices him does not remain, but passes away, then it is like the river of Babylon, the deceptive river of this life. He should sit on the bank of that river and weep.[94] But people disagree with St. Augustine. The worldly disagree even when they know that the river of happiness flows away, for they prefer to throw themselves into the waters and continue downstream, rather than sit weeping on the banks. After all, they think, a river is beautiful from the shore, but it is also beautiful when we are on it. What they do not discern is the bitter sea into which the river empties its waters.[95]

Many Christians likewise disagree with St. Augustine, for they never quite believe this claim that the pleasures of wickedness pass quickly. He replies that created things surely pass away quickly, but we are like feverish patients who want things immediately. They pass away quickly, for man's days, too, are quickly fled.[96] Besides passing quickly, the things of this world do not extinguish the desire for them. And he who has no hope of drinking in happiness when the right time comes, need not drink of the fountain of worldly pleasures, for he will thirst again.[97] When anyone comes to feast on the happiness of this world's pleasures, whether it be in food, drink, recreation, displays and ostentation, sexual excesses, will he not again feel thirst? [98]

But let us not lay all the blame on created things. Their inconstancy, together with their profound deception, is only one of the ingredients of unhappiness. Besides this, there is sin, and sin is always bitter. Often the worldly individual does not believe in sin, but God will take care that it embitters him. The parable of the prodigal son contains this teaching. In the *Confessions*, which are his commentary on this parable, St. Augustine frequently makes this statement. He repeats it throughout, as if he still feels the dulling of taste which an excess of temporal sweetness caused him. The sweetness of this world for a time leaves a good taste in the mouth, but afterwards a cloying bitterness ensues.[99] Even granted that some worldly things may be sweet, they are digested with a large admixture of acidity.[100]

It is impossible for true happiness to dwell in the heart of the worldly individual, since he does not have within him that which confers hidden graces and gifts. The worldling places his happiness in what he has in his treasure. The Christian has his joy in God, whom he possesses in his heart. Now compare the gold with God, the treasure chest with the conscience. But observe that we do not have recourse to our conscience in order to drink of ourselves, for thus we would speedily dry up, but of God.[101] To enter there, into the conscience, this is one of the most uncomfortable habitations for the worldly individual. It is precisely his conscience—if by the grace of God it still functions—which is shrieking at him, torturing him, so that he cannot digest his happiness in peace.[102]

St. Augustine argues still more convincingly. It is not enough for him to prove that the digestion of worldly pleasures is acid and tormenting; and he frequently returns to the words of the Gospel to express something even more critical: "You tell me that the rich Epulon ate and drank and enjoyed himself while poor Lazarus was dying of hunger. . . . Well, I tell you that now he is digesting what he ate at that time." [103]

Consistent with his Christian principles, then, he asserts that there is no true joy in worldly diversions; not in money, fishing, hunting, or lust,[104] but true happiness abides in God. All the rest is a diseased swelling,[105] a dream (which Christians who love this world's happiness share, if not continually, at least they give it a nod).[106]

As a consequence of a principle which he had previously stated, namely, that God gives or refuses things with a view to eternity, he states that this world's happiness is a snare into which the careless put their head, or a cave in which God traps them. The trap may be set by the devil; and we are like birds. Sometimes there are those who stretch out their neck to consume the food of iniquity, and the trap springs, thus catching them. But God makes a shout with the fear of hell, and the bird flies free. By the mercy of God we are freed from the snare of this world.[107] Again, it is God Himself who prepares the trap. In the case of rebellious sinners, knowing that it will profit them nothing to give them further time for penance or to warn them, He digs for them the ditch of the joy of their sins, and they fall into it as into an abyss.[108]

Lovingly and tirelessly St. Augustine repeats to his people: "All this has its pleasure, but it is not true happiness." He knew this from personal experience; he had stated it at length in his *Confessions*. But if they do not believe it on his authority, despite his full experience, he tells them at least to give their attention to Isaias, who also experienced what the glass of wine, the pleasures of table and bed, lustful worldly joys can offer. For he also knew what happened to men who frequent places of diversion, the lusts of a thousand kinds, heavy drinking, etc., and in the face of all this he says: "There is no happiness for the wicked, saith the Lord." Perhaps you will say that you can see no other happiness except what Isaias enjoyed within himself. It is a question of purifying your inward eye, the eye of the heart, so that you may behold true happiness. Perhaps it is diseased, perhaps it is disturbed by anger, avarice, the appetites, unreasoning sexuality. Cure it, and you will see.[109]

D) CRISIS OF THE OPTIMISTIC VIEW OF LIFE

I don't know, but sometimes it seems to me that we have taken too seriously this happiness of worldly persons. St. Augustine never took it seriously. If we observe his earlier unequivocal statements, I believe there can be no doubt as to his thoughts. "If the joys of the wicked seem to you to be genuine happiness, the reason is that you have no faith." [110] And more emphatically: "Let men know that God will never permit the wicked to be happy." [111] I say this because, after arguing at length with the worldly that their happiness is not true happiness, they now come and tell us that the whole subject of happiness is a myth. It is they who again have raised the two disturbing questions: Does happiness exist? What is happiness? It is they who now say that there is no substance in what we are arguing about, because the whole world is embittered, and no one possesses happiness. Then they begin to take refuge in despair and bitterness as the only possible human answer. It is they who now have seen that the licentious case of Augustine in his *Confessions* is the only reality of life.

But perhaps we may now have to change the subject and begin to prove to many persons that happiness does exist. For this purpose we have abundant doctrine and experience in the works of St. Augustine. He never denied absolutely the existence of happiness in the natural life, and he always affirmed the existence of interior happiness, though in a limited measure. Moreover, he never tired of pointing out the roads to this latter kind of happiness; roads which, if not followed correctly, will not lead to happiness either. He knew that in both the natural and the supernatural order of life God draws us onward by means of happiness, as He also attracts us by the intellect. For God draws the whole man.[112]

But this phenomenon (which appears as a universal theme) that happiness is a myth, has extraordinary depth. Basically, it has shaken the entire optimistic theory of life, which has been the indisputable attitude since the Renaissance. It was one of the pagan notions revived at that time, and now it is again being buried. We should note that in St. Augustine's works contemporary optimism always was considered pagan and worldly. He knew that it would end badly. Not only in relation to the other life, but also in this life, he saw no cause for so much optimism. In his position as a clear thinker he did not see reasons for such optimism and from the depths of his Christian soul he pitied them. It seemed to him that truth provides much firmer grounds for rejoicing than does error, and worldlings are a living lie. It seemed to him that a person must be stupid and perhaps emotionally upset to feel happy in the external world, while utterly forgetful of the conflict within. He was convinced that such "happy" persons were hypocrites or madmen. Therefore he told the faithful to pray for "the happy worldlings." If they wish, let them think that Christians are sad. It is certain that Christ's teaching has made our life serene and peaceful, and cured it of the madness which formerly possessed it when men found frenzied pleasure in the vanities of this world. In the same sense the Christian's life can appear sad. In other ways, even more profound, it is certain that we do have sadness and anguish, but "our sorrow is of more avail than their joy. . . . Let us send up our sighs to God for those who still are sick." [113]

For the rest, Christianity has never been hedonistic. Let us strengthen ourselves through humility.[114] We are pilgrims, and we know that God is our happiness. "We are God's planting and His harvest"; in His fields He cuts and plants, makes grow or dries up, as He wills.[115] We have received no promise of earthly happiness from Christ, but we do not complain on this account. We do not complain, for we are satisfied with nothing less than Himself.[116] We know that when we possess Him and see Him, our joy will be complete and everlasting. In this hope we proceed along our way, wounded in heart.[117]

ARTICLE 4. *Fear as the offspring of carnal prudence*

There remains a final aspect to be discussed with respect to the goods of this world: the fear of losing them. Carnal prudence, the guiding compass in this world, is a special perspicacity for acquiring these goods and living our lives with respect and regard for such goods. This very prudence causes us to fear the evils of this life, to fear the loss of these possessions.[118] It means fearing inordinately. It is fear which arises from our attributing excessive value to the goods of this world and not perceiving the supernatural meaning of life's trials. It is a question, then, of a worldly spirit which impedes the Spirit of God, and as long as it remains, there is no way that Christ's Spirit may quicken us. Here we merely point out its existence, its folly, its opposition to the Spirit of Christ; later, when we discuss the dehumanization of the Christian, we shall discuss this subject at length.[119]

9

A Characterization of the World

IS THE WORLD ATHEISTIC? There are few persons who openly claim that they do not believe in God. Even fewer are intellectually convinced that God does not exist. But in men's *hearts* there is an atheism, whether acknowledged or not, which is one of the world's fundamental principles. "The fool hath said in his heart: There is no God."

St. Augustine notes all these particulars and describes the atheism of the world as one of its significant *practical* characteristics: atheistic at heart (*in corde*). The lost, the wicked, the shameless—and they are numerous—all have in their own way some idea of God. It is a false idea, whence arise all their misfortunes; and in the practical order they deny God. From the false notion of God which they have formed, come their broken lives, and they end in the deepest iniquity.

They begin by feeling that their life is boresome: "Come, let us crown ourselves with roses. Let us eat and drink." "Is there anything more delightful than roses?" asks the Saint. "But lust is intermingled with eating and drinking. What follows? 'Let us destroy the poor just man.' Would you expect that from something as delightful as roses would come the torments of the just? But such is the way of the wicked. When they said to Christ, 'Come down from the cross,' they were still saying, 'There is no God.' Indeed, in crucifying Him they were saying the same thing. Do not be surprised, brethren; the base of the thorns is soft and tender, but he who grasps them is pricked by the points." [1]

Nor is this necessarily an intellectual atheism; it is enough that it be atheism in practice. It begins with erroneous thinking (*a mala fide*) and then assumes a multitude of personal and social variations, in which are found the same historical constants which we have observed up to now. In this multitude of variants one can perceive the degree of worldliness which afflicts an individual or a social group. However, we should not apply these norms to every case, unless we wish to err in our characterization of the world. The multiplicity of variants is frequently noted by St. Augustine, although pessimistic descriptions are more abundant. "In any class of life, not all are elect, and not all are reprobate." [2]

A need imposed by the instinct of self-preservation and by those who more or less seek justice (although it be justice in the sense of the Kantian norms, with laws for individuals) has brought it about that the world also has its standards. Not all life is warped and corrupt; there are also standards. And worldlings glory in these standards. One of them is that which St. Augustine describes in himself when he was young. In spite of his being surfeited with sex, he liked to appear elegant.[3]

The world indeed has its standards, and it permits no one to infringe upon them. Those who go beyond the "temperate" norm of malice pay for it. Yet this comes about, not through any love of justice, but because they do not allow to others sufficient peace for their own wickedness. One can do anything in the world, but according to certain standards. Whoever exceeds these standards is considered an enemy and ostracized. Then the world administers justice with maximum cruelty so that men may see its outstanding love of peace and justice.[4] The fact is that in certain situations the malice of the world has all the pharisaical hypocrisy which is narrated in the Gospels. It boasts of its exquisite solicitude for justice. It repudiates whatever is undisguisedly diabolical, but within . . . whitened sepulchers. Nor is it pure coincidence that on the same day they crucified both Christ and the thieves—the thieves because they disturbed the peace, and Christ because He would not permit them to enjoy *their* peace. They acknowledge a golden mean of their own, but for those who exceed the prudent mean of this world (*excedunt mundi medietatem*) there is proscription and perhaps punishment.

St. Augustine draws attention to the fact that all the rules and standards which worldlings apply to things human are not going to avail them anything.[5] They will not profit from them because, not possessing faith, they are separated from the true order of justice and from God.[6] The fundamental requirement is that there be a standard, but it must be a standard from God and not merely one which always vacillates to the disadvantage of some men and to the advantage of a few, although such is not stated or cannot be proved. The Saint points out several of these miscarriages of justice in favor of particular individuals or personal interests, taking as an example the attitude of the Pharisees, who would not allow a man to be healed on the Sabbath, yet permitted him to be circumcised on the Sabbath, even though both acts were for man's healing.[7]

The fact that they had "personal" ideas about God and justice caused men to organize *their city* according to *their* standards and to establish their classifications. One of their specific categories is *possession.* "You are worth as much as you possess." This is the world's motto: "You *are* what you possess." This is the slogan of the avaricious, of thieves, of oppressors of the innocent, of the envious, of those who betray what was entrusted to them. All such persons do not consider God as their helper, but trust in their own riches. But do not think that I refer only to those who hold possessions, because it may well happen that those who have nothing also think this way. "Of what profit is it to you if you lack power and burn with covetousness?" (*Quid prodes si eges facultate et ardes cupiditate?*) It is not the possession of things as such which is condemned, but avarice.[8] Basically it is the problem mentioned earlier: of believing that possession is equivalent to happiness, which in practice is to deny the whole order of God and to reject God as man's happiness.[9]

The result has been that the world is not exactly a garden of paradise. It seems to St. Augustine as bitter as the sea, and there, quite appropriately, the laws of the sea prevail, for the big fish swallows the little one. By analogy the world is called a sea, bitter in its deception, turbulent in its storms, where men devour one another as do the fish. How they enslave, and if possible consume one another! And when a big fish swallows a small one, the former, in turn, is consumed by a still larger one. All this happens daily before our eyes.[10] Boasting of their wickedness, men devour each other.[11] Nor could it be otherwise. To start out on the roads of egoism is to start out on all the roads of wickedness, for love cannot stand still. If we do not love God, we will love what is not God; and what is not God is evil. Evil begins on the level of love and readily becomes the love of evil. Therefore, because men started out on the roads of iniquity in their love, they ended by running the whole gamut of prostituted affections: "Infamies, adulteries, crimes, murders, all kinds of obscene acts, do these not arise from love?" [12]

The fact that, practically speaking, people do not believe

in God is responsible for their failure to trust in God's justice. But they know through experience that they cannot place full confidence in the justice of their fellow men, and hence vengeance is one of the world's characteristics. This is a result of hatred, which the world cherishes. It is the logical consequence of having separated itself from charity, which is the very foundation of Christianity. Whoever loves the world will hate; whoever hates will seek revenge.[13]

Whoever does not believe in God practically, will not believe in His providence either. Therefore, he will not believe that the events of life are regulated by God, who always draws good from evil. And because they do not believe that evils can become blessings—since they believe in no values save those of this world and do not believe in divine providence which governs all—they rebel against God when things turn out badly for them.[14]

Neither do they believe in grace, and in this respect they act foolishly. Sometimes they credit themselves with a long life-expectancy, which spurs them to seek recreation and pleasure in the world.[15] At other times they are so distrustful of the power and efficacy of grace that they despair of being healed, and throw themselves still more feverishly into sin.[16] Then, with no less ignorance of the true nature of grace, they presume that they will be saved without any merits, for they do not believe that God condemns those who have been happy in this world.[17] This second explanation is the one which St. Thomas gives for the sin of the angels, and the catechism defines as a sin against the Holy Ghost.

It appears, then, that in all this there is a logic which should be examined from its beginning, in order to understand it, because if we do not elevate our vision, then what appears before our eyes is often a contradiction. Let us consider examples of this contradiction. Worldly persons not only come to do evil, but spend the whole day thinking about evil, preoccupied as they are with wickedness. They even come to glory in evil.[18] Yet, on another day they are railing against injustice: "What criminal does not find it easy to speak of justice? Or what person, on being interrogated, even if he does not live thus himself, cannot easily define what is just and right?" For if he does not speak of justice, he is afraid that men may consider him unjust.[19] Such persons speak authoritatively of justice, even when they are not at all interested in observing it. They appear to be very righteous persons. And they are even more partisans of justice when they are insulted or injured. Then they say that "the others" are such and such. But they do not consider that justice should be the norm of their own life.[20] Nor is it difficult for them to come to Church, to join their blows to hers in combatting those whom the Church is combatting at the moment. They do this so enthusiastically that they almost appear desirous of showing us how they defend justice and truth, freedom, etc. In reality they are following their own interests. We are friends only because of a temporary coincidence [of interest], not because they have ordered and directed their lives and objectives in accordance with supernatural norms.[21]

There is an internal logic and consistency which give unity to this perplexing conduct: it is self-love. Like centrifugal force, this self-love drives man in the direction which always becomes more distant from God. Yet sometimes it transpires that even the worldly individual understands that the best defense of what he is seeking is in God. Then he has no hesitation in allying himself with Him, to defend himself against other men. This is a temporal, selfish, superficial, and deceitful alliance. It is an alliance, moreover, which does grave harm to truth, because the truth which is defended by these men remains limited in its depth and extension. Moreover, all the other truths which they do not defend are compromised by this act of worldly prudence and condescension to one particular truth. This is not an alliance of righteousness but of self-love; such is the combination which overcomes contradictions that appear in such conduct. When this does not actually occur, the fact is that someone has exceeded the established norms of prudence, and then he has no hesitation in repudiating such behavior. However, he does not reject the vice itself, but only the exaggeration of the vice.

10

The World as a Social Unit

UP TO THIS POINT we have observed diverse aspects of the world, but we have fixed our attention especially on phases which are of an individual character: the worldly person as an individual. There is another aspect of the world, that is, the world as a social unit or society. Nor are these two aspects completely unrelated to each other, for we consider the world as society and in this respect it possesses aspects which are quite distinct from those previously investigated.

This did not escape St. Augustine, and he divided men into two cities, which are equivalent to two societies. The world as a society also has its own spirit, its laws, its government, its ruler.

With respect to procedure, it should be noted that in investigating and studying the world as a social unit, I shall insist on studying it under aspects which almost always are different from the previous ones, in order not to repeat the same thing. Yet almost all that has been said earlier has its social application, and hence almost all the aforesaid can be applied to the world as society. All in all, I prefer to combine the theme somewhat, and to concentrate directly on phases of the question which previously have not been treated in detail. Specifically, I refer to the fact that up to this point I have insisted almost exclusively on the opposition of the world to God as Creator, and I maintained in the second place, as a hidden reciprocity, the extension of this opposition to God as Redeemer. Now I prefer to concentrate on the opposition to God as Redeemer, while the other antagonism becomes the theme which is implied. This prepares us better for the second part of this study, and for understanding all the malice which exists in the world, all its ingratitude. But I repeat that it will not be an exclusive study of the first phase. This would be curtailing the dimensions which the theme possesses by its very nature, both as to its extent and its depth.

The world as a social unit or society is a closed corporation where God is not admitted, except, for some "practical" reason. He is brought in to swell the inventory. The two principal traits which mark the world's attitude toward Christ are that "they received Him not," and that they hate Him. Basing himself on St. John's Gospel, where these two attitudes are clearly enunciated, St. Augustine contrasts the attitude of the world with the mercy of Christ who came to save it. The overwhelming majesty and grandeur of Christ, which the Saint felt so profoundly, is contrasted with the hostile world. It is a masterful picture, filled with light and shadow, where the light is Christ and the shadows are the world. It is a light which attains its fullness, and shadows which also reach their plentitude—that of absolute blackness. The light is life and love; the darkness is hatred and death. It is a vast antagonism, if we consider what is at stake. It is also vast and extensive because step by step it follows the course of history. It is an antagonism which possesses a constancy in its light and love which only the divine mercy can uphold, and a constancy in its darkness and hatred which only a superhuman force can resist. Thus the mystery of love and the mystery of hate come into mortal conflict. It is a struggle which already has its history, though we do not know very well all the depths and details of that chronology. It is a conflict which God directs, which will always redound to the welfare and blessing of His elect and to His glory. For if one day the wickedness of this world were so great that His elect would not have the probability of being saved, on that day the conflict would end, to reduce the world to everlasting darkness, to subjugate the wicked to God's righteousness, that righteousness which they refused when He appeared as their Friend and Teacher.

11

And They Received Him Not

ARTICLE 1. *Pride as the world's principal vice*

WHEN ST. AUGUSTINE SPEAKS of Jesus Christ, his style takes on all the nuances of tenderness and all the impatience of love. Just as when he speaks of those who are obstinate in heresy or sin, he is terrible, harsh, aggressive, so when he speaks of Christ he becomes serene, profound, ardent. It may be said that the words which come to his lips then are glowing with fire, yet do not express all that he intends to say. It can be asserted (he himself makes this claim) that in order to speak of Jesus he frequently plumbs the very depths of words, yet finds them inadequate. That Jesus, whom St. Augustine presents with such magnificence and all the depths of his thought, is in synthesis the Doctor of charity, the Doctor of truth, and also the Doctor of humility.

One of the constants in St. Augustine's works is the contrast between the humility of Christ and the pride of the world. It is the divine response to human stupidity. It was a disturbing response, transcending all prudence of the flesh, reaching the very roots of man, because it attains even to the edge of nothingness ("He humbled Himself"). It reaches to the very limits of humanity. Such a disturbing reply shook the foundations of the world.[1] It is so vast, so comprehensive, that it filled all history and changed it. Christ's humility, says St. Augustine, wounded the devil, freed men, and blotted out with His blood the indenture of our slavery.[2]

In its turn, the world's pride, already a separation from God—converted into a more or less open hostility as history progressed—is changed into a rebuttal and is the world's answer to the miracle of Christ's humility. There are two colossi which confront each other in history: the prodigy of Christ's humility and the diabolical prodigy of human pride. Few things are more frequently repeated in the works of St. Augustine.

With respect to the world's pride, he knew its trajectory and recorded its history when he stated that the "City of Man" is founded on self-love and contempt of God. This contempt found—and still finds—its most extreme and frantic expression in scorn for Christ and His work. Laconically St. John states: "He came unto His own, and His own received Him not" (John 1:11). St. Augustine is not so laconic or calm when he comments on the insanity which this represents. "Through diabolical pride it came about, and still occurs, that the humility of Christ Crucified appears base and vile to those who love the excellence of this world."[3] Never have awe and stupidity been so widely separated. This is the final state of that desire to know good and evil: the inability to know Christ.

There is an offspring of this incompatibility. Those who do not understand Christ nor wish to know Him, belong to the devil. The wicked are members of Satan; and as the devil is proud, so his members also are proud: "As Christ is the Head of the good, so the devil is the head of the wicked. . . . And the whole body of Satan is concisely described in the Psalm: 'The proud have laid a snare for me' (Ps. 139:5). They are proud to the point of becoming loathsome, as their sins clearly indicate. . . . They are envious to the point of envying whatever is considered good or lofty in the world. Besides all this, they wish to be considered just men. . . . Finally, as the devil was proud and therefore grew envious, so also his body." [4]

Pride is the daily temptation which the devil presents to his own: "The proud one tempts the proud with pride . . . and he tempts only the proud." It is an incorporation which quickens its members in hate, an offensive hatred of God and all God's works.[5] With this the cup of iniquity is filled to the brim, and dynamic impulse is given to the wretched persons enmeshed therein—a perversion of the vital spark essential to every human being. This is a blasphemous parody of God which appears in men who are thus incorporated, in varying degrees of intensity, from the elegant man of the world who, because he has exquisite manners, categorically denies that he is proud, to the arrogant, irascible individual who considers himself a personal enemy of Christ. These are attitudes which differ in their intensity, but are identical in the formal aspect of their pride.

Since pride is the source of every sin and the constant element in every sin, it should not be surprising if the Saint attributes all kinds of sin to pride. Excluding those sins which are not the product of pride as a particular sin, we find in the works of St. Augustine a complete list of the children of pride. When he sees a poor wretch, half drunk, stretched out on the street, content with his poverty and his drink, he becomes absorbed in the reflection that it is precisely pride which drives men to worldliness.[6] Thirst for one's own fame is what drives men to bold undertakings, in order to be considered great men of the world, to be lauded by their fellow citizens, thus seeking glory before men rather than in God's sight. With such acts they pass as prudent, strong, well-adjusted and virtuous.[7]

But the pride of these men is such evident pride that little proof is needed to recognize it. St. Augustine is especially concerned about their negative attitude toward Christ. But the ones whom he studies in detail are those who presume upon their own justice, in order to dispense with divine grace. However, in his sermons he does not inveigh against these proud spirits so much as against others. Perhaps because some were in good faith in their allegiance to Pelagianism; perhaps because some of his hearers were related to Pelagians through family ties.[8] Yet he speaks the whole truth, and one can readily deduce all the consequences which he has expressed regarding other proud individuals.

Besides, his invectives against one and the other class of proud individuals appear either in the same discourse or on consecutive days. Speaking of the latter, he almost always employs the example of the Pharisees who slew Christ, because they were satisfied with their own righteousness and thought that they had no need for the physician. Is there, he inquires, anyone who is stronger than the maniac in his frenzy? Those who assaulted Christ and killed Him were strong enough for this because they trusted in themselves; they placed themselves between Christ and the multitudes who sought Him as their physician. They subdued the crowd, and murdered Him who was the physician of all men. But precisely because He had been slain, this physician prepared from His own blood the medicine for those who were ill.[9] They rose in rebellion against Him, because they did not wish to apply to themselves literally the words of the *Our Father*, for they considered themselves sinless.[10] The fact is that fundamentally they rejected a basic concept of Christianity, since they rejected grace and expected to receive everything by virtue of their own merits.

This is the *active* principle in all who do not believe in grace and expect to receive everything because of their own good works, because they do not hope in God. They do not believe in a certain Christian passivity which leads us to prayer, to hope, and to humility. They prefer to *keep busy*. St. Augustine uses both terms in their transcendental sense when he remarks: "Truly it is termed *activity*, because it denies to us the leisure of *inactivity*. . . . With good cause our Lord expelled them from the Temple, saying to them: 'It is written, My house shall be called a house of prayer; but ye have made of it a den of thieves' (that is, a place of business), meaning that presuming on their own works and despising leisure (synonomous with prayer), they were contemptuous of Him who said, in contradiction of their hectic life and business sense: 'Be still and know that I am God' " (Ps. 45:11).[11]

Now if with respect to God, pride consists in fundamentally refusing to recognize His handiwork either in the natural or the supernatural order, with respect to our fellow men pride is always inconsiderate and despotic. Men begin by acknowledging that they owe everything to God, but they despise their fellow men, even insult them, because they do not act like the proud. Such is the pride of the Pharisee who prayed in the Temple (Luke 18:10–14).[12] The fact is that the person who loves the world cannot love his fellow man.[13]

This is both imprudent and ridiculous, because each group seeks to delude itself, pretending that it possesses superlative qualities. But inasmuch as both use the same language, they no longer deceive themselves so readily. In its foundations it is a failure to take cognizance of God, who knows authentic truth, who also knows the absence of love behind their actions.[14] And this stupidity reaches its height when, as we continually observe, this lie, this deception which all see through, is rewarded with wealth and honors.[15] The result is that it not only separates man from God, but also divides men and sets them at war against each other, establishing here and there a Tower of Babel where confusion, conflict, vengeance and slavery appear as men fight among themselves.[16]

ARTICLE 2. *Unbelief as the world's basic sin*

But the gravest element in this situation is the blindness which pride produces. There is a blindness resulting from pride, in the sense that pride is the source of every sin; and as every sin darkens the soul, pride indirectly means darkness for sinners. There is another pride which immediately darkens the soul, for this pride is itself sin. In both ways sinners are pure gloom and darkness. St. Augustine repeats this continually, basing his statements on St. Paul, who calls all the descendants of Adam darkness because they are sinners, and describes the demons as rulers of the darkness of this world (Eph. 5:8; 6:12).

This community of gloom, formed simultaneously by demons and by sinners, is the black night which opposes Christ. St. Augustine says: "Every fool, every wicked person, is blind of heart." [17] Oh men, do not seek darkness, do not desire to be incredulous, wicked, thieves, avaricious, lovers of this world; these persons are darkness.[18] The darkness becomes so substantial a part of the world that the Apostle calls the world simply darkness, ruled by the prince of darkness.[19]

The immediate result of pride was the creation of a race deprived of truth. The pilgrimage of the wicked is horrible, because they perish of hunger and thirst for truth. The only drops of truth we have on this pilgrimage, given to us for our help and comfort so that we will not falter and faint, are those we drink of the fountain which is Christ. For of himself man is only sin and deception.[20] This is the tragic journey through life during which the worldly are continually beset by new errors, finding only hunger and more hunger once the false satiety of novelty disappears. They will not be satisfied, because they have within them a thirst for the supernatural which they ignore, and as a punishment they are rejected from the truth.[21] St. Augustine himself, when he comments on the journey of Augustine the prodigal, exclaims: "Alas, alas, down what steps did I descend to the lowest depths, filled with fatigue and dying of hunger for the truth! [22] Thou didst humble me as a proud man who is wounded; I found myself separated from Thee by my swollen vanity, and my face, extremely inflated, did not cease to behold the truth before my eyes." [23]

But if they possess such hunger for truth, it should be logical that when Christ appeared, the Truth and the Life, they would follow Him with enthusiasm and fervor. But quite the opposite has happened. They want nothing to do with Him. They are too important, and God became too insignificant for them. He appeared small as a stone which breaks loose from a mountain; and they stumbled on that stone. They have no excuse, for they had been clearly informed beforehand that He would be as a stone dislodged from a mountain. The stone that was dislodged grew and became a veritable mountain; and they were blocked by that mountain. They stumbled upon Christ, who is humble and lowly. They stumble upon the Church, which is great and majestic as a mountain. Their blindness is too all-encompassing.[24]

This sin is so vast that after Christ's coming it is the world's greatest sin, the one which Holy Scriptures consider the world's peculiar sin. For this sin there is no excuse. The world's sin, without which it would not be the world, is unbelief.[25] There will be no excuse for those who did not believe in Christ, neither for those who heard Him in person nor for those who have heard Him in the person of His disciples and His Church.[26] All the light which Christ brought is rejected by this darkness which continually seeks to blot out the light. And for them the mission of Christ, who came as a physician that they might see, remains of no avail.[27] Bound by ties of kinship to the devil, who is their head, their father, rejecting Christ and the work which Christ has wrought, these wretches will ally themselves with all that is diabolical, with anti-Christ himself when he comes.[28]

We have reached one of the central thoughts of our investigation, and should halt a moment, attempting to synthesize the entire thought of St. Augustine. To this end let us probe the waters farther upstream in order to measure the total pressure which now bore down upon events.

The one whom the Jews crucified, our Master and our Physician, He who humbled Himself and died, was one whom the Jews could not destroy, nor was He annihilated by their brutality. That Man was the Eternal Word, who before all ages was the Word. Life does not disappear. He is life, the life of all creation. He is wisdom; and according to this wisdom, according to His plan, all things were made. He is the life of all; but among things created there is one creature who occupies the apex, and this is man. For him that light is also life, the life of men, not of animals, since only men possess a mind, intelligence, the part of their nature on which they bear the image of God. This is the attribute which definitely raises man above all other things of earth. Now the Word is the light of human minds, the light which is above all minds and excels them all. This is that life by which all things were made. . . . The light shone in the darkness; but the darkness rejected it.[29]

He came as one sent by God, a messenger with a message of love. God so loved the world that He gave His only-begotten Son. He came not as judge, but as Redeemer. Yet men loved their darkness more than the light. But not all! When He came, all were in darkness. But some loved their sins, while others confessed them. Those who confessed their transgressions did so because God enlightened them. "It would not be displeasing to thee unless God enlightened thee" (*Non tibi displiceret, nisi Deus tibi luceret*). That is, God gave man light; and then he began to be displeasing to himself, to confess his sins. Those who rejected God refused the light, and Him who sent it to them. The individual who is admonished because of his sins, and continues to love them, hates the one who admonishes him. He hates the light, he flees from it, in order that it may not convict him of the evil deeds which he loves.[30]

Here Augustine describes life as two roads going in opposite directions. One belongs to those who have received the light, those who should so walk that the darkness will not encompass them;[31] the other road is that which worldlings travel, running ahead of the light so that the light will not show up their wicked deeds. It is a tragic route, this road which leads head-on, fleeing from truth and the light, the light always at their back. They are forever in fear of that light, hungry and tortured as they undertake the most shameful and desperate of flights.

And because He is merciful, God follows them!

"If He had not come and had not spoken to them, they would not have sin." St. Augustine tells us that this refers specifically to the Jews, and in their person, to the world, because the Jews are part of the world. At that moment they are the most active phase of the world in their opposition to God, with explosive hatred, with the blindness of a poisonous cobra. But the assertions of Jesus apply to everyone. Can it be said that when Christ came the Jews were not in sin, so that it was necessary for Him to come and speak to them in order that they should be guilty of sin? Who will assert this foolishness? It is a question of a great sin hidden beneath the general classification of sin; a sin which, if one commits it, makes him guilty of all other sins. And if one is not guilty of this one sin, he receives forgiveness for all the rest. This incalculable sin is that they believed not in Christ, who came into the world for precisely this purpose, that they might believe in Him. Had He not come, they would not have been guilty of this sin. Hence, for the believer His coming is salutary, but for those who do not believe, it is death.[32]

Christ's coming effected a demarcation of areas in our world. It compelled each individual to define his own position in relation to the supernatural and eternity (predicated on this new light shed on the problem). There is no use hesitating, because the very advent of Christ defines our position. In assuming its position, the world has chosen its own—the position of unbelief. Its new attitude is so grave that it eclipses all other sins; all the rest become of lesser weight in comparison to this. Previously, in the relationship between the world and the Creator, the expression was that of a proud, forgetful individual. Through pride it proclaimed itself independent. In its independence it forgot God. Then its situation became worse. The world is twice a renegade. It is an unbeliever; it has rejected all Christ's light, all His love, all His solicitude, even though He came to cure the world. Its sin is so vast, so grave, because it is a sin peculiar to the world.

As we already have stated, there is no excuse for this sin, neither for those who heard Christ nor those who heard Christ's disciples nor those who now have the Church.[33] And by this the Holy Ghost will convince the world of sin. It is a relationship different from the mission which the Holy Ghost will have in the world, to call it to faith. This is the mission of a judge to the criminal, of a ruler to the rebel, [a judgment pronounced] in the name of the light which was despised, personifying that love which impelled God in His wondrous plan of redemption.

He will convince it of sin, says St. Augustine, because it has been unwilling to believe. He will convince it of justice because if so many men believed Him when they saw Him, those who saw Him but did not believe will have no excuse. Further, if there are such untold numbers who have not seen Him, yet have believed, then those who have not seen Him will likewise have no excuse for their unbelief.

He will convince it of judgment. If it has imitated the prince of this world, then by those same standards and judgments by which his conduct is condemned, the world's also will be judged and found guilty. Nevertheless, so that the worldly will not have the excuse that God is relentless, God's mercy followed them throughout their life, surrounded them, called them, enlightened them, touched them on the shoulder. The person who was unwilling to take refuge in His mercy must bow to His righteousness, since we must all submit to God.[34]

But until this definitive judgment is pronounced, they will not cease to make war against God, to antagonize and oppose His plans. In perpetual alliance with all that is diabolical, they will continue to prepare the paths of iniquity until they finally become the best servants of anti-Christ.[35]

Such is the tragedy and mystery of darkness in all its scope and baleful wickedness. This is the world's formal sin.

Manifestly we can also talk of occasional and partial incredulity—practical states of unbelief experienced by persons who believe. These individuals do not belong to the world, for they believe, but they perform worldly actions. These are worldly Christians in the sense that they perform worldly actions but they themselves cannot be said to belong to the world. Their actions are not permeated by faith in the practical order but are influenced by worldly standards and are separated from that supernatural goal which faith restored to us when it again linked our life with the supernatural. These will not be actions which are called sins, in the sense of a prevailing supernatural pathology. This is something more tenuous; it is something so simple that people no longer understand that it is evil. Nevertheless it is something so wicked that to a certain extent it unhinges time itself, as well as dislocating some of the heartbeats of the supernatural element, with the result that faith no longer informs one's actions. While these intermittent sins persist, the door is open for the devil and for even more serious actions to enter. So long as worldly qualities remain in the Christian soul, there is no way in which it can achieve perfection.

12

The Hour of Darkness

ARTICLE 1. *Hatred for Christ*

THE DARKNESS IS ACTIVE, and its activity is crystallized in sin. Its sin at times takes the form of hatred, a hatred that began by unleashing itself against Christ, and which, more or less disguised, more or less unrestricted, appears each day throughout recorded time. It employs various excuses, manifests itself in various ways; but it continues always as hate. This is the hour of darkness, the hour of the enemies of light, "the dark hour, the nocturnal hour," which comes to destroy faith or at least to weaken it. It has received power over the flesh, but not over the spirit. It can slay the body, but it cannot blot out faith.[1] Jesus stated this plainly to His disciples: "If the world hates you, know that it has hated Me before you. If you were of the world, the world would love what is its own; but because you are not of the world, but I have chosen you out of the world, therefore the world hates you" (John 15:18–19).

The hatred of the Jews—and we already stated that for

Augustine these people are representatives of the world—led, as we know, to their slaying Christ. Thus from that time onward there will be two attitudes toward Jesus: the attitude of those who seek Him in order to love Him, and that of those who seek Him in order to hate Him. The Jews inaugurated hate as a way of life.[2] The Saint insists upon the worldly aspect of this hate and murder; he asserts that when they perpetrated their crime they were filled with the world's iniquity.[3] The deep-seated malice and blindness of this hatred are presented by the Saint in these same quotations, when he informs us that this hate consisted specifically in despising and rejecting the only one who was able to save them.[4] They rejected and killed Christ at the very moment when He was doing everything possible to save them. He says that the Jews, filled with the world's malice, were like a strong vinegar, the corruption of the generous wine which they had received from the patriarchs and prophets. When Christ cried out that He thirsted, He was saying to them: "What I have received from you thus far is little. What I want from you is yourself. The blindness of this hate is horrible: in order to please God, they kill Him who is pleasing to God, who is the temple of the living God." [5] It is impossible to find in Christ one single trait which irritates. But actually irritation resides not only in the one who provokes it, but in him who is irritated. Light irritates a person who has weak eyes; the serenity of truth irritates the liar. This is what happened: they were children of darkness, children of lies, and Christ was for them a living witness to their darkness, their falsehood.[6]

St. Augustine points out sharply the gratuitous character of this hatred for Christ. If He had not wrought for them deeds which no one else had done, they would not be guilty of sin. But they saw them and hated Him, so that there might be fulfilled that which is written in the Law: "They hated Me without cause." [7] The Saint analyzes this idea in detail: to hate gratuitously without cause means that this hatred seeks no advantage, does not seek to avoid some difficulty or inconvenience. Thus, the impious hated the Lord, and so also do the righteous love God gratuitously, not seeking anything besides Him, nothing distinct from Him.

But Augustine is especially illuminating in his exposition of the words, "If I had not done among them the works which no other man did, they had not had sin; but now have they both seen and hated both Me and My Father" (John 15:24). Make an historical survey of the miracles which holy men and prophets of Israel wrought, in order to prove that Jesus excelled all the rest in the magnitude and majesty of His deeds. The quantity of the miracles which Christ performed is unique. No one else thus placed himself at the disposal of the sick and the infirm, curing them one after another, irrespective of the nature of their ailments. "When it was evening, and the sun had set, they brought to Him all who were ill, and who were possessed. And the whole town had gathered together at the door. And He cured many who were afflicted with various diseases, and cast out many devils; and He did not permit them to speak, because they knew Him" (Mark 1:32–34).

The Evangelist himself narrates how the people gathered together in the villages and cities and squares, how they set before Him those that were ill, beseeching Him that He would at least touch them with the hem of His garment; and as many as touched Him were made whole (Mark 6:56). Further, these words are to be interpreted as His actually healing them, not merely as describing some act which He performed before their eyes and in their presence. For He worked His miracles not only to impress them with awe, but to heal them. In return for such beneficent acts they owed Him, not hate, but love. He wrought other miracles which were even greater, like that of being born of a Virgin, and rising again from the dead, but these He did not actually work *upon them.*[8] The explanation becomes clear in the first lines of this treatise "Whoever hates the truth must necessarily hate the Author of truth." With this statement St. Augustine again has reduced to a synthesis the whole perplexing entanglement which men's acts can create.

St. Augustine's final thought confronts us with a serious question: Do worldly persons hate God directly? Is the world's hatred for God so diabolical a hate that it selects God Himself as its formal object? Or is it an indirect hate, to which some previous action impels it? The Saint answers this question in the following way: We can suppose that an individual thinks of God as being what He is not, and that thus he hates what he mistakenly believes to be God. It can also happen that there is no error or mistake, but that one hates God directly. Then why does the Gospel tell us that they hated Him whom they knew not? It may happen that we think a certain man is impure, and avoid his company. If it transpires that this individual is not unclean, in reality we will love him. We love him without knowing that we love him, because what we really love is the purity which dwells in him.

The contrary may also occur; a wicked man loves a good man since he believes him like himself; but in this instance he does not love the just man, but what he believes the just man to be. For thus the wicked man hates the righteous, hates him because he does not know what he is, and loves that which he does not believe the man to be. And as happens among men, so also with God. The Jews hated that truth which condemned them and their works. How can they love the Father of truth? Nevertheless, if you should ask them, they would respond that they love God. They do not wish to condemn their own deeds, but the truth condemns them. Therefore they are compelled to hate the truth as much as they hate the condemnation of their own acts and the punishment which will accrue to them on this account. *They do not know that it is the truth which condemns them.* Therefore they hate that which they do not know, and thus hate Him who is the Father of truth.[9]

It is not a direct hatred which we here encounter, but an indirect one; they hate what condemns their wicked deeds. This is the direct hatred. Then it transpires that what they hate is none other than Truth itself. Within the Augustinian system the final result is also quite logical: God is the source of truth. It is the Word who activates the truth within us, who teaches it to us, and therefore of necessity they hate the source of truth.

There are many Christians who sleep peacefully because they have heard that the world hates God, and they have not the least hatred for God; therefore, they are not worldings. St. Augustine calls attention to the fact that the Jews would have made the same response. Yet they hate the truth which condemns their actions. In another passage, St. Augustine discusses this at length: If the evil deeds of the wicked are tolerated, then all of us are good. If they are criticized, or rebuked, then they say: "How wicked that other person is!" The word which rebukes their conduct has been spoken; and therefore they hate God's word. If you are silent when they steal, then they consider you to be good; if you rebuke them, then you are bad. Whoever condemns the thief is wicked; and he who robs is good! Avarice commands, and you obey. God commands, and you hate.[10]

This is not a direct hatred, though it can be such. When it reaches this extreme it even displeases the world which, as we remarked, does not like excesses, even excesses of evil, because they disturb that tranquillity which the world has manufactured for itself.[11]

ARTICLE 2. *Various types of hatred for Christians*

Before Christ's coming, hatred for Him already existed in the attacks on Abel, the patriarchs and prophets; and after His coming this hatred continues for us Christians. The history of the Church is a tale of persecution on the part of those whom she has the vocation of loving and saving. Christ gives us the explanation: "But because you are not of the world, I have chosen you out of the world, therefore the world hates you" (John 15:19). The grace of divine election has placed us in a realm apart. They are not acquainted with that kingdom, even as they know not Him who founded it. They belong to the kingdom of evil, and it is impossible for these two realms to have harmonious relations. Scarcely was the Church born, the Saint tells us, when the sea (the world) lashed against it with its furious waves.[12] And in another passage: When Christ infused His Spirit into those who believe, He changed them into rivers which move through the earth, crying out. It was then that the sea raised up its foaming waves against them, the frightful shouts of its persecutions.[13]

All this is rooted in the world's ignorance of Christ. It is a culpable ignorance, but ignorance nevertheless. The election which God has made among us, changing us into His children, "that we may be called and may be the sons of God," this election causes the world not to know us, because it did not know Him who called us. This is the most stubborn lack of comprehension. Two classes of men have lived in the world for so many centuries, and the world has been incapable of understanding us. Citizens of the world—citizens by virtue of their love of the world—do not possess a sufficiently penetrating love to see and understand those that have set their love beyond this world. The world knows nothing beyond its own frontiers; therefore it did not know Christ who came to cure its ills. And loving what their feverish delusion set before them, they wounded the physician.[14]

But we should not think that this was the result of infantile simplicity. If they had not had the roots of iniquity within their hearts they would not have unleashed persecutions against Christ.[15] This is the explanation of so much wickedness disguised in the vesture of righteousness, of patriotic appeals, defense of the State, of democracy, and other songs which the children of Babylon sing. These are songs sung at the instigation of the devil who, in the last analysis, directs the drama: he is the only one who knows the plot.[16]

All that the world has comprehended of this tremendous confusion is that two classes of men, having placed their affections on different worlds, are two races divided at the roots of life. Two forms of existence—one of which is focused on money and selfishness, the other on God and things eternal—these are two forms of existence, two banners facing in different directions. One looks for everything here on earth; the other looks for everything from God, and not necessarily here. These are not harmonious or compatible lives.[17] Yet it does not follow from this that these two forms of existence should be hostile and at enmity. It is only the world which assumes a hostile posture, because it is disturbed by the attitude of Christians, by their righteousness, their detachment, their contempt for all that the world holds dear. They believe that what the Christians hope for is pure phantasy.[18]

This is the accusation which Communism levels at us today; because we look for everlasting blessings, they believe that we are incapable of achieving the good things of this life, which for them are the only reality. Indeed, the history of persecutors is an old story! It is only one step from persecution to believing that Christ, since He instilled contempt for earthly good in the hearts of Christians, is a malefactor. And this step has often been taken throughout the course of history.[19] Basically, as we already have stated, it is a narrowness of heart, the inability to understand and to love those who are not as they. The breadth of heart which they lack is precisely what Christ required; it is that which He has made possible for us by His grace. Whether perspiring and in agony, as Nietzsche asserts, or not perspiring, we love those who persecute us, because we do understand all that they are and all that they can be.

Not all make a philosophy of persecution; there are those who are satisfied with ridicule and contempt. The basis of that ridicule and contempt is the same: pride—pride which despises whatever is not like itself. This is the source of the ridicule which worldly persons direct toward those who seek to be good. This is the reason for their mocking those who do not wish to find their pleasure in this world.

It is curious to observe the pattern of those who ridicule Christians or despise them. We have already observed that St. Augustine grows impatient in regard to these wealthy worldlings who, when they are surfeited by their own illusions (because they dream up the delusion that they are really rich), argue against God and inquire contemptuously: "Who are these Christians? And Christ? They must indeed be stupid to expect something they have never seen." "You sleep and you bleat," St. Augustine says to them. "Shout against God to the limit of your ability! But how long shall the wicked glory . . . ? When will they consume themselves and let Christians live in peace?" [20]

St. Augustine notes something which occurs daily: that many of these persons despise us because they consider themselves to be at the culmination of their desires. If they were to become miserable, they would not despise us. Now they insult us because they are happy, boasting of the nothingness of their deceptive possessions (*in ventositate falsorum bonorum*). "Let them leave me in peace," the epicure says in a deprecatory tone, "those who promise me what they cannot show me." But if he should become miserable and wretched himself, he would not utter insults. And they will grow wretched, and their insults will turn against themselves.[21]

St. Augustine cautions Christians (since it is useless to warn the powerful, because up to now they have not understood it): "Don't think that they are really so happy, lest you yourself become shipwrecked. Either [his earthly] possessions will depart from him or he will depart from his possessions. Could his father or his grandfather take the family home with them when they died? Neither can he take it with him. We know that we live, as it were, in a temporary dwelling, and that happiness is in the other life. And because the hour has not yet arrived, we sigh and bear the disdain of those who are happy in this world.[22]

"We are despised even by those who have no possessions or who suffer the punishment of their evil lives in prison. They revile us, because somehow they consider themselves wealthy. If they did not think they were rich or privileged, they would not be proud. This person possesses a vast sum of money; and therefore he is proud. Another is covered with honors; and he too is proud. What is much worse, still another individual thinks that he abounds in virtue and righteousness; and he also is proud. This last, indeed, classes himself with God; and since he never recognizes his own wicked ways, he wants to give God lessons in the government of the world or to arrogate this to himself, to distribute honors and sufferings, rewards and punishments. Don't be surprised; even on the cross one, who was a thief, hurled insults.[23] They insult us because we do not wish to get drunk, because we don't go to scandalous public spectacles, etc." [24] Today we have a picture of people leaving the theater or the stadium, who meet others coming from church. Within themselves the former are saying: "Poor fools! What they are missing!"

"Brother," St. Augustine says with irony and pity, "let us

pray to the Lord for such solicitude as they have for us, because they think their attitude is good. They love you indeed; but he who loves iniquity hates his own soul." [25] With such variants of hate, contempt, or pity, it is apparent that the history of persecutors is the same since the world began.

The measure of irrationality inherent in many persecutions deserves to be stressed. Frequently St. Augustine notes this. "Now there are many who multiply their sins daily, who have lost their sense of shame; the mystical body groans aloud when it comes into contact with such persons. Listen to them: 'We are bored. Come, let us eat and drink, for tomorrow we die. Let us crown ourselves with roses before they wither, and let us leave a remembrance of our revelry. Then let us go off and slay the poor.' Who could expect that punishments would arise from so delicate a thing as a rose?" [26]

The fact is that the world considers Christians to be kill-joys; it does not want Christians to interfere with its happiness. They are saying this when they complain that our laws forbid their complete abandonment to pleasures.[27] We have seen that this was one of the principles in the constitution of the "City of Man": that brothels should abound; . . . that luxurious mansions should be built, with many parties held in them; that within these mansions whoever so desires, whoever is able, may drink, vomit, waste, and celebrate. Everywhere there should be dances, theaters in which thunderous applause resounds in appreciation of obscene programs or performances. Whoever is disgusted with so much frivolous joy should be considered a public enemy. And if he attempts to deprive them of these, they should cast him out from among the living.[28] We have already seen how up-to-date are these accusations which indict Christianity of wishing to make those who now are happy, unhappy, so that Christians may then have the pleasure of consoling them.

It is appropriate to observe that there are worldlings who seem quite friendly and understanding. Such persons are, in their own way, another instrument for destroying the soul. The Saint lists and classifies such individuals. Not all worldlings are persecutors, but all are wicked, because in some way they are lustful, drinkers, licentious. Do not say that they are not harmful to you, since whoever is harmful to himself will not fail to harm you. Immediately, by his example he incites you to that very thing which you must combat within your own heart. Strive to extirpate these evil roots in them, and if you are unable to do so, be sure that other thorns will sprout forth. If you cannot do this, be assured that you will have them for your enemies. And he who cannot love you must necessarily seek to harm you.[29]

But what earthquakes shake the world when a Christian strives to become more perfect! When a Christian strives with determination to raise himself above the world's standards and conditioning of time and space, to take flight like a bird and mount ever higher, surrendering himself more and more to God; what things are said, what looks are directed at this serious Christian! These range from sophisticated criticism and irony to slander! [30] To be sure, they do not tell him that what he is striving for is wrong, because today people no longer would dare to assert that Christ taught evil. Instead, they tell him his goal is too high, that he cannot succeed in what he is attempting, etc.[31]

Along with this we have stated that there is a type of worldly persecution which comes from Christians themselves—Christians who know not the spirit of Christ, or Christians who utter insults because they wish to continue their own heavy drinking, their fornications and obscene conduct.[32]

It is a question of making salvation impossible, whether by one route or another, of digging up the seed which the Holy

Ghost has planted in our hearts, or causing thorns to choke off the tender shoot which God has planted.[33] This is accomplished by a strategy that takes cognizance of specific circumstances in place and time, immediate family situations, one's physical constitution, etc. At other times it is the result of a temptation arising from within: that we will lose our friends, our social influence, the means of earning a livelihood. Again, the obsession that we will die of sadness if we renounce worldly things, or that we will be unable to get ahead. Besides this come ridicule, slander, persecutions. St. Augustine has seen the alternative course of action, the one which the world chooses when it persecutes us. Sometimes it threatens us with misfortune and with its hostility, and if it sees that with this it does not succeed in overcoming us, then it tempts us with its joys and successes.[34]

The very scandals which are constantly caused by the lives of the worldly are a kind of persecution that makes the mystical body of Christ groan. And this kind of persecution is worse than a bloody persecution.[35] Further, scorn and slander are as bad as these.[36] St. Augustine is irritated when he observes that worldlings claim that Christians seek worldly honors, and that he himself preaches only for applause.[37] With respect to scandals, there are two kinds which the Church suffers: scandals from the worldly and scandals from Christians; those from within and those from without.[38] Obviously, the scandals from the secular-minded do much harm, but the scandals coming from Christians are much more serious, because many who are not Christians will at once cite the bad lives of Christians as excuses for not accepting Christianity.[39] There is evidence that this latter argument still has not lost its importance, since undoubtedly the greater share of the criticisms which contemporary enemies of Christianity direct at us have a basis in reality. The Saint says to Christians: "Since it is necessary that the world should hate you, let it hate you without cause, as it hated Christ when it nailed Him to the cross." [40]

These last words are not merely a comparison, but rather the foundation of Augustinian thought on this subject. We are the mystical body of Christ, in which He completes the sacrifice He began in His physical body. Therefore this also must be a gratuitous sacrifice, without cause. "Two thieves were there, and the Lord was there. They were crucified and the Lord was crucified. The world hated the thieves, but not without cause. It hated Christ too, but without any justification. . . . This is the meaning of being hated gratuitously. 'I repay what I have not stolen; I suffer punishment, and I have not sinned.' "[41] We must be a holy sacrifice, in order to complete the sacrifice which was inaugurated in the first-fruits of our human nature, in the physical body of Jesus, since that sacrifice is to be consumated in all those who are to rise again with Him.

But before continuing this profound concept of the consoling mystery of redeemed sorrow (provoked by the world), let us analyze the shadows of this subject, in order to plumb the very depths of this darkness.

ARTICLE 3. *Diabolical aspect of this hatred*

All this is the superficial aspect of a great torment which is quite intricate. It is only the human phase of a drama in which Christ Himself personally plays a role, the part of characters with secondary roles. This suffering and drama, which embraces all ages and all men, confers diabolical or divine transcendence upon human actions. It is the struggle of Satan with Christ. First the personal, the physically personal struggle against Christ; then the battle against the mystical body of Christ. The Saint gives us this summary: "Because the enemy pursues my soul, he humbles me to the very earth. Here we are included, and Christ our Head, who represents us, is included. For the enemy pursues my soul. The devil pursued the soul of Christ; and Judas pursued the Master's soul. Now, in the persecution of the body of Christ, the demon continues at his post, while Judas has been relieved by other Judases. The body does not lack reasons for saying also: 'Because my enemy pursues my soul, he has degraded my life, cast me into the dirt. . . .' What is every persecutor attempting to accomplish, except that we should renounce the hope of heaven and, instead, prefer this earth? . . . Openly, by means of cruelty, secretly, through guile, they try to crush our life to the very ground. Let us be alert, so that we can say: 'We languish for heaven.'[42] And if anyone is looking for our soul, let him find it united to Thee."[43]

This is the struggle which has always existed, in which all our souls are at stake. Moreover, it is a fight which is replete with mysteries, inasmuch as human and superhuman powers are so intermingled that they transcend any possible estimate of their extent and efficacy by the unaided intellect of many. It does not matter; we are not struggling in order to understand, but because we love. The rest (and the rest is the whole complex of human activity) does not interest us; only love: "You should know that no road is loftier than the high road of charity, and only the humble travel on it," says the Saint. "And Thou knowest, Lord, that for Thee I suffer, that I suffer for love; Thou knowest that love makes all things bearable for me; Thou knowest that if I deliver my body to the flames, it is because I have charity, without which naught else would profit me"[44] (I Cor. 13:3).

ARTICLE 4. *The mystery of redeemed suffering*

Jesus stated it clearly: They will hate Me *in you,* they will persecute Me *in you.*[45] They will hate you for My name's sake; not for your sake, but for Mine, St. Augustine comments.[46] This is the fundamental and consoling distinction which exists between persecutions that Christians will suffer, and those which the rest of mankind will bear. "How shall we prove," the Saint asks, "that Christ suffers in us? By that voice from heaven, 'Saul, Saul, why persecutest thou Me?' (Acts 9:4) . . . and by that reply which the Judge will give: 'I was hungry, and you gave Me to eat; I was thirsty, and you gave Me to drink. . . .' We should rejoice and give thanks, brethren, for He not only has made us Christians, but He also has made us other Christs!" [47]

The immediate explanation of this mystery is our consecration by grace, but the final source lies in the mystery of the Incarnation. When the Word assumed human nature, He sanctified it, personifying it. This was a twofold personification, mysterious in both manifestations, but as real in the mystical personification which He effected with the redeemed as in the physical personification which He effected in the human body in which He became incarnate. St. Augustine, whose intellect was proficient at contemplating problems from the standpoint of their marvelous unities, could not miss this thought which throbs at the basis of all Christological discussions within the Church. The nuptials which the Word celebrated with humanity, so often mentioned by the Church Fathers, is something more than an analogy; it is really the sanctification of humanity by means of the flesh which He assumed. This espousal is the beginning of a mysterious unity which extends to our manner of life and our eternal destiny.

St. Augustine correlates the strands of this mystery by commenting on these words: "All flesh shall come to Thee" (Ps. 64:2). Why shall it come? Because Christ was made man. How will men come? Christ assumed the primacy among men in the virginal womb. Having taken the primacy, all the rest would follow so that the holocaust might be complete.[48]

Every predestined soul is joined to Christ by the eternal decree of predestination, in the concrete likeness of a holocaust.

"I will go unto the altar of God"; from His holy mountain, from His tabernacle, from His holy Church, I will go unto the sublime altar of God. Of what sacrifice is he speaking? The very person who enters is chosen for the sacrifice.[49] Yet this sacrifice is not fruitful so far as it is human, nor is it great because it involves human suffering (this would be returning to the world by a pathological route), but rather because of the mystical union of the predestined with Christ their Head. This is a sacrifice in which the world acts as executioner, and love as immolator, the same as on the cross.

It is a total sacrifice, not only in a personal sense but also in a quantitative sense, including all the predestined. Without such totality in every respect the sacrifice is not consummated, since by its nature it is a *total* sacrifice. Nor will this totality reach all its amplitude until those sacrificed are absorbed by life: the body by resurrection, and the soul by being cleansed of every particle of evil. "I will go into Thy house in holocausts" (*Introibo in domum tuum in holocaustis*). What is this holocaust? When all is aflame, but with divine fire. There are other kinds of sacrifice, but when all is aflame, when all is consumed by the divine fire, it is called a holocaust. If it is only partial, it is called a sacrifice. But a holocaust is promised and it is the body of Christ which speaks; it is Christ's *unity* which speaks: I will go into Thy house as a holocaust. I am completely consumed in Thy fire. Let nothing of self remain to me; let all be for Thee.[50]

In the previous section he stated that this fire, which here is specifically divine love, had begun as a persecution by the world: "Now that the first-fruits of the Spirit are already born within us, by which we desire the everlasting Jerusalem, many elements of corrupt flesh make war against us, which will not war against us when death is swallowed up in victory. . . . But how we struggle with death now! Carnal suggestions abound, inviting us to unlawful pleasures. Do not consent to them. In not consenting we struggle against them. First, concupiscence of the flesh carries us into the street; afterwards it drags us down even as we complain. But at last, having received grace, it neither carries us away nor drags us down, but still it wars against us." Yet after the struggle will come victory. "I shall keep my vow." What vow? That of the holocaust, when the fire consumes all. "May the holy fire of Jerusalem consume us completely. Let us begin to burn with charity, till all that is mortal is wholly consumed, and whatever opposes us is turned into a holocaust." [51] It is certain that St. Augustine is thinking especially of the martyrs when he writes these transcendental lines (frequently repeated in his commentaries on the Psalms). But the words which I have just cited refer to all Christian states of life, to all the situations which the Christian encounters.

Before continuing, let us observe the profound meaning of the Christian idiom which considers the religious vocation as indeed a total holocaust of the individual, describing it as a "flight from the world," thus uniting these two basic concepts of holocaust and hostility to the world.

As we were saying a short while ago, all the hidden meaning of sorrow resides in the union which exists between Christ as Head and Christians as His members. For us this marvelous unity contains mysteries and perspectives which transform what is human, exalting it, without its ceasing to be human. In explaining this holocaust and the suffering inflicted on Christians by the world, St. Augustine's mind is immersed in the mystery of the mystical body of Christ, with a profundity and intimacy which scarcely admit a comparison. St. Augustine does not hesitate in his assertions, which are much more daring than all we have heard from a certain decadent asceticism which is far removed from the Patristic tradition. And let us observe in passing that these claims were made in public sermons, because St. Augustine believed that one cannot be wholly Christian without knowing all the depth of the Christian mysteries. And one of those mysteries is that of our own sorrow-laden existence.

In his commentary on Psalm 85, he gives an impressive summary of what he thinks about the suffering of the mystical body.[52] Having established the unity of all men in one single man who has Christ as Head, St. Augustine draws his conclusions and also unifies the prayer of that man as well as the suffering of that man. This unification is the personal accomplishment of Christ, who has made us His members or, as is stated here, it is the work of God. "God could confer no greater blessing or gift on men than to give them the Word, through whom all things were made, as their Head, and to give them to Him as His members." When this man is crushed to earth by tribulations, persecutions, scandals, temptations to evil which the devil implants by means of the worldly[53] ("See how the chaff murmurs and complains on the thrashing floor"[54]), then his whole self cries out to God in sorrow and in anguish.

The voice of this man is prayer. God is present in this prayer, not only because it is He to whom we address it, but also because it is Christ Himself who prays in us and with us. God wrought this union, "that He might be the Son of God and the Son of man; one God with the Father and one man with men, so that when in prayer we speak to God we will not separate ourselves from the Son, and when the body of the Son prays it will not be separated from its Head; that the Savior of His body may be one, our Lord Jesus Christ, Son of God, who prays for us, who prays in us, and to whom we pray. He prays for us as our Priest; He prays in us as our Head; we pray to Him as to our God. Let us then recognize our voices in Him, and His voice in us."[55] This mighty voice of prayer, which synthesizes all the prayers of the elect, has its greatest power and true hope in this unity. Finally, it is this which puts anxiety to flight. This unity of prayer is what the Church continually recalls in ending its official prayers with the liturgical formula, *per Christum Dominum nostrum,* etc.

Christ also personifies the groans of suffering in His mystical body. All the laments and anguish of the predestined throughout history will be the suffering of that man. Thus, as it is Christ who prays, so it is also Christ who suffers, who sheds His blood throughout time. When He grew sad, when He tired, when He was hungry, when He slept in the boat, when He was thirsty and spent the night in prayer, there were we. And when drops of blood stood out on His body and ran down, what did this signify except that His body, which is the Church, already was suffering the martyrdom of blood? [56]

But so far as they are individuals, not all voices will have the same tone or know the same suffering. He receives some members, He scourges others; some He cleanses, some He consoles, some He nourishes, some He calls, others He calls again; some He corrects, others He again incorporates in Himself. But it is the body which cries out, which suffers, which has but one voice, one voice with which He cries out all the day long. He has one voice through this mystical unity because charity prevents the voices from degenerating into meaningless sounds.[57]

The voice of this Man of sorrows, since it is the voice of one man alone, is unique in history, endures as long as the world will last, transcends the human members as the science of suffering. It is an outcry which moves us by reason of its intensity, its constancy, its depth and its mystery. Christ's voice sounds a chant of anguish, Christ's voice alone, which still moves through life, sorrowing and striving onward, fighting the battles of life and death which each Christian experiences. For death and evil must be given as many opportunities as possible for conquering, so that when their defeat takes place, they shall have no excuse. All the resources of evil must be exhausted, so that its condemnation will be infinitely just. This test to which the predestined are subjected may perhaps seem cruel to us, or at any rate fill us with fear, but this battle is not measured by human standards, nor do we need to struggle with human weapons. Good and evil, victory and death, come from beyond. Yet our anxiety does not arise merely because we bear the evils of this life—this is a good for us—but because we still are pilgrims and exiles. Thus, we continue sorrowful by reason of our exile in the desert; we are held as hostages by the children of darkness. Often we are abandoned by God, with hunger and thirst, as a further test.[58]

Compared to such pain and anguish, the sorrow of despairing existentialists is small indeed. Beside this cry of pain which embraces all history, the cry of a solitary Man who is suffering both without and within, who suffers in His life and in His soul, who prays, groans, hopes and goes His way, already sensing in His soul the light of dawn, the pain and anguish of "pure humanists" is like the whining of little babes.

If this phenomenon contains a mystery, we should also recall that we men are weak. Just as we do not believe in the world's persecution because of an inferiority complex, so we do not believe in our own victory because of a belief in our own strength. We always look to God for help, and it is by virtue of the solidarity of the mystical body of Christ that we hope for victory. The example of Christ's victory encourages us to imitate Him in the struggle. "He did not will to come down from the cross because He wanted to teach us to bear insults . . . , to drink of the bitter cup now, and afterwards to receive everlasting happiness. Drink this bitter cup. . . . Do not tremble, since the Physician drank first, so that you would not hesitate."[59]

It is certain that as long as the world endures we shall have to live side by side with the wicked, but we should not attach too much importance to this disturbing company. We are like a quantity of unthreshed grain on the thrashing floor, both chaff and wheat. They eat, they labor, they exist at our side. Thou knowest, Lord, those whom Thou dost crush, and Thou knowest those whom Thou wilt not crush. All will be brought to light when they are winnowed.[60] "Let not the persecution by the wicked terrify you. They are like storms of winter howling down from the crags. They cannot last long, since they must drive onward to their appointed place and end."[61]

It is certain, however, that not all are of equal strength, even though they consider themselves powerful. This is what happened to St. Peter. Those who are not strong should pray. The perfect as well as the imperfect are written in God's book. The imperfect should not fear. Let them but continue along their route. . . . Let them advance as far as they can. They should progress each day, advance each day, and not separate themselves from the body of Christ.[62]

It happens that one of the temptations which the devil most frequently insinuates is that God does not provide timely help, so that we should look for other assistance, and then find ourselves unarmed in the hour of combat.[63] However, it is certain that God does not abandon us.[64] It is as when the apostles were foundering in the boat, and Christ was asleep in it;[65] when it was time to give aid, He gave it. Your faith must not fall asleep. It is true that persecutions do not cease as soon as we pray for their cessation, but God waits until the number of the elect is complete.[66] One thing is sure, that the bark of Peter can go on shifting for itself, but it is the only one which can continue navigating, continuously on the alert, carrying its passengers along a safe route, for they already have set their hopes on the port.[67]

13

The Father of This World

ARTICLE 1. *The devil's mastery over worldlings*

"THE DEVIL'S SIN DOES NOT CONSIST in drunkenness or adultery, but in pride. And since envy is the companion of pride, the devil envied men who were entering where he had been cast out forever. Therefore he tempts us and makes sin alluring." [1] The devil tempted Adam through pride and envy. In making common cause with him, Adam fell under the tyranny of the demon. This is the diabolical extension of original sin which revelation shows us in its two sources.

St. Augustine explains the scope of this dominion. It is not a question of rule over the physical world—this latter is subjected to God—but of domination in the moral world. Therefore the Apostle states that Satan is the prince of darkness, the prince of sinners, of unbelievers.[2] His is a dominion which is consolidated in the possession of the hearts of sinners. All the children of Adam were dominated by the demon. After Christ, those who believe are liberated from this tyranny. Before Christ, a few of the just were also freed, but they were an exception, whereas today it is common.[3] It is a question of the devil's influence in the heart of sinners, corrupting them and leading them to do his will in this world.

To illustrate the profoundity of this rule, St. Augustine resorts to all the similes and comparisons which indicate dominion. Employing concepts of government expressed in the New Testament, he constantly reiterates that the devil is the prince of this world and the prince of sinners.[4] Also, in commenting on one of Christ's thoughts, he asserts that the devil is the father of sinners. Sinners are his children, not because he has begotten them, but because they imitate him in lying, in pride, in impenitence, etc.[5] In another passage he completes the genealogy, stating that worldly individuals have the devil as their father and Babylon as their mother.[6] He attributes an especially degrading character to this rule over the worldly when he explains the devil's dominion over sinners as a response and a parody of Christ's rule in the souls of the just.

The pride of sinners is indeed a consequence of this rule, for the wicked are *members* of Satan. The devil is depicted as the *head* of sinners, even as Christ is the Head of the elect. The body of which Satan is the head has a very special response of its own, which is pride.[7] This effects a mutual penetration and reciprocal influence between the head and the members of this wretched body, which parallels that between Christ and His members in the realm of goodness. In a certain sense the devil appears before sinners as their judge, even as Christ appears before the elect.[8] And as Christ left a vicar in the world, who is to be His representative and personification, so at that time the devil also was personified in Judas. In this representation both were respectively the heads of the two "cities," each in his own category.[9]

Satan's dominion is limited and restricted, for he does not

possess the absolute power of destruction,[10] neither is his a dominion which signifies complete suppression of actual graces. But it is a dominion which shows us the depths of the "mystery of iniquity." The punishment for rebellion against God appears in all its terrible seriousness in subjugation to the demon. And man, who wished to be like God, has ended in being like the devil. He has terminated by being a member of Satan, in the sense that the devil has power over him, corrupting his heart and inclining his will to do evil. Whatever is consoling in the truth of the mystical body of Christ, of the mutual influence of the members and their dependence on Christ their Head, a dependence which is translated into vital influence and assistance in virtue, becomes shameful and depressing when it is a question of dependence on the devil and a society of those who are perfect in evil. This is the measure of the gravity of wickedness, but above all, the seriousness of the world's opposition to Christ. With an obstinacy which exceeds the constancy of the stars in their orbit, the forces of evil continue to oppose Christ and the elect from the beginning of the world. Employing all the coincidences of history and all the mistakes of human nature, in deed as well as in reasoning, they stubbornly persecute Christ, the Truth and the Light.

Yet, since there is no specifically diabolical manifestation, but rather since all the manifestations of this kind of evil are simultaneously human (pride, envy, hatred, etc.), the children of the devil are not conscious of such relationship and slavery. As Christ stated that the Jews were children of the devil, so the Church is compelled to say the same thing of worldlings. Nevertheless, they paid no attention to Christ, nor do the worldlings of today take seriously what the Church says to them.

St. Augustine repeated all this "in season and out of season." With comparisons to the dog, the dragon, the wolf, etc., he tries to show Christians the power of the demon. By his similes of wars and kings he attempts to instruct them regarding their constant hostility toward unbelievers. The two cities, he says, are like two kingdoms. All who prefer earthly joys to God, who seek what is not of Jesus Christ, belong to the city which is symbolically called Babylon; they have the devil as ruler. Those who have set their hearts on the things that are above, who meditate on heavenly things, who reflect seriously on not offending God, who are careful not to sin (but who, if they fall into sin, are not ashamed to confess it), who are gentle, holy, just, pious, good, all these belong to the city which has Christ as King. Babylon is older in the world; the other began afterwards. Cain was the founder of Babylon, Abel founded the other city. These two cities, like two armies under their respective leaders, are at war with one another until the end of time, until those now locked in deadly combat are separated, with one group placed on the right hand and the other on the left.[11]

Though it may seem otherwise to those who worship the liberty of man, there are no mere guerrilla fighters in this war. All operations must conform to an over-all strategy; and only the leader knows their tactical value.

Employing the serpent metaphor, he comments on Psalm 103, where it is stated that God gives to all animals their nourishment. He says: "He also provides food for the devil. If you live well, Christ will be your nourishment. If you separate yourselves from Christ, you will become the food of the devil. What was said to the serpent? That he would eat dust all the days of his life. You indeed know what the serpent's food is—dust. Do not desire to be dust, do not desire to take pleasure in dirt, for then you will become dirt. If you are not dust, the serpent will not devour you." [12]

In speaking of the treatment which Satan accords to his

own, of the courtesy which he reserves for them, St. Augustine likens him to a shepherd. He insists that he does not have absolute power to dispose of his own as he wishes, but his power over them is that of a master over his slaves, a shepherd over his animals, and he treats them accordingly.[13]

But St. Augustine carries the parallel beyond this life. Just as Christ will be the shepherd of the elect when they receive the reward of their toil, so also the devil will continue to be shepherd of the damned, of those who prosper now and ask what advantages they could derive from believing in Christ and not loving the things of this earth. Christ is life and Satan is death. Not because the devil is himself death, but because through him death came. In the next life the faithful will have Life as their shepherd; and the damned will have death as theirs. It will be death, not as separation of soul from body, but as separation of the soul from God.[14]

The means he employs to establish his rule are, in the first place, the pain and suffering which the human race endures since it sinned and permitted itself to be led by the devil. Man rebelled against God, and he was punished by becoming the devil's prisoner. This is the truth which Holy Scripture and the Church Fathers repeat continually. And Satan continues to expand the scope of his rule in every man, using diverse methods. St. Augustine names many of them: pride,[15] refusal to believe in Christ,[16] attachment to material things.[17] And these methods of control are the same that the devil uses to penetrate into the hearts of the faithful.

ARTICLE 2. *Temptations which the devil uses to secularize the faithful*

As prince of this world, the devil also has his influence on the faithful, even though they are not of the world. It is an influence which is fundamentally quite different from the one which he employs toward his own subjects, because this latter is that of a master toward his slave, a shepherd toward his own flock, whereas the former is exercised only because God permits it in order the better to purify His own children.[18] Satan's action is not an act of sovereignty but a trial or test. Nor is this an indiscriminate testing, but one which has its measure and reason. For St. Augustine the typical example is that of Job. By divine permission he was stripped of everything except his wife, in order to tempt him. Job did not lose his patience, nor his insight into the true nature of his situation: "The Lord gave, and the Lord hath taken away; blessed be the name of the Lord" (Job 1:21). St. Augustine cautions us that Job does not say, "The Lord gave, and the devil hath taken away," for all these trials of the righteous are permitted by God for the purification and coronation of His elect.[19]

In this same passage St. Augustine informs us what the devil really can do against us by divine permission. He can deprive us of everything except the virtues. What God desires of us is the sacrifice of a good conscience; and into that hidden sanctuary the devil cannot penetrate. Satan can deprive you of everything by his violence, but he cannot take away your faith without your consent. The demon makes war against us in two ways: in our *inner selves,* by arousing us against God's law; and *outside* us, by means of other human beings or things. The inner warfare is more distressing and is planned in a crafty manner. Each individual is tempted where he is most vulnerable. When Satan sets up an outward temptation, it is because he knows he has allies and accomplices within. Avarice rules you by means of love of money. The devil knows this, and he suggests to you here, in your external acts, some sharp piece of business (the Saint uses the word *fraud,* but today it is called sharp business practice).[20] St. Augustine thinks the devil can also take a hand in cases of illness. In these outward trials he uses the wicked in order to see whether he can make us worldly, and he uses the good, who at times by their ridicule or language attempt to prevent the Christian from fervently following Christ. Usually Christians bear quite well the temptations which come from illness, but they become upset by temptations which come to them from their fellow men. They forget the true meaning of the temptations and who is their author. They also forget that through such temptations they may receive a crown.[21]

Speaking of Christians who test their fellow Christians, St. Augustine classifies them among the devil's allies, as were Eve and the serpent.[22] Furthermore, the aberration of such persons remains unexplained. The devil knows well what he is seeking to accomplish in tempting Christians; he is anti-Christ and will always be a persecutor of Christians. He knows that he is persecuting Christ. But you, a Christian, what are you persecuting in your fellow Christian? [23]

St. Augustine considers it so impossible that the devil should cease to persecute Christians, that he asks those who believe that definitive peace already is here (because the Roman emperors have become Christian), whether perchance the devil himself has become a Christian.[24]

St. Augustine, who frequently notes the opposition of the two kingdoms, also calls attention to the opposition between the two rulers. He frequently explains that the devil has no relationship with Christ, since Christ, who without sin assumed our flesh in the womb of Mary, has nothing which belongs to the demon. From this pure principle of light arises an offensive against the darkness and the kingdom of darkness which the devil rules. The struggle occurs in every man and in every aspect of man's nature, in all men and in every type of individual.[25] It is a war which, as we were saying, the devil wages through his members.[26] Although outwardly it appears that Christ abandons His own—as in the case of the martyrs who cry out for justice when it seems that justice nowhere is visible—it is certain that He does not desert His own.[27]

The cure for all these miseries and wars rests with God, not with us. We pray so that we may obtain help. Close the door of your heart, and there pray to God. Satan does not cease pounding at the door, but if he sees you have locked it, he goes his own way.[28] In this same passage the Saint recommends the remembrance of hell. In other passages he speaks of the remembrance of Christ who became man, to teach us how to endure the sufferings and attacks which the devil inflicts upon us through our fellow men. To teach us this lesson, he refers especially to Judas.[29]

Nor could he fail to recall the Christian's response to this struggle which the devil's members inaugurate. Later we shall consider it in more detail, but it is well to take note of it now: "Pray for help against the devil who incites, and pray for those whom the demon incites and moves." [30]

Among the numerous deceptions which Satan prepares for his own flock, St. Augustine points to certain ones which he describes as "the devil's sacraments" (*sacramenta diaboli*). In reading his works I have come to the conclusion that he does not refer to any permanent method of deceiving, but rather to certain well-concealed snares, such as the remnants of pagan rites and practices or popular superstitions. Since the Saint does not consider these regular or permanent tactics of Satan, I have not included them in my investigation of his wiles.[31]

14

What God Thinks of the World

THE "CITY OF MAN" believes that, geographically, the "City of God" is *there*, like any earthly kingdom; one is *here* and the other *there*. This is a kind of horizontal view of life. As a consequence, the most important worldlings respect what those of the "City of God" think, because they are two kingdoms with different latitudes, but *within the scope of humanity*.

But God arranges these two kingdoms vertically; one is below, the other is above; one is inferior, the other is superior; one is earthly, the other is heavenly. The Ruler of the heavenly kingdom is above all created things; He transcends them all. He is above material bodies, above spirits, above time, above all. He is the apotheosis of excellence, the very apex of being. On the other hand, the citizens of this world are miserable reptiles who eat dirt, who gorge themselves with filth and dust. Indeed, they themselves are dirt. The distance between these two kingdoms is as great as that which obtains between light and darkness.[1]

Looked at in this manner, vertically, from God's height

and by divine standards, what are worldly persons? St. Augustine has a rich collection of comparisons; he has a clear idea of their wretched existence and their fatal future.

THE DEGRADATION OF THE WORLDLY

Considered as a human being, the worldly individual is a poor slave, like the Jews whom the Egyptians subjugated and forced to make bricks for them.[2] Such a person is classified as a slave, like Abraham's bondswoman.[3] Perhaps all this seems insufficient to Augustine, and he pursues it further: the life of the world is a bestial existence, because beasts live by what they find here below and take their pleasure in what is here below.[4] As beasts we already have observed that he compares them to the fish of the ocean which consume one another. He also compares them to falcons because of their haughty attitude and arrogance, to mules and donkeys because of their lowliness. They are tied to the treadmill of material things as to a millstone.[5] What worldly individuals desire is the same as what stupid brutes want; and when they ask God for anything they ask for health, which they hold in common with all brute creation, as if they were asking Him for some great gift; and in life they seek the things that animals seek.[6]

RELATIONS WITH GOD

All this is the result of a much worse situation. The true state of worldly persons is their status in relation to God. Everything else serves to demonstrate their degradation, but this is their true personality. The worldly individual is an enemy of God. "Lovers of the world are enemies of God," is the expression which St. Augustine so often repeats. And he resorts to a parable to substantiate it. The soul is the spouse of

God and owes Him all its love. If it loves someone besides God, it is an adulteress. Now every adulterous woman is the enemy of her husband. So also with the soul.[7] Because of this enmity, therefore, God hates the soul which loves earthly happiness.[8] Christ did not wish to pray for the world, because those whom He has chosen are not a part of it.[9] Indeed, they are considered as anti-Christs.[10] Therefore, too, the Holy Ghost will convict the world of sin, because it has not believed; of justice, because it had no reason for not believing; and of judgment, condemning it with the same sentence by which He condemned the prince of this world.[11]

IN THIS LIFE A REIGN OF TERROR

One of the temptations by which the demon deceives the world is to make man think that God's punishments are reserved for the next life, but that in this one he will enjoy himself stupendously.[12] This notion is completely false. It is certain that at life's end they will receive a special punishment, which is well known, but in this life also they will be punished. St. Augustine touches extensively on this point: concupiscence is like a burning fire. Now then, if fire burns your clothes, will not concupiscence also burn your soul? If you place live coals on your breast, they will burn you; if you are planning an act of adultery, will it not burn you? But to more than one person this probably will appear as a delicious, sweet fire, and you may claim that there are few indeed who think of it as punishment.

Precisely for this reason the Holy Ghost insists on saying that He will punish sinners by delivering them over to the desires of their own heart. It is like a dissolution, decomposing them by the heat of the fire. It is a dissolution and destruction which results from their inconstancy in chastity. When they surrender to their own desires they are melted, liquefied, as it were, and hence have no firmness of constancy. The first sin is pride and apostasy from God; the ultimate punishment is damnation, but everything in between is likewise sin, and simultaneously, punishment for sin: avarice, frauds, etc. Men began by thinking themselves wise, and their hearts were dried up in folly.[13] If we were to express this in our present-day speech, we should say that the punishment of the wicked is an inward restlessness and dissatisfaction which consumes them, carrying them to the verge of madness.[14]

Outwardly we observe that class of men who are of no use in helping others, who do not even have the stature of men. The *Confessions* of St. Augustine is a study of these happy worldlings and these impoverished individuals. One would have had to live indoors constantly not to recognize the daily reality of this observation by St. Augustine. We already have touched on this subject earlier in discussing the anguish and boredom of the worldly and in evaluating their form of happiness. Now we repeat the idea in order to emphasize that in all these situations it is God's hand which is meting out punishment.

There is a second punishment: blindness of the mind. Such persons are established in the world; they judge by worldly standards and ultimately they understand nothing but worldly standards. They consider the Commandments meaningless because, in truth, they are not made to satisfy man's desires. Moreover, the Commandments have the temerity to brand as evil what the worldly consider happiness. Basically the matter is very grave. Here it is a question of nothing less than that God hides Himself from them and they do not perceive the truth. For them the sun has set. They go their way, guided by their own desires, their pride and their anger. These are all fire which emit much smoke; but the sun has not yet risen for them.[15] This is no exaggeration. Daily we encounter more and more men who believe that worldly values are the only ones; they understand nothing else. On such standards they have built governmental policy, a system of justice, business. And according to these norms they plan wars and evaluate victories. When these blind men assemble to arrange the world, we know beforehand how they will arrange it.

The Saint describes another punishment: the way in which such persons, deceived by the attraction of immediate appearances, become unaware of their own future. They are deceptive sins, like those thorny plants which have thistles when they are no longer tender. When they were sprouting they were soft and beautiful; later they became thorny. So too with sins; at first they give delight, as if they would not prick. But we should note that the thorns already are in the plant, because this species bears them. Thus, sin of its very nature bears the thorns of damnation.[16]

But God is not nervous, and hence His punishments do not have the quality of impatience. What we call God's wrath is not tumultuous and emotional, but rather a serene anger. It does not resemble a streak of lightning or a hurricane.[17] It is eternal, and always manifests itself at the right moment. Indeed, this actually happens when it seems as though nothing is happening. But then the symptoms of punishment begin to appear, and even the near-sighted can see that God has lowered His hand. At other times His punishment is scarcely audible; it can only be perceived from within, where we experience a coldness, without light or warmth, an exile from God and an insensitivity to the things of God. If His punishments do not have the quality of impatience, they often bear the mark of power and might. Occasionally they discharge a squall of misfortunes upon the proud, and this shakes them to the very foundation of their being, if it does not entirely dislodge those who seemed firmer than the mountains themselves.[18] Yet even then He is not impatient, and judging from human nervousness it seems that His chastisement has arrived later than expected.

Let us remember that punishments are in proportion to men's pride and their trust in their own possessions. Therefore when a man is worldly, not through perverseness but because of weakness, punishment always has a medicinal function, and together with this more or less bitter medicine, God continues to supply completely supernatural remedies, such as charity.[19] Finally, when an individual loves the world, this is a sign of illness which should be treated.[20]

But all this represents aspects of a permanent economy which the Saint calls the regimen of fear. But Christianity is the regimen of love: of God's love for men and of men's love for God. The world, however, is subject to the rule of fear. St. Paul says that Christians have not received the spirit of fear, but rather the spirit of adoption by which we cry to God and call Him Father. Explaining these words, St. Augustine states that the spirit of fear was the rule in the Old Testament, and in saying that the New Testament possesses the spirit of adoption of children, the Apostle is showing us the profound difference which exists between the two Covenants. In the New Testament we are under the rule of love, but God subjugated the Jews to the regimen of fear. They feared Him, for He held death in His hands.

The Saint notes that this was the Lord's providence, because they were devoted to acquiring the things of this world for themselves. Here is the connection which exists between worldly possessions and the rule of fear, and not simply because they were under the Law. This regimen of fear is the rule of slavery. But this did not cease with the coming of the New Testament except for those who had been adopted as God's children, for those who satisfy their carnal desires and augment their sins by their lies are following the same rule. And it is the Holy Ghost Himself who torments them with terror so that they may be converted and depart from Satan, who is resolved in any case not to release them.[21]

With reference to this fear and terror, St. Augustine has written definitive pages and it is regrettable that we can do no more than summarize them. He divides fear into chaste and unchaste fear. Unchaste fear is fear of God because He can send the soul to everlasting torments. "If you fear God because of punishment, you still do not love Him whom you fear." Chaste fear is apprehensive lest God leave us, thus depriving us of His friendship. It is a fear born of love. The former fears the punishment; the latter loves the good, loves God. Then the Saint explains his thoughts by means of a comparison. Let us imagine two married women. One has a will which inclines to evil; she longs to commit adultery, she delights in wickedness, but is afraid that her husband will catch her. Since she loves evil, she fears her husband. For such a woman the presence of her husband is not agreeable, but rather disagreeable. But if she behaves sinfully, she is apprehensive that her husband may return home. Such also are the persons who fear the coming of Judgment Day.

Now let us consider another married woman, chaste, loving her husband, a wife who would not commit adultery for anything in the world. Her desire is to live at home with her husband. Actually both wives are apprehensive. One fears that her husband may appear; the other fears that he may disappear. One says: "I am afraid he may punish me"; the other says: "I am afraid he may go away." [22] The fear which tortures the adulterous woman, which will not leave her in peace, subjecting her to anxiety and suspicion within herself, this is the fear which racks the worldly. Those who cherish their own sins, who run after the world, are subject to this reign of terror. It is these who use God's "absence" to commit adultery. Finally, the world as creation has its master, and the human heart, too, has its master. The day will come when the heart must render its account. That fear of a reckoning is what the worldly constantly experience in their hearts, if indeed God's mercy confer upon them this gift of salutary fear.

Such is the regimen of terror and death, for the world is the death of the soul. We have stated earlier that this is always a disease; if this disease becomes serious, it kills the soul. It destroys the soul as surely if it clings to temporal possessions as if it loses grace through other vices and sins.[23] As a consequence, it will not surprise us that a worldly life is disqualified and is considered a false life; in fact, no life at all. We have touched on this point previously.[24] It is a thought which St. Augustine constantly repeats. In the passage which we cited earlier, to enumerate the punishments of sinners in this life, he adds: "Why did he not say simply 'the living,' instead of 'as if they were living,' except because the life of the wicked is false?" They are not really alive, but it seems to them that they are very much alive. Those who do not wish to reform seem alive, but they are not really living.[25]

This is exactly what they were looking for—to be alive, in a completely independent sense; yet now it transpires that in God's sight this life is reputed false—with the further deception that it appears true, so that their injury is even more grave.

ITS LEGACY IS DARKNESS

We have already stated that one of the world's shortcomings is that it does not look ahead. If it would look to that which will definitely come to pass, it would be cured of its malady. When things are viewed in their present state, in the pomp of their existence, they are capable of deceiving. When we survey the world's broad highway, filled with wayfarers who invite us, we could readily believe that this is the better route. St. Augustine also once knew this blindness, and prescribed for it: It is not foolish that you should consider what is going to happen to the wealthy who prosper in this world, what will be their ultimate destiny if they do not reform their lives. For those who now thunder loudly will then be struck by lightning.[26] And that other statement: "Perhaps you like the way of sinners because the road is broad and crowded. You observe that it is wide, but you do not see where it leads. At the end there is a precipice . . . ; and those who travel this way joyfully and confidently plunge down at the end." [27]

The Saint has one formula and example which he continually reiterates in an effort to impress upon the faithful this last end of the world. The formula is that the worldly flourish in time but perish in eternity.[28] The example is from the Gospels: The world (like a panorama of human life) is a thrashing floor where wheat and straw intermingle. The wheat is the elect, and God will preserve them in His granary without losing a single grain. The straw is the worldly. So long as the world endures, God continues to thrash the corn and winnow the grain. The straw blasphemes because it is being crushed. The wheat patiently bears God's thrashing, and hopes that it may enter the eternal granaries. Before all is over, the day of winnowing will come, when the straw will be separated from the wheat. Afterwards all the straw will be burned.[29] This is the final result of the attitudes and loves of these two "cities." The city established by Cain, which always seems to excel Abel's city, which has its heart always fixed on the earth, living the life of man, which so nourishes human pride that they love their darkness more than the Light who came to illumine their lives, this city will have darkness as its enduring heritage.[30]

This is what we said earlier when we defined the world. The world is the aggregate of moral evil and of all iniquity.

The world is the congregation of the damned and of those who must damn themselves, including the very devils. Therefore Christ did not pray for the world, and therefore, too, it will not see Him. It rejected Him; and now the world also is rejected.[31]

TWO

I have chosen you

JOHN 15:16

15

Two Victories over the Human Element

ALL THAT WE HAVE CONSIDERED up to this point concerns the human enigma in its roots and its transcendence. This human enigma presents only two types of problems: the problems of man as an individual and those of man in society. We have considered both of these. We have seen man fleeing from God, restlessly gathering his flock and departing from his Father, in order *to live his own life*. When the prodigal son left his father's house, the Gospel records the character of his life and activities: "He lived in lust among prostitutes." We have noted that man's whole life has this characteristic and this preoccupation with baseness—with adultery, as St. Augustine often expressed it. We have also seen what man has achieved: anxiety, torment, bestiality. In the same category we find those who wanted to slay God in order to provide a new set of values for things human, truly to discover man. [E.g., Nietzsche, *Jenseits von Gut und Böse*.] What they have succeeded in doing is to bring man to the gates of despair and madness. Together God and man were walking along life's highway, but it seemed to these "humanists" that God was overshadowing man, so they fired their shots in order to destroy God. What happened was that they destroyed man. And yet they claim that they can see!

When man fled from God he was changed into darkness, because apart from God there is only darkness. But even in the gloom God's merciful eyes followed after that fleeing shadow, until one day He grasped man by the shoulder, turned him around, and brought him face to face with God.[1] This was the victory over the humanism attempted by the rebellious; turning man back to divine support, which is the only way in which man can continue to be man.

But man bears in his nature a social instinct which transcends the narrowness of his personal horizon. For this phase of human nature, too, it was an unquestionable tragedy that man separated himself from God. An unwelcome ally, the devil, assisted at the gathering of the rebels. After the "City of Man" was established, one always had to reckon with Satan, since he was one of the founders. Thus it transpired that the "City of Man" was doomed to fail because it was founded on egoism and because it would have to give place to the diabolical city. Whoever loves the world cannot love his brother.[2] Even the blind can see this, and by means of Communism they have tried to provide a social solution to man's selfishness. But what they have succeeded in accomplishing is to form, not a human but a diabolical society, which is exactly what happened in Paradise at the creation of the world. God has also provided for this human necessity, sublimating man's need for the society of men and changing it into a divine fellowship in which He Himself is King and Head, Lord and Father. Had this human need for fellowship not been provided by the "City of God," then one of the noblest human tendencies would have been frustrated.

God never deceives, and He has been wondrous in providing for this need. The foundation of the Church is an answer to the world, and as the fellowship of all the elect it is not only a mercy of God but also an act of mercy which is singularly in accord with what the human heart longed for. But His mercy has shown forth in such abundance that He has given them much more than they asked for. The following pages continue as a further study of the world, but from the standpoint of the divine response. Since there are only two areas, that of the world and that of the elect, in studying the latter we shall understand more clearly the nature of the citizens of the world. If previously we have examined the dark aspects of the picture, now we shall see the luminous parts. Only thus can we truly evaluate the *chiaroscuro* of a work of art, and thus will the values of the light be made known.

16

The World's Frontiers

WHERE DOES THE WORLD END and Christ's kingdom begin? Are there clear, objective boundaries which allow us to indicate with precision the limits of the two "cities"? Before specifically responding to this inquiry, we should thoroughly consider what this question comprises, as well as its implications.

The world is out of joint, and for that reason man remained separated from God as his supernatural end. This, then, is a human problem, for its object is man, raised to a supernatural level, and it is there that the dislocation occurred.

Since it is a human problem, any answer to this question will have to take the human element into consideration. Specifically, as God preferred to let man fall rather than to deprive him of his freedom, so now his restoration, if it is to parallel his fall, will likewise respect his freedom.

Whatever establishes the dividing line between the two kingdoms must be something which, while continuing to respect the human element, will once again center man in God. However, none of the moral or cardinal virtues unites us with God immediately. They all presuppose another virtue, which binds us immediately to God. Therefore it must be a theological virtue. It seemed (and for many worldlings it still seems) that temperance was enough to draw a line of separation from the world. Yet this is not a virtue which unites, but one which divides. It separates from worldly things and from their improper use. It is not a virtue that joins us immediately to God; and this after all, is where the disruption exists.

It must be a virtue which centers man in God and radically destroys the entire anthropocentric tendency which sin introduced. It must be a virtue which takes into account man's intellectual pre-eminence with respect to the rest of creation, which touches him through this, the loftiest aspect of his nature. Yet it must not be exclusively intellectual, a virtue which neglects the fact that man, as a person, is something more than mind. He is life, and transcendent life. He projects this transcendence by means of the mind, but not by the mind alone, for love also is transcendent.

It must be an answer which solves the problem of human happiness, or it will be no solution, because men will not accept anything which does not restore happiness to them, whether this be an immediate restoration or a trustworthy promise.

It must also be medicinal—at least this appears fitting—and accordingly a remedy which eliminates pride, the cause of man's fall, and includes humble submission to God.

It must be something so advanced in God's dominions that all else is predicated upon it.

It must be something so clear and lucid that it allows no doubts, and yet so accessible that all men can find it.

ARTICLE 1. *Faith defines the limits of both kingdoms*

What is it that marks the boundaries between these two domains? What determines that from here to there is the extent of the world and from here to there the limits of the Church, the realm of the elect? Is there one element or are there several which fulfill all these requirements? St. Augustine has no doubt as to the answer, and he repeats it many times. What delimits these two zones is *faith*. "The wicked man is justified, not through the merits of previous works, but by faith, as the Apostle says: 'But to him who does not work, but believes in Him who justifies the impious, his faith is credited to him as justice' (Rom. 4:5), in order that afterwards faith itself may begin to work by means of love." [1] Commenting on Jesus' words, "He that believeth in Me, although he die, yet shall he live," St. Augustine says: "Believe; and though you die, yet shall you live. But if you believe not, you are dead. . . . Why is the soul dead? Because it does not have faith. Why is the body dead? Because there is no soul there. Therefore the soul of your soul is faith." [2] He expresses the same thought, but in other words, when he says that the demon wants to dwell in men's hearts and there to take advantage by his presence to whisper seductions to them. But what did Jesus Christ say? "Now will the prince of this world be cast out" (John 12:31). Cast out of where? Cast out of heaven and earth? Cast out of the believer's heart. He has cast out the invader, so that the Redeemer may dwell therein.[3]

It is not necessary to multiply texts, for this is something evident. Earlier, St. Augustine informed us that what the Holy Ghost will charge against this world of sin is unbelief. And this sin is so basic that if the world were not guilty of unbelief, it would have no other sin.[4]

But a difficulty arises. Faith is not always understood in the same sense in the New Testament. And since St. Augustine depends on the New Testament, in what sense does he understand it?

In the New Testament one can observe a certain breadth

of concept in speaking of the virtue of faith; and the limits of this virtue with respect to hope and to charity are not always defined with precision:

1) Sometimes faith means all the virtues, at least indirectly. It is called faith *in sensu praegnante* and then is used either to include hope and charity or only one of these virtues.

2) At other times it is used in the strict sense of faith and belief.

3) Again, it signifies a tendency or inclination toward God in general.

4) Lastly, it refers to an inclination centered on Christ and God.

Evidently, since St. Augustine depends on the New Testament for all his statements on this matter, we find all these meanings in his writings. But beyond each of them, transcending each of these variants, we can affirm, *a priori*, that St. Augustine will place the boundaries of the world at that point at which the supernatural begins as justification. Speaking of the attraction which the Father exerts so that we will approach Christ ("No one comes except the Father draw him"),[5] he insists at length that faith is a theological virtue which is proper to the intellect. There he denounces heretics at length because of their false interpretation of the truths of faith. And if one has a false opinion of the truths of faith, it is not the Father who has drawn him. He ends with an exclamation concerning the knowledge of truth: "What does the soul desire more ardently than to know the truth? Why should man have his mouth ready and his sense of taste untainted for the recognition of truth, except to eat and drink wisdom (which, for St. Augustine, is knowledge of God), justice, truth, eternity?" This is the uttermost limit of the supernatural, faith as knowledge of God and His truths.

It is faith which puts us on the true path to God. Afterwards it is a question of who will or who will not travel along that path, but one is then already on the right road. St. Augustine further clarifies the limits when he states the following in explaining the meaning of the Epistle to the Romans and its clarification by St. James' epistle: "The apostle James wrote to correct those who, presuming on faith, did not want to perform good works. . . . He praised the great work of Abraham, but faith was its foundation, the root was in faith. For if Abraham had made his sacrifice without faith, it would have profited him nothing, nor would anything else that he had done. . . . But is it possible that prior to faith we can perform any single act which we can say is good? All works which are performed prior to faith are useless, even though they may appear praiseworthy in the eyes of men. They are like great efforts or a strenuous race along the wrong road. Let no one presume that the works he performed prior to faith are good. Where there was no faith, there was no good whatsoever. An act or work is good by virtue of the intention with which it is performed; the intention is the faith which directs it. . . . Imagine a man, a great mariner, who has lost his compass direction and his route. Of what avail is it for him to confront the waves skillfully, to strike a balance and keep the ship on an even keel when the waves break over the side, to use all his talent for sailing, if when you ask him where he is going, he answers that he does not know or that he is going to hit against a reef? Is it not true that all his knowledge and skill become handicaps since they more readily lead him to shipwreck? Now such is he who travels outside the right road. . . . Much better is the man who takes the right road and progresses satisfactorily along it, . . . who does not lose his way completely, or halt, even though he may make some slight error in his course." [6]

The least that can be expected of a man is that he travel

in the right direction. The direction is anterior to the work, anterior to everything. Before the direction of our course toward God we have nothing, nothing. There are, if you wish, says the Saint, acts and works for which a man will receive honor or will avoid being hanged, but all this pertains completely to the world. But prior to possessing faith, there is nothing of God's kingdom.[7] On the other hand it is evident that St. Augustine clearly distinguishes faith from the other theological virtues, asserting that faith can exist without hope and charity, and that such faith is the beginning of our personal redemption.[8]

As a practical example there is the conversion of St. Augustine, where the transition from the world to God is described in detail; and the transition is brought about by faith. St. Augustine took the Scripture and read: "Let us walk becomingly as in the day, not in revelry and drunkenness, not in debauchery and wantonness, not in strife and jealousy (the whole picture of worldliness, and now comes God's portion) but put on the Lord Jesus Christ, and as for the flesh, take no thought for its lusts" (Rom. 13:13–14). "I had no desire to read any farther," continues St. Augustine, "for no sooner had I finished the sentence than it seemed as if the light of certainty had entered into my heart; all the darkness of my doubts vanished."

What is the name of that light? We need not resort to syllogisms: "Alipius asked to see what I was reading. I showed it to him, and he noted what follows: 'Him who is weak in faith, receive' " (Rom. 14:1).[9] I believe I should not insist on this, but I thought it opportune to mention it, in order to point out that the doctrine of justification defined by the Council of Trent had already dawned in St. Augustine.[10]

It is not necessary to point out that St. Augustine also teaches that faith without charity is merely the direction, but does not necessarily mean that one is traveling along the way. So useless, in the last analysis, is faith without love, that it does not save. Stressing the question of the direction which is achieved through faith, he amplifies this concept, stating that the Christian has an obligation not only "to have the right direction" but also to make progress on the road. We make progress by means of charity, by "living faith." Because to believe and not to act or to have a dead faith does not establish any definitive difference from the demons. In order that we may not presume on faith, St. John himself joins it immediately to love; because faith without love is sterile. Faith with love is the faith of Christians; faith without love is the faith of demons. And those who have not faith are even worse than demons. Let us suppose a person does not want to believe in Christ. Such an individual is not even imitating the devils. Let us imagine another who believes in Christ, but hates Him. Such a person's confession of faith consists in his fear of punishment, but not in the love which crowns faith. This is precisely the faith of the demons, who likewise fear punishment.[11]

ARTICLE 2. *Faith in Christ as the immediate bond with God*

We have stated that in the New Testament faith sometimes has its polarization in Christ. "To believe in Christ." This is the most constant element in St. Augustine, because it is this which best explains the pattern of God's work. In the very passages from his commentary on the Epistle of St. John, which I have just cited, St. Augustine explains this subject by amplifying the parable so dear to him, that of the prodigal son. As fugitives we had strayed far from God. Moreover, we were sick. Then the Physician Himself came to us; He who is the Way offered Himself to pilgrims.[12]

The continual repetition of this idea, always unsatisfied, achieves a majestic synthesis in the book, *De utilitate credendi:* "One cannot deny that human wisdom is an intermediary point between the foolishness of man and the purity of divine truth. So far as his human capacity allows, the wise man imitates God; on the other hand, the ignorant person, so that his imitation may bear fruit, has no model as near as the wise man. But . . . as the ignorant person finds it difficult to understand abstract concepts, it is appropriate that some miracles should be presented to his sight, for the ignorant use their eyes better than their reason, in order that by means of the previous purification of their life and conduct, under the guidance of learned men, they may be prepared to accept what is reasonable. If, then, it is necessary to imitate man—and we cannot place our whole confidence in man—could the divine goodness show itself more generous than when the pure, everlasting, unchangeable divine Wisdom, to whom we must of necessity join ourselves, condescended to assume human form, thus offering us in His life examples and stimuli to follow in His way?" [13]

St. Augustine repeats this constantly in his public sermons: "What is your life? Faith. 'The just man lives by faith.' And those who do not believe? They are dead. . . . Now the hour is come, and it is here even now, in which the dead shall hear the voice of the Son of God. And those that hear it will live. Whence will they live? They will live by life. By what life? By Christ's life." [14] What a marvelous way of curing man, eliminating his egocentric tendency, and at the same time causing him to continue in the loftiest human lineage! Faith touches man in the noblest aspect of his nature, and subjects him to God. Man's center is no longer man, but God. Yet it touches him by means of Jesus Christ, the flower and glory of human flesh; by means of the wisdom of God, and not through any angel, which would present another parallel step to that other angel who brought about the fall. Faith is the re-establishment of that order which was broken at the original fall, and in all other falls. It is the recovery of the right direction. With faith there no longer exists that humanistic sense of "having lost our way" along the road. We have recovered our right direction, but not only intellectually. We begin there, but the recovery is more profound.

Faith impels us toward God not only as the source of truth announced in His word, but as the supernatural end of human life, joining us immediately to the divine link which is Christ. It draws us out of ourselves, impels us toward Him with the speed and assurance of an arrow which is shot from a bow stretched taut by Christ Himself. Something like this, it seems to me, is the Redemption and the outstretched posture of the Cross.

Thus we have stated that faith is no mere mental exercise. Let no one confuse faith with a wretched method of avoiding science in order to continue to presume on one's brains. Faith is something more profound. When it is restricted to the mind it becomes paralyzed. Faith is an adventure in salvation, and is as absorbing as life itself. Men who have faith but do not actualize this concept of salvation and vitality, end by not knowing whether or not they believe. Rather than inner illumination—which it also possesses—and clarity of orientation, faith is the certitude of obtaining the things we hope for. It is an interior dialogue with that which we have within and has not yet been fully revealed. "And you entered into His abode, sweeter than any light, deeper than any secret, more sublime than any honor." [15] "Let the *faithful* become the body of Christ, in order to *live* by the Spirit of Christ . . . , for the body of Christ can live only by the Spirit of Christ (as your body lives by your spirit). . . . O mystery of mercy! O pledge of oneness! O chain of charity! Whoever desires to *live* now has a place to live, a source of life. Let him come, *let him believe* so that he may be incorporated, and he will be *quickened*. . . . Let him cling to that body, let him live through God, for God. [Let him live] now on this earth, in order to reign in heaven." [16]

Faith has restored to his life the divine dimension. It has restored him to "God, . . . that third dimension in which man finds his profundity." [17] Those who have tried to withdraw into their own depths, devoid of God, have ended by saying many stupid things or by going mad. But if we abandon God, can we continue speaking of man's "interior"? Many people respond thoughtlessly; they have preferred to flee to the "exterior." Communism, for example, thinks that man possesses naught within himself, that he has nothing to do here. Actually, we are on a completely animal level here, for neither do animals have an "interior." It is God who restored man's "interior." What previously was a "vacuum dripping sadness" is now a temple illuminated with harmonious life of the dawn. "For you have died, and your life is hidden with Christ in God. When Christ, your life, shall appear, then you too will appear with Him in glory" (Col. 3:3–4). And we also, who believe and possess the first-fruits of the Spirit (because by faith we are joined to God in spirit, no longer as mere creatures, but as God's children), "groan within ourselves, awaiting the adoption and redemption of our body." This adoption already is a reality in them that believe; but it is of the spirit, not of the body, because the body has not yet experienced that celestial transformation which the soul already has received by the reconciliation of faith, laying aside its errors and returning to God.[18]

We shall return to this discovery of man's inner depth. Let us insist for the moment that faith brings the answer to the problem of happiness; not in this life, where it never will be perfect, but in the next. Yet we should observe that the distribution of happiness is as inexact as that which we noted earlier in speaking of worldly happiness. If it was not completely correct previously to state that the wicked are happy here and that afterwards, in the other life, they will be unhappy, so also it is false to assert that the believers will be happy only in the other life. The words which we have just quoted speak to us of a spiritual adoption, of an interior life. They allude to a sweet and luminous intimacy. In those words which we cited, when Augustine was describing the progress of the faithful as a pilgrimage through the desert of life, he was also careful to recall that the faithful have some drops of refreshment along their route. Better still, as travelers they have before them the majestic figure of Christ with arms outstretched, reminding them that He is the Way and the Source of life.[19] It is but natural that a happiness too long postponed would exhaust man's limited patience. An answer which did not include happiness would not even be human.

ARTICLE 3. *Faith and human freedom*

Finally, faith is a sublime consideration which God shows for human freedom and at the same time it involves our subjection to God. In various passages, but especially in a well-known text, St. Augustine touched on the question of grace and freedom in the initial act of faith: "No man can come to Me except the Father, who hath sent Me, draw him." The Saint comments: "What a powerful commendation of grace! No man cometh if he is not drawn. Whom He draws and whom He does not draw, why He draws one and not another, do not attempt to determine these things unless you wish to fall into error. Have you not been drawn to Him as yet? Then pray that you may be drawn." And he alludes to a difficulty: "If we are drawn, then, when we believe, we no longer are free. Therefore, we are under compulsion, and we do not believe of our own free will." This is a serious matter, for such an act destroys the entire human foundation, and accordingly it is without merit. The Saint replies: "One can enter a church without desiring to do so, can approach the altar without so willing, can receive the sacraments without willing this; but one believes only when he desires to. If one believed with the body, it would be possible to believe under compulsion; but we do not believe by means of the body. The Apostle states this: 'We believe with the heart, unto justice.' The act of faith proceeds from the roots of the heart." [20]

The question of freedom and faith became sufficiently clear, in its basic lines, through principles given by St. Augustine. Subsequently, the human mind exerted itself to the maximum in order to justify this reconciliation. Today, nevertheless, it seems that many do not formulate the problem this way in practice. It appears to me that all are convinced that if they believe, they do so because they will it; they believe with the full freedom of their decision. Afterwards the problem arises; they think that if they believe they will be compelled to be consistent, and that they will lose their freedom. This is a fear, more instinctive than reasoned, that they will not continue to live as free men. In other words, it is a question of a worldly reaction which, despite all arguments for believing, despite knowing that truth is found in the faith, still wishes to continue without being subjected to anyone. It is the same as in Adam's day.

However, faith never possesses the quality of anti-human repression, but as worldlings themselves acknowledge in their flight from it, faith demands subjection. The Saint replies in two ways to the charge of coercion. One is by explaining that

God, in attracting us, is evidently seeking a pleasant method and one which suits us best. He does not draw us to Himself through a cold syllogism, but in another way, which is pleasing to us. This is one more of God's mercies. St. Augustine explains the other characteristic by saying that faith is precisely a restoration of freedom and a liberation. Explaining the former, he states that if we show a green branch to a sheep, we attract him, or if we show a bauble to a child, he comes at once. If this happens with material, corporeal things, what will occur in Christ's dispensation, when the Father draws us? If a man is powerfully drawn by truth, righteousness, wisdom, eternity, then will he not be drawn by Christ, who is all these things? [21] And the Saint turns to qualified witnesses: "Give me a man who loves, and he will know what I am talking about. Give me one who desires to love, give me one who is hungry, give me a wanderer in the desert, thirsting for the fountain of his everlasting homeland, and you will see that he knows what I am saying. But if I speak with a cold individual, he does not understand me." [22]

The second kind of liberty contained in faith is based on the Gospel assertion: "The truth shall make you free"; or another statement, which is an equation: "If the Son free you, then shall you be truly free." He studies the grades of freedom and in what this truly consists. But he also notes that the Jews, proud of their freedom as children of Abraham, disdained the liberty of believers.[23] In the next chapter we shall discuss this subject at greater length.

To conclude, when St. Augustine places the frontiers and limitations of the world in faith, he has sensed perfectly the whole doctrine of justification and its antecedents. Historically, the grace of the Law did not justify men. A second grace was needed—faith in Christ. For the individual it is of faith that justification, too, begins with faith. St. Augustine saw the problem in its two dimensions.

By establishing the frontiers of this world in the faith, God has freed us from all the pride of humanity. No longer will any race be able to boast presumptuously of its peculiar racial merits as ponderable categories in God's kingdom. All nations and races have been called to faith; and faith is completely gratuitous. No human merit earns it.

In this way God has freed men from their enslavement to professional intellectuals. The principle by which men will be selected will no longer be that of knowledge, but that of grace. In the presence of this grace no human value possesses importance, neither those of blood, nor of knowledge, nor of money. The poor and ignorant are in the same class as the powerful. God has definitely answered the "wise," placing human salvation in something which surpasses man's control and knowledge, in something which appears to man as foolishness, in order more effectively to confound man. It is a mercy of God that life escapes the analysis of science and enters into the realm of mystery and the heart, because the man and the life that are completely polarized in the intellectual domain have the repulsive effluvium of a sick room.

If man, as a human entity, is more than filled by faith when he receives it, so also he overflows in his expression of what faith does for him. Faith unites these two members of a binary: 1) God as the object of our knowledge; 2) God as the end of our life, because faith is a knowledge of God as man's supernatural end. Knowledge of God which is disconnected from the second element is mere speculation or sterile science, if you wish. It is a knowledge which does not engage anything. Faith is wisdom, as knowledge of God, but God as the final end of our life involves the whole man, impels him toward the intimacy of union with God and life everlasting. In these two projections human nature achieves its fullness, precisely because it has not remained confined and limited to human narrowness and insufficiency.

17

Christianity as Emancipation

IT HAS BEEN NOTED that during the first centuries of the Christian era, when men accepted this teaching, they had the impression that they had passed from a state of oppression and slavery to freedom.[1] St. Augustine studied this liberation in detail, and now we can say that he found a liberation which is greater than that which they described or visualized as a mere liberation from cosmic terrors.

Granted the existence of liberty, which was the point of departure, and having corrected the false notion of freedom as synonymous with living unrestrained by any law except that of personal caprice—whose manifestations we considered at length in previous pages—we can reduce the subject to two aspects: liberty as a state of emancipation, and liberty as the actual liberation of the individual. Or, expressed in another way, the emancipation of man with respect to the world and his liberation with respect to himself.

ARTICLE 1. *Man's emancipation with respect to the world*

In preceding pages we stated that the consequences of sin were to subject man to the devil, to subordinate him to his own passions, and to enslave him to the exigencies of the external world. As prisoner of all these things, we have seen him groan and yield to despair, become anxious and bestial.

His relations with God, when he maintained them, also bore the mark of slavery, because they were exclusively relations based on fear. He considered himself a guilty and indebted creature. In this respect the Old Testament was also like other religions. It was a religion of slaves, a cult of fear.[2]

Christianity is a liberation from all these fears, from all these forms of slavery. Faith frees us from the world and gives freedom to those who believe, because faith is the regimen of truth and "it is the truth that makes us free." [3] It is not a freedom which dispenses us from good works, as was falsely asserted by those who did not understand Christianity, but a freedom which is based radically on serving God out of love, doing those things which faith teaches us. "Serve God with joy.

"All slavery is filled with bitterness; all who serve by reason of their condition of slavery, serve and complain. Do not fear the service of this Master. Here there is no groaning, no murmuring or indignation. Let no one believe that he is merely a paid servant, because it is sweet that we should be redeemed. It is a great joy, brethren, to be servants in this great house . . . ; actually there is no slavery here, since we do not obey from necessity, but out of love.[4]

"Love has made you a servant, after truth has freed you. . . . At one and the same time you are a slave and a freeman;

a servant, because you are a created being; free, because you love Him who made you.[5] But it is not we who have freed ourselves. Christ, who has no need of anyone, has freed us from the world, the devil, and the wild beasts that formerly threatened us." [6]

Therefore, the main division of freedom is not in freedom as a personal and vital function, but in liberty as a state. Men either are of the world or they are not of the world, and consequently they are not free or they are free. In this sense freedom extends beyond what is simply personal and egocentric, which is all that the rebels have been able to see, raising it to an absolute category in humanism. Freedom now embraces the entire transcendence of man and his eternal destiny. It includes truth, the truth and its realization in human life, both in thought and in action. It connotes a fundamental change in our relations with God, whom we now regard in the new relationship of a father toward his children. Finally, it involves a new social status in the citizenship of life: we belong to the "City of God," where righteousness (God's righteousness) is the norm and the true liberation.

ARTICLE 2. *Man's emancipation with respect to himself*

But the whole of Christianity is personalized with respect to salvation. Therefore it does not mean a mere collective or mass emancipation, but also a personal liberation. It is personal in the sense that each individual in particular is freed from the world and in the sense that each person individually is freed from himself, which is the most characteristic expression of the world. It is a liberation from the anxieties of fear.[7] It is a functioning freedom, since it has restored to us a devoted will, causing it to act freely without exercising its freedom in sin.

It is a liberty which has its gradations, from the most basic—which consists in being free from crime and serious sin—to that which frees us from following the invitations of the law of sin, which still remained within us after baptism.[8]

The Saint considers that two wills still exist in man, the human will of Adam and the supernaturalized will. Man's true liberation occurs only when God frees him from the will of Adam, from his own self-will, in order to do the will of God. In the situation in which Christ prays in the Garden of Gethsemane, asking that not His will but God's will be done, St. Augustine always sees the collective prayer of Christians, praying that He may free us from this rebel will of Adam and grant us the grace to do His will,[9] because man's true mastery is to conquer himself and not to be enslaved by any appetite or lustful desire. (Cf. *Imitation of Christ*, Bk. III, chapter 53: "The perfect victory is to triumph over self.") [10]

This liberation from self and from the world raises the question of grace and freedom. To the immoral concept of absolute freedom the Pelagians opposed a lofty notion of human dignity and duty, but they eliminated the supernatural element of grace which effected this liberation. In so doing, they removed the essence of a religion which is above all supernatural life and not an ode to duty. In history we can observe perfectly this tendency to return to an elevated concept of duty when men wish to combat the supernatural. Protestant countries, which generally have such a confused notion of grace, retain a lofty concept of duty. Pure humanists hope to preserve men from a state of pure savagery because they think that human dignity and a sense of duty can be superimposed.

St. Augustine studied human dignity conscientiously, both in itself and in its present state of impotence. He studied liberty, which is evident, and he analyzed its relations to grace, which is not so evident. Man's freedom is the work of grace;

but the human element never will be wanting, because even as God preferred that man should sin rather than deprive him of his freedom,[11] so He prefers that man should not be saved, if this means taking away man's liberty. Liberty is the basic element in order to be a human being. It enters into all that is transcendent in man, both in order to attain faith as well as to enter heaven, but it is always subordinated to the divine element, which is grace. God calls us before we can call Him. It is we who respond to His call because, by using our freedom, we desire to respond.[12] Once we believe, it is He who continues to liberate us along the way, so that wild beasts will not devour us. And if a person does not feel that he is called, he should humble himself and pray that God may draw him until he is changed into a humble beast of burden for Christ.[13]

Nor does it cease to be a paradox that liberation from freedom should constitute true freedom. But from the standpoint of this paradox we see the broad horizon that Christianity opens to us, we breathe the fresh air of open country which Christ gave to life when He became man.

18

The Prince of Freedom

THE RULE OF FEAR AND SLAVERY was ended through the personal intervention of Jesus, whom St. Augustine calls the Prince of freedom.[1]

The feast of that liberation begins the moment He assumes a human body. The divine Person, assuming human flesh in the holy virginal womb of Mary, accomplishes something more than joining Himself to a particular portion of human flesh. In a certain manner His Incarnation is a union with all humanity, by virtue of which it infinitely transcends the relationship we have with Adam.[2]

For St. Augustine the Incarnation is most fruitful and productive in its consequences. From this he deduces that all of us human beings are capable of sanctification, because the Word, in His espousal with human flesh, hallowed His own and began to sanctify all the rest. Whence he deduces the place that man occupies in the universe. The Incarnation is a call to intimacy and a pledge of resurrection.

The Son, who is the first and most spiritual expression of

the Father's nature, is sent into the world to take possession of all creation as Chief and Head and King (a place which was vacant because of Adam's defection). He is established in its center, which is man. And from this center He draws men, as members of Himself, in order to communicate to them, so far as possible, His divine nature. This central, comprehensive function of the Son of God vastly transcends that of one who merely reforms conditions externally, as some heretics say of Christ.[3]

In the thought of St. Augustine the significance of Christ and the purpose of His work resides in the defection of Adam: "Because Adam fell, therefore Christ came to earth."[4] Any other theological interpretation of the Incarnation is absent from his writings. For Augustine, too, Christ is no mere reformer, but the center in man's new relations with God, the author of a new life. It is He who, by means of His divinity, raises us to a new status as God's children, and by means of His humanity He is the cause of our resurrection.[5] This is the *whole* work of the *whole* Christ. In his treatise on St. John, he does not tire of giving us formulas concerning these ideas, to see whether the faithful committed to him are holding fast to what is the essence and summary of the Christian religion. Jesus Christ has willed to infuse into us the true greatness of our soul, of the rational soul which is within man, and not in animals. He tells us, moreover, that man does not grow into or achieve happiness, that he is not illuminated, except by the very substance of God. The soul occupies a place between the body and God. And though it can receive certain pleasures through the body, its happiness does not come through the participation of any other holy soul or that of the angels, but rather through participation in that ever-quickening, incommunicable and everlasting substance which is God. But Christ, the eternal Word of God, became man. If man is the pinnacle of creation, and above man is none but God, the Word that was made man took unto Himself our flesh and also a rational soul, and not the soul without an intellect, as is characteristic of animals, as some heretics thought. Without ceasing to be God, He became man.

Here you have a cure for your illness, something conducive to your perfection. Let Christ raise you up, so far as He is man; let Him guide you so far as He is God; let Him bring you to the realm of the divine. This is Christ's whole preaching and mission, and nothing more than this: to raise up souls, to raise up bodies. Both were dead (the body by reason of its infirmities, the soul by reason of its iniquities), and who will raise up the soul except Christ our God? Who will raise up the body except the Man, Christ Jesus? Indeed the truth is that God the Father does some things through the Son as man, and not through Christ as His consubstantial Son. Thus, His birth, death and resurrection, these things do not pertain to the Father; so also with respect to the resurrection of the bodies, because the Father effects the resurrection of souls through His own substance, availing Himself of the substance of the Son, which is equal with His own, and thus souls share in His unchanging light.[6]

According to this remarkable passage, the Redemption is not the tortured task of Christ as emissary of the Trinity, as one who travels far from His homeland to spend some years in suffering. This was not the task of a diver submerging himself in human misery, seeking to bring afloat a man who was shipwrecked and drowning. This is the work of the entire Blessed Trinity, placed in the center of creation, which is man, in order to communicate to him the very spirit and substance of the Godhead. Manifestly, this is something more than a simple answer to the tragedy of the fall.

In the Gospel of St. John, Christ is presented as in constant opposition to the world; and as a consequence of this opposition Christ is victor over the world. It is St. Augustine who perhaps has best explained this thought of St. John, and in his commentaries he refers to it constantly. Because he has penetrated accurately into the thought of St. John, St. Augustine has carried this thought to its ultimate conclusions and has seen the irreconcilable antagonism between the world and Christianity, between the world and the Christian. The conflicts between the world and Christ are well known, but let us summarize them, following the thought of St. Augustine.

Christ's opposition to the world in general is that of light to darkness. In His person He is the light; and the world is the personification of darkness. Here is the antithesis which exists between flesh and spirit, heaven and earth, and the higher and lower. He is from above, He is light and truth. He is sent by the Father but the world rejected Him. He is the clear manifestation of the Father among men, but the darkness has no love for light. The actual distance is measured by the fact that the world derived from Adam, and Christ came from the Father.[7]

Opposition to the prince of this world has the same origin: "The prince of this world hath no part in Me," because Christ has no sin, St. Augustine comments.[8]

The world rejects Him. Therefore, in view of the embassy which Christ bears and His mission to make known the Father, to communicate the divine nature to men, the world rejects the Father, ignores the Father. "Where is Thy Father?" the Jews asked Him when Jesus told them that He was giving testimony of the Father who had sent Him. St. Augustine comments: Since they interpreted Christ's words in a material, carnal sense, they also thought of the Father materially. He who spoke to them was visibly a man, but in a hidden manner He was the Word; visibly man, but internally God. They saw His vesture and despised what it covered. They despised, because they did not know; they did not know because they did not see; they did not see because they were blind; they were blind because they did not believe.[9] The Holy Ghost will undertake to convince the world of this blindness, because the mission which Christ now comes to fulfill is not that of Judge but of Redeemer.

Christ came to save the world, and though the world rejects Him, He carries out His mission; He founds the Church, His kingdom, His extension. He endows it with riches, gives it His peace, His life, His blood. His peace, St. Augustine comments, is the result of keeping His commandments, and it is Himself, for Christ is our peace.[10] He establishes His kingdom, which is not of this world, but will endure here in the world as long as there are human beings. All that believe will enter into this kingdom, all those who, being citizens of the world as Adam's offspring, come into His kingdom through faith.[11] Even though everything indicates the contrary, He overcame the world (John 16:33). And St. Augustine draws the conclusion: He would not have overcome the world if the world had overcome His members.[12] It is a victory all the way down the line; it is a victory because of which only Christ can glory, the true and only victor. With what forces have you conquered? With your own. But who gave you the strength? Note well who conquered first and who made you victor afterwards. "But take courage; I have overcome the world" (John 16:33). Let us indeed rejoice because we have conquered. We who were vanquished *in ourselves,* have conquered *in Him.* Therefore He crowns you, for He crowns His own gifts, not your merits.[13]

Thus, for St. Augustine the conquest of the world pertains to a field as broad as the world itself, as sharply defined as the individual—"to be defeated in ourselves." Consequently, Christ will draw all men to Himself, and each individually.[14] He will draw all men, so far as He will attract all classes; and each one is drawn individually as regards that which he comprehends, that by which he lives, and that through which he has a visible, tangible existence. This is the same humanistic formulation of the question which runs through all history from Adam, and Christ could not overlook it if He was really to overcome the world.

Morever, this victory over the world, this curing of the sick, this liberation of slaves, appeared in an act which in a special manner summarized all else: the Cross. St. Augustine's statements relative to this subject can be taken from any part of his writings, for it is an idea which he expounds "in season and out of season." The world was like the paralytic at the pool of Bethesda; and the sick at the pool are cured only when the waters are agitated. The Father aroused great restlessness among them. With the coming of the Lord the waters were troubled, but He who disturbed them remained hidden. Yet in the agitation of the waters a great disease was to be cured; by the passion of the Lord the world itself was to be healed.[15] With respect to humanism, the same thing transpires: Christ gave battle with fire and sword. "I have come to cast fire on the earth" (Luke 12:49). "Do not think that I have come to send peace upon earth: I have come to bring a sword, not peace" (Matt. 10:34). He brought fire and sword. And this havoc was wrought for us that we might be renewed. . . . Thou hast destroyed us in order to build us anew. Thou hast destroyed us because we were poorly constructed. Thou hast destroyed vain antiquity in order to build the new man, an edifice which will endure forever.[16] Let us cease accumulating texts to substantiate this doctrine—a very easy matter—and let us observe the reaction in the world.

In the first place, the world has never understood the drama of the Cross. For the secular minded this is a mere historical event, a brutal act, but nothing more. St. Augustine warns that if men knew—those who truly want to be men—how Christ Crucified "has become for us God-given wisdom, and justice, and sanctification, and redemption, so that, just as it is written" (I Cor. 1:30), they would not glory in the purely human.[17] This they knew not, and hence the Cross appeared to them as a vile thing. "Through diabolical pride it transpired . . . and it still transpires that Christ's humility, humbled even unto the death of the cross, appears contemptible and wretched to those who love the praise and prestige of this world." [18]

Recalling once more all that enters into this world's list of combat, who are fighting and what they are fighting for, we shall come to recognize perfectly the voice of the world, perhaps even the prince of this world, when we read that "the tree of the Cross is the most poisonous of all trees," and that "it blasphemes life itself." [19] Nietzsche understood that the true significance of the Cross is the destruction of a proud, rebellious, diabolical humanism. The devil himself saw this first, as do all those who would be a law unto themselves, all proud individuals. The only difference is that Nietzsche sought to formulate this as a philosophy. But in reality there already had been many philosophies that asserted the same thing. It seems to me that the prodigal son acted more honestly when he simply went away, without seeking justification in philosophies.

Among the virtues which Christ displayed in redeeming us, and more especially upon the cross, St. Augustine seeks particularly those qualities which are an answer to worldly vices. Love, humility, patience are constantly mentioned in his sermons. We shall speak of love presently. During his whole life he remained in awed wonder at Christ's humility. He himself acknowledges that so long as he was not humble, he did not understand Jesus, and he did not know that his cure was the very medicine which God prepared: wisdom mingled with the flesh, because God's wisdom was made flesh.[20] The path Christ chose to refute the world's pride was the most profound humiliation. Indeed, it was so awesome that it made the very foundations of the earth tremble.[21] Christ's abasement wounded

Satan, depriving him of the option he held on us.[22] It is certain that this very Jesus, humbled even unto the depths of the earth, has risen again, now is placed as Judge of men. But the Church is in love with this humility and does not presume to know more than Christ humbled and crucified, as St. Paul proclaimed.[23] Therefore we Christians continue to follow this pattern of humility, even though all about us exults and triumphs.

Patience is associated with humility. If we are to be persecuted by the world, then we need the example of patience. For this reason St. Augustine insists so much upon it, recommends it to Christians: "They gave Him blows and exclaimed: 'Hail, King of the Jews!' In this way Christ fulfilled all that He had prophesied of Himself; thus the martyrs were encouraged to suffer whatever their persecutors chose to visit upon them; thus with His omnipotent power concealed for a time, He first of all commended patience; thus the kingdom which is not of this world triumphs over the world, not by the fury of its assault but through the humility of its suffering; and so too that grain was sown in the horror of blasphemous insult, in order to be increased and multiplied in glory." [24]

The world is like an ocean. Many did not know that there was a route across this sea. Others who know the way do not know how they should travel, or toward what port. Then Christ came and made of the Cross a vessel to sail the sea of this world. . . . Many disdained to enter such a small boat. Don't you see that the way to your homeland has been cut off, that you will not arrive there unless this boat carries you? [25]

Not only is Christ our way through this ocean; He is also our light and our life. God has lighted many lamps along the path of men's lives, that they might not lose their way. It is a wondrous gradation of light: first it is the prophets, then Christ and the Church, that have illuminated the soul up to now. When finally we arrive at our homeland, all these lights will be extinguished, for the very Sun [of righteousness] will be born in our soul.[26] Christ, this unique light who is come into the world to enlighten men, illuminates man in every possible situation: the bestialized individual who seems to lack all understanding,[27] the individual who believes he has enough light, but actually resides in gloom.[28] Here it is a question, the Saint exclaims, of Christ, the Light of the world, who enlightens the darkness, the darkness of conduct and habits rather than that of the eyes; not the eyes of the body but those of the soul, by which we distinguish, not white from black, but the just from the unjust.[29] And as eyes which receive no light cannot see, so also souls, if they receive not Christ's light, see nothing, since they cannot come to know what justice and wisdom are.[30]

This light, which is Christ, establishes the line of demarcation between the zone of light and the zone of darkness. Where this light fails to reach, there is only the region of gloom, even if it seems to the dwellers therein that they possess some other light. And as light unifies things within a frame, a distinct area, so this light unites the concept of justice in our hearts and in our minds.[31] This is a profound observation, because as long as Christ does not influence the fields of politics, government, business, etc., we are speaking of the justice of this or that individual, of this type or that type, but men cannot even agree on the definition of justice.

This Sun differs from the physical sun, in that the latter departs from us each day; but the former will not abandon us if we do not abandon Him.[32] Without metaphors, it is faith which makes Christ our light, which illuminates our route and the destination toward which we are traveling. It is faith which is the light and life that we receive immediately from Christ. "He that believeth in Me, abideth in Me. He that abideth in Me, possesseth Me. What is it to have Me? It is to possess life everlasting." [33]

19

I Have Chosen You

THERE IS NOTHING SIMPLE about this theme. At its root lies the whole mystery of grace and predestination. Whether one is of the world or not of the world has its ultimate cause in God. Moreover, it has its crowns and termination in God as Judge and Prosecutor, so that the entire Blessed Trinity is involved in this action.

St. Augustine realized this when he noted in his *Retractions* that in repudiating the sensory world he did not act thus in order to seek refuge in a Platonic, "idealistic" world, but to find refuge in Christ's kingdom.[1] And in the long run, to be nauseated and repelled is not to save oneself, and what is really involved here is the problem of salvation. In saying this, we are stating that at this point is involved the entire problem of initial grace, of perseverance in good, and final perseverance. We are not going to deal with these problems except from the point of view which we are studying, from the precise aspect which shows us the mystery of election and its amazing contraction when projected in glory.

There is one undeniable historical fact: those who are of the world do not realize their profound misery. Humanity's response to Christ did not consist in the fact that some already were just, and these received Him, while others were unjust and rejected Him. No; all were unjust. But some began to repent of their sins, while others contentedly continued therein. Those who experienced sorrow and confessed did not do so because of a more or less prudent reflection. "You would not be disgusted with your sin unless God had enlightened you and shown you His truth." [2] One might cite the case of a man who already knows that the world is wicked, yet wishes to continue to be "sweetly burdened" by the weight of this world. It is a situation that St. Augustine experienced personally and he tells us about it. Therefore he acknowledges that had it not been for grace he would not have emerged from the dream which seemed so sweet to him.[3] The Saint refers to the struggle which ensues, which shatters man's inner self. The greater part of the *Confessions* record and analyze this struggle. In another place he summarizes the matter by saying that when the soul observes this ambivalence in its interior, when it sees that the world now is displeasing to it, but notes also that its sick soul still has an attraction to the world, then it should pray and weep, in order that the Lord may heal it by His grace.[4] Thus, not to be of this world is more than man's decision; it is God's mercy.[5]

St. Augustine thus explains the mystery of the election of those who are not of this world: these elect are the portion and possession of the Eternal Father. The Father gives them to Christ, and Christ calls them. They are not the Father's possession in the sense that the Son, as God, has no claim to them, because the Son, as God, also chose them, and they are His. But the Father delivers them to Christ as man; He entrusts human beings to "the Man." And fulfilling the office which this implies, Christ calls them. "I have chosen you" (John 15:19). He prays for them, not for the world (John 17:9), and He sanctifies them.[6] Yet this election touches the very foundation of the mystery when, as St. Augustine tells us (following St. Paul) that in the same everlasting love which Christ has for the Father, He loved us, and then He predestined us.[7] From these everlasting heights comes our wondrous union with Christ and the mystery of our predestination. As a result of the Father's predilection and His loving commendation, as a consequence of this unity, Christ will glorify the Father, revealing His name to those whom He has chosen; that name which was hidden, but afterwards was clearly revealed to the elect. He glorifies the Father, teaching His name to the elect, not only to those who knew Him personally here on earth, but also to all the elect who will ever exist in the world, for His spiritual presence will remain as long as the world endures.[8] We are the treasured possessions of the Son, and He is pledged to lose not one. This is a great joy for the Christian! Yet it is no reason for pride, since no one is chosen for his own merits, but rather by God's mercy. No one cometh to the Son if the Father draw him not; therefore do not boast of what you possess.[9]

We said that this mystery of our election is an event in which the whole Blessed Trinity shares. This is apparent in the Gospel itself. St. Augustine observes that the grace of election "is regeneration, not a generation."[10] We do not participate in the very nature of God in the way that the only-begotten Son is of the Father's nature; nor should we visualize it after the manner of a natural generation, as Nicodemus understood it. Our regeneration is parallel to the temporal generation of the Son, and it is by the power of the Holy Ghost. And as the Son, though taking the form of a servant, was never of this world, so also those who are reborn in the Holy Ghost are not of the world.[11]

But birth is not everything. The life of the elect should grow and develop. "Sanctify them in Thy truth," Christ prayed, when He saw that He was leaving them in the world. What Christ prays for, the Saint explains, is that those who are sanctified may advance in holiness of life. But neither can this be accomplished without grace. "We possess the patrimony of truth because we have Christ Himself as our inheritance, and in this truth, which for those of the Old Testament was given only in the form of symbol and shadow, we sanctify ourselves; we sanctify ourselves in Christ." [12] We effect this sanctification by our cooperation with grace, the active force within us, but basically we should visualize it as active on the part of Christ, in the sense that it is Christ who sanctifies us in sanctifying Himself. "Through them do I sanctify Myself." What does all this mean, asks St. Augustine, except that "they are I [Christ]?" For it has been said of them that they are members of Christ, that He is the Head; but Christ is one. . . . I sanctify Myself; I sanctify them in Me, for they are I.[13]

This sanctification involves a certain casuistry which transcends human calculation. Each individual confronts particular situations; and it is difficult to formulate general rules without losing that which in a particular situation was the loving and personal mystery of God as it touches each person. Leaving aside the hidden, personal mystery, the Saint takes up the subject of sanctification, giving realistic advice in order to help and also to avoid mistakes. As we have seen, one of these is not to lose the attitude of the pilgrim. With hunger and thirst we are traveling through the desert. To those of us who were toiling in Egypt, in our worldliness, serving Satan, Christ said: "Come to Me, all you who labor and are burdened, and I will give you rest." [14] Another means that we have is prayer, so that He may help us overcome the world. The soul that truly wishes to be pure, commends itself to God so that He may assist in its total purification and emancipation from the world.[15] The soul that follows Christ knows that this hour belongs to the world, and therefore the soul suffers and hopes. It knows that its hour will also come. Yet it does not wait in apathetic expectation, which leads to weariness; instead, it has hope activated by love, because here within, the best of its life is associated with Christ.[16] Therefore, since love always possesses a certain urgency, it pleads with the soul to withdraw from the prison of this life, from struggles with this malicious flesh. At the same time the Saint observes that love does not consist in cherishing excessive longing for death.[17]

I stated earlier that all this has a contracted and diminished appearance as projected upward from below. St. Augustine reminds his followers that he personally did not intend to desire cucumbers, melons or onions, as the Israelites did in the desert, who preferred these to the heavenly bread which rained down upon them from heaven. His sole intention was to gratify his desire for glory, which is the inheritance of the New Testament.[18] This thought has more depth than its analogy of vegetables would suggest. He meant that in the New Testament there exists a fundamental counter-proposition to the Old Testament, in the concept of the reward for virtuous living. He told us several times that the Old Testament was an economy of material rewards, inasmuch as the hearts of the Jews were materialistic. Now men's hearts have changed through the regeneration which the Holy Ghost has wrought in them, and their hearts have become spiritual. Now everlasting glory is life's end and reward. To be sure, some persons describe this goal and reward as egoistic—this is not the place to argue the point—but it is time to assert that it is the New Testament which has disclosed heaven to man in a vital manner.

I mean that there are two ways open to man in this election of which we are speaking: one is from the world to faith;

the other is from this life to glory. By God's decree and in His election these are one and the same, although transpiring in two periods of time. St. Augustine becomes enthusiastic as he explains this second phase of election. If faith means for us the elevation of our life, a joining with the supernatural, then our bond is with Christ. And what is this except our attainment of life everlasting? "He that believeth in Me, walketh in Me. He that walketh in My way, abideth in Me. What does it mean to abide in Me? To possess life everlasting." [19] This projection of faith into the next life, this need for eternal life, which faith contains within itself, did not escape St. Augustine's attention. He had penetrated deeply into the subject of justification; he knew that this includes a restless desire for self-perfection. And this perfection is glory. We may dissociate ourselves from the Saint's exegesis when he explains these ideas, but we cannot neglect his meaning, his idea. Commenting on Christ's prayer to the Father, "That all may be one; even as Thou, Father, in Me, and I in Thee, that they also may be one in Us; that the world may believe that Thou hast sent Me" (John 17:21), he says that as Mediator Christ asks for glory for His followers, because perfect union does not exist as long as we see God through faith alone, but only when we see Him face to face. Hence the text adds, quite reasonably, *that it may know* (John 17:23) and does not state *that it may believe*. Here we understand the world of the elect; those who already believe.[20]

It should be stressed that all this becomes reality not only at life's end, but it is a reality even at the beginning of the supernatural life. However, it is a manifest reality only at the end; at present it is a reality only in the form of a pledge. From the moment that the Holy Ghost breathes into our souls the gift of justification, God's greatest blessing, charity and faith are in themselves concomitants of glory, a beginning of glory. At the same time they are an escape from what surrounds us, what presses in upon us and causes anxiety. He that believeth in Me, let him come and drink; for there shall gush forth within him rivers of living waters, vital currents demanding more life, aspiring, leaping toward life eternal.[21]

As yet we have not beheld this everlasting life for which we feel such a strong desire. But in order that we may somehow see it, Christ manifested Himself in the majesty and glory of His resurrection, because this is what He asked for our sake: "And the glory that Thou hast given Me, I have given to them" (John 17:22). By the immutability of predestination, says the Saint, Christ now speaks in the present tense of what is still in the future. And this glory which the Father will give Him when He raises Him up is the glory that Christ will confer on us when He raises us again from the dead.[22]

Christ came into the world, assuming leadership and primacy with respect to every creature, "that to those whom Thou hast given Me, I may give everlasting life." He also holds unbelievers in His power and will visit everlasting death upon them. To those that have believed, He gives life eternal. Let us open our hearts to hope, let us rejoice in this hope, for He has pledged His word. It is not the promise of a mere man, which is always undependable, but the pledge of Him who is co-eternal with the Father, who became man for our sake, who is the way, the truth, the life. Believe, hope for, desire what He says: "Father, I will that where I am, they also, whom Thou hast given Me, may be with Me" (John 17:24). What this great shepherd promises is that all His sheep will be with Him. What the Head promises to all His members is that they shall be where He will be.[23] This is the synthesis of Christ's whole task, His whole work of emancipation, a liberation in two periods of time, but joined together by a changeless ordinance. In this liberation He shines forth and triumphs as Prince of freedom, yet fundamentally He joins in an act in which the entire Trinity participates.

And we, since the day that Christ sealed us with His blood, also are set apart in a fundamental way from other wanderers in the desert. We are sanctified, and already we bear within us the flame of a life which "burns eternally with longings to burn yet more"; and it waits only for the clay of this flesh to break in order to appear in its fullness.[24]

20

For They Are I

WE CAN OBSERVE A PHENOMENON among Christ's elect. In a certain sense they lose their personality, and in another sense they acquire a new one. Although these appear to be two distinct phenomena, they are one and the same. The personality which they lose is their "I." (We are not here attempting to determine to what extent the ego is lost, but we shall study the phenomenon in a general way.) In parallel fashion another ego is acquired, an ego which is common to the members of Christ, transcending the individual without destroying him. On the contrary, it strengthens him. Thus, for example, we observe historically that a series of important acts of the liturgy have no known author. Who has formulated those beautiful prayers which serve as official worship? The Church. This is the new "I" which we shall now attempt to investigate.

Since the development of pure humanism necessarily leads to an all-absorbing and oppressing egoism, to the point of making human society difficult, and perhaps impossible (St. Augustine already said that the world prevents one from loving his fellow men), and since it has been necessary to react against that individualism which disturbs the peace and order of that same worldly society, the kingdom of Christ, established apart from selfishness, apart from humanism, must necessarily culminate in a society which transcends the individual and personal ego. In today's atmosphere there is a need to transcend such individualism with something that will join men together in communities that are above the personal. Today, in the "City of Man," that tendency, basically noble and necessary for life, is directed toward Communism, a new Pantheism, and other diabolical substitutes which have never failed to cheat men. But Christ satisfied this tendency from the first moment of His earthly life: "The whole Church is the bride of Christ; its origin and first-fruits are the flesh of Christ. In the Church, bridegroom and bride are joined together." [1]

This is a mystery and a divine mercy. It is also a reply to the world as society, as we have examined earlier. It is a city built by God, to survive in the ocean of this world. Even though the sea, with its waves and furies, continually surges against it, God will preserve it from being submerged.[2] This is the ship which God has built to navigate in the world's flood.[3]

It carries a special citizenship with its own name, which the habit of repetition has perhaps induced us to neglect or minimize. When Rome wished to confer the privileges of citizenship upon an individual, it named him a *Roman;* this was the greatest civil distinction. Now Christ, as God, possesses an everlasting kingdom. All things were made by the Word (John 1:3). Yet He also has His kingdom as man. This kingdom the prophets foretold: the kingdom of Christ as man. He made its citizens *Christians.* The kingdom of Christians which now is assembled together, which now is won, was purchased by Christ's blood, and it will appear to the whole world as His kingdom when He comes amid the brightness of His saints.[4]

This is a citizenship of the living, not of the dead. I mean that it has its own life; and this is conferred by love. It is love which integrates the members of this community, giving them life, causing them to be one society, with one heart and one soul. This unity is achieved, not by re-evaluating the human element (that will be a consequence), but by drawing closer to God. In approaching Him, those who before were many are now one single soul.[5] Considering this vital aspect of Christ's kingdom, the Saint says in another place that love is what distinguishes the children of God from the children of Satan.[6]

The Saint attempts to explain this whole transformation to us, commenting on St. Peter's vision and the words which he heard: Kill and eat. No one enters into the body of the Church unless he first dies. He dies to what he was, to become what he was not. But if he does not die, is not consumed by the Church, he may continue as one of those citizens who are counted by the physical eye, but he cannot be among those citizens whom God recognizes. The pagan comes, in whom idolatry still dwells, and he must be grafted to the members of Christ. For this, he first must die. He cannot be consumed by the Church unless he first be dead. Let him renounce the world; then he is dead. Let him believe in God; then he is consumed.[7]

When this incorporation has been completed, he belongs to a body, and that body has a soul, and that soul possesses life, and that life has an ego. But the ego of the Church is Christ. "They are members of Christ, and He is the Head; but Christ is one. . . . I sanctify Myself; I sanctify Myself in them, for they are I." [8]

If this is true, the consequences are transcendental. The ego of a subject is the receiver of the relations which come from other subjects, and it is the source of activities which proceed from itself. It should possess unity throughout time;

it should be one, in contradistinction to the variety which exists outside of it. St. Augustine frequently substantiates this permanent unity of the Church's ego, together with the responsibility which we have described. The proof which he often adduces is that of Jesus' words to Saul when he was persecuting Christians: "Saul, Saul, why dost thou persecute Me?" (Acts 9:4). If Christ were not one person with Christians, Jesus would not have spoken these words, says the Saint many times over. He finds another proof in the words which will serve as a contrast on judgment day, in order to know who will be glorified and who will be condemned. "Come, blessed of My Father, take possession of the kingdom prepared for you from the foundation of the world; for I was hungry, and you gave Me to eat; I was thirsty, and you gave Me to drink" (Matt. 25:34–40). In expounding these words, the Saint adds another personification of Christ, that of learning when His members learn. Likewise, he says, we too, like those on judgment day, can ask Christ: "When hast Thou been a learner, Thou who teachest all things?" And at once, in our faith, He answers: "When one of My children learns, I learn." [9]

St. Augustine discovered this great truth of the ego of the mystical body in St. John and St. Paul. I do not mean that before Augustine no one observed it within the Church. On the contrary, the tradition of the Greek Church abounds in this truth, in many ways penetrating it more deeply than St. Paul's words. But it is St. Augustine who makes constant reference to it, until it becomes the most frequently repeated theme of his sermons. The majority of his commentaries on the Psalms begin by recalling the doctrine of the mystical body, and they show masterly insight into our unity with Christ. The sufferings which martyrs will bear, all are personified in Christ. All the sorrows which Christians will experience, through persecutions, scandals, temptations and slanders, will become Christ's sufferings. He will raise His cry of pain, the cry of one single man, which will echo sadly through history as long as the world endures.[10] It is Christ who prays when we are praying. "Let us listen to the poor Christ who is in us and with us. . . . Today you are in tribulation, and it is *I* who suffer; tomorrow another will be in pain, and *I* will suffer; after this generation, others and still others will suffer tribulation, and then too it will be *I* who suffer. Thus it will continue to the end of the world; no matter who is suffering, *I* will be the one who suffers. Daily I am tormented. 'Incline Thine ear unto me,' Peter prayed, Paul prayed, and the other apostles prayed. The faithful prayed in those days, they prayed in later years, they prayed in the age of martyrs, the faithful pray in our own times, they will pray in years to come. Hear *Me*. I ask not for what is earthly, like an earthly individual. Rather, as one redeemed from the first captivity, I pray for the kingdom of heaven." [11] This is the impressive majesty of Christian suffering, of which we already have spoken several times. Here it is definitely sanctified and exalted. The power of the Christian's prayer, in this personification, gives us hope. It is the sanctification of the Christian which, as a sanctification which Christ accomplishes as in His own person, is changed into a mysterious inner efficacy. And the Father has this love for us because He loves the Son.[12]

One of the essential conditions for this union of egos is that there be an inner union of life. Our life not only will be where Christ is, but it will be in Christ by means of the theological virtues.[13] Moreover, in this final enumeration he summarizes the doctrine by saying: Christ's manner of abiding in us, so far as we are His temples, is one thing; His dwelling in us, so far as we are He (even as He became man to be our Head, that we might be His body) is something else.

The Saint explains this unity by all kinds of comparisons,

so that Christians may understand and sanctify their actions with the quickening power of this mystery. The unity of marriage serves him well. As in marriage there are two persons, but after marriage there is only one person who speaks, so also there is one person in Christ, whether it be the Head or the members who speak. There is one who speaks, since we hear only one, and in Him we also speak.[14]

We are His members. In another passage he states that Christ is our Head and cannot be separated from the body.[15] We are one body which raises its Head on high. As the members of the body support the head among themselves, so also with the mystical body, there is nothing higher than the Head, and the Head is borne by all the members, so that thus the body becomes the support of the Head.[16]

Actually these truths have often been stated in theology. We now repeat them to emphasize their position in St. Augustine. They are God's answer to the world, the victory over the diminished human personality which now is incorporated in the transcendent person of the mystical Christ. By this embodiment man enters into a holy company with Christ Himself, into a vital fellowship where, with respect to its worldly nature, the human ego disappears in order to be transformed into the ego of Christ.

We repeat these truths in order to draw attention to the unity which this whole ocean of mysteries has in St. Augustine. It is a unity polarized in Christ as God and man, who comes to cure man, who had ignored God when he became a citizen of the world. From this center several questions of theology derive their urgency as immediate problems, for they now acquire a scope as vast as life itself. The questions of God's life in men and the life of men as such are reduced to a single problem, rather than being analyzed within a framework of pure logic.

21

The Mystery Within

IN THE PRAYER WHICH CHRIST directs to His Father for those whom He has chosen out of this world, He develops in synthesis the entire mysterious life of the Christian. In this prayer the curtains hiding the supreme realities of our inner life are drawn aside; it is here that Jesus summarizes all He has given to those He has chosen from the world. St. Augustine's commentary on this prayer of Christ is gentle and profound, intensely profound. In it ideas and feelings mingle serenely with realities and hopes, mysteries and intimate experiences. And the predominant note in this melodious exposition of mysteries is the grateful joy of feeling that one is chosen by Jesus.

Man's restoration achieves its eminence in the act of the Cross, and it acquires its mysterious depth in the fact that we are members of Christ. But Christ is a divine Person who has a vital relationship with the other two Persons; consequently, we have been introduced into the company of the whole Trinity. Here, where all is mystery, let us be led by Augustine's skillful hand.

"I have manifested Thy name to the men whom Thou hast given Me out of the world" (John 17:6). St. Augustine comments on this. He has not shown them that He [the Father] is God. The Jews knew this well before the time of Christ, as did those men whose nature was not wholly depraved, because all creation led them quite clearly to this conclusion. What Jesus made clear to them was that God is *His* Father, the Father of Jesus.[1] It is necessary to keep this relationship of the Son in mind, in order to understand the measure of greatness of the new children adopted by the Father. The fatherhood of God is a special gift which Jesus' elect also receive; we too are God's children in a sense which we did not know. But not in the same sense as Jesus, who possesses His own individual, personal sonship.[2] Without apparent depth, St. Augustine relates this new paternity to separation from the world, and in this manner: Whoever follows Christ is poor; poor because he has disdained the goods of this world and placed his hopes in Thee alone. And "Thou art He who helps the orphan"; him to whom the world as father has died, that world of which he is the carnal offspring; and now he can say: "I am crucified to the world, and the world to me" (Gal. 6:14). For such persons, God is indeed a father.[3]

I say that at first glance this way of describing God's fatherhood apparently lacks depth, since it appears here that God is Father only by reason of His providence, which He also demonstrates in regard to animal creation. But such is not the case. The fatherhood which God acquires over those who have died to the world is precisely a paternity related to the Father's love for Christ. "And Thou hast loved them (whom I have chosen out of the world) because Thou hast loved Me" (John 17:23). St. Augustine states that the Father loves us in the Son because He chose us in the Son even before the world existed. To be sure, He does not love us on an equal basis, for we are not equal to the Son. Yet He who truly loves His only-begotten Son also loves His members, whom He adopted in Him, for His sake. Nor is there any other cause for the Father's love for us except this fact, that He loves His Son. In divinity He loves His Son, because He has begotten Him equal to Himself. He loves Him as man, because this same only-begotten Son is He who was made flesh, and for the sake of the Word, the flesh of the Word is precious to Him. He loves us because we are members of the one whom He loves; and that we might be such, He loves us even before we existed.[4]

This love of God is incomprehensible and endless. It has not come about as when two enemies are reconciled after hating one another mutually, but rather, before we were reconciled by the blood of the Son, He loved us already, and He began to love us before the world existed so that we also might be His children, together with the only-begotten Son. Thus, when we hear that the death of the Son reconciled us, let us not understand this in such a way as to think that only then did God begin to love us.[5]

The reason for all this mysterious and gracious love is simple indeed. Why does the Father love us with the love wherewith He loves the Son, except that we are His members and beloved in Him, for He is loved completely—Head and members? This is a new fatherhood, exclusively for those whom He has chosen out of the world, for He has communicated His nature to them by means of His Son, making us His adopted children. Or, to state it better, man as Christ, the whole Christ, no longer has the world as father, but God.[6]

We have already examined some of the relations which the elect share with Christ. Let us add others, which St. Augustine now elucidates as being more closely related to the Trinity. The elect were delivered by the Father to the Son as His special possession, with a particular and complete title. We already belonged to Him in His divine nature, because man, as a rational creature, is subject only to God. This new title of possession is a sanctification of our being and our action. Nor can any other way than this be logical for the saints to belong to Him who has created and sanctified them. Therefore all that is theirs belongs by right to Him who is their lord and master.[7] This attribute excludes the Christian from any partial loyalty and dedication, whether this be by reason of counting the hours of the day or by reason of counting the actions of one's life. We belong wholly to Christ; all that is ours is Christ's; and anything that we take away from this Lord is a partial compromise with the world. The malice of many acts which lukewarm Christians think are not wicked is this: they are acts which are independent of Christ.

The surrender of the justified souls to Christ elicits a special watchfulness on His part, to deliver them from evil and to assure their everlasting salvation. "While I was with them, I kept them in Thy name" (John 17:12). This is a guardianship which Christ as man exercised in a physical manner while He lived among us. This guardianship He now continues to exercise in a spiritual manner, understanding spiritual as opposed to bodily. In His turn, Christ, at the time of returning to the Father, commended His own to the Father, that He might keep them in His name. And St. Augustine stresses that we should not understand this as if the Father and the Son alternately kept guard over us. This is a style in which the Scriptures speak, as adapted to our ways of understanding. In reality, the whole Trinity stands guard over us, because even when the Son undertook the task of watching over us, He did not relieve the watch which the Father exercised over us, nor did God transfer this responsibility to the Son in such a way that He [the Father] is no longer concerned.[8] This is certainly an efficacious protection, and a valid prayer that is heard, for not even a grain of wheat will be lost, no matter what storms arise in the world, no matter how the skies are darkened and the day overcast so that confusion reigns and they see not. The prayer of Christ is for all who will be joined to Him by faith, because through Him they will have been rescued from the patrimony of perdition which Adam established. The world will be destroyed without a single straw remaining unconsumed. They were not chosen. (The Saint has told us not to judge why one has been chosen and not another, if we do not wish to fall into error). And Jesus did not pray for the world, because it was not chosen.

This prayer, indeed, contains an express petition of Christ as man, as Mediator between God and men, asking the Father that He gather together the predestined and elect where He is. The absolute assurance of His resurrection and ascension empower Christ to speak of things to come as though they were now present: "Father, I will that where I am, they also whom Thou hast given Me may be with Me" (John 17:24).[9] Evidently from thence forward believers possess a vast infused hope, so vast that it could be no greater.[10]

But there is also a relationship of possession, a possession derived from God's abiding presence within us. The whole Blessed Trinity loves us. The Holy Ghost likewise resides within us, for He is God just as are the Father and the Son. St. Paul's words are clear and definite. But St. Augustine's exposition of the prayer with which we are here concerned is interesting: "Father, I will that where I am, they also whom Thou hast given Me may be with Me." Manifestly, He is referring to the happiness which is possible only with God. And as God He prays that we may be with Him. It is a question of being present with Christ in glory, because by faith believers are already there.[11] Receiving these words of Christ, uttered as Son of God, co-equal with the Father, we also are in the

Father with Christ—He as Son and we in our own fashion, no matter where our body may be. If we take the word "place" and apply it to that which is characteristic of physical bodies, it has the meaning of a "place where something is." Now the everlasting place of Christ, where He ever abides, is the Father. The Father's place is in the Son. He testifies to this Himself, saying: "Do you believe that I am in the Father and the Father in Me?" (John 14:11), and in the prayer, "Thou, Father, in Me, and I in Thee" (John 17:21). They are our dwelling-place, for He continues: "that they also may be one in Us," and we are the dwelling-place of God because we are temples of God. As He who died for us prays for us, so He lives for us, that we may be one in the Blessed Trinity.[12]

This is the central mystery of the Christian life, that which transcends and transfigures it. It is a mystery which displaces man's center of gravity (which the rebels had situated in man himself) in order to establish that center in God's mysterious life within us. When our whole inner self is filled with this majestic presence, the individual can return to his home, to his own inner self, not to return to that "perfect solitude" which Nietzsche desired for man, nor to go mad (as Nietzsche also went mad, though he did not desire this), but to be active in loving and adoring, as man's first activity when he has such guests within his home. And the rest will follow, without life or love ever being absent themselves from his dwelling.

Let us observe briefly that in this presence of God within us, Christ holds the first place, for He is our "I." "That they may be one, even as We are one; I in them and Thou in Me, that they may be made perfect in unity" (John 17:22–23). As in verse 21, He presents to us the unity of all the elect in the Blessed Trinity: "That they also may be one in Us." Now this unity stands forth by means of Christ. This is the function of the Mediator, so often repeated by St. Paul, and even more often by St. Augustine.[13]

Our association with the Trinity fills St. Augustine with enthusiasm, compels him to seek more refined ways of stating it. He also grows sad, since he does not yet fully possess his guests, because his mind cannot fully penetrate the vastness of this gift. But now this presence impels him to bear patiently life with its inconveniences, until faith purifies him completely and he deserves to dwell with God.[14] He acknowledges that he finds his enthusiasm already expressed in St. John.[15]

Such enthusiasm leads him to seek brilliant, expressive similes in order to make us understand the magnitude of the mystery that abides within us. We are the heaven where God dwells. What is heaven without holy souls where God abides? We are temples of God. What were the apostles, if not God's thrones, where the Lord rested, where He moved through all the earth? [16]

But for St. Augustine all this has an unworldly, anti-mundane significance. Christ is going to depart, and the world will behold Him no longer. St. Jude Thaddeus asks Him why He is not going to show Himself to the world. And Jesus answers him that the manifestation which He now will reveal unto His own is the indwelling of the Blessed Trinity. This is an antagonism which is rooted in the fundamental opposition of the world to God. The world does not love Him; He does not give Himself to the world. It is love which singles men out, prepares them to be God's dwelling-place; love changes men into God's mansion, where He lives.[17] This is a contrast which St. Augustine is not the first to point out, for it is well expressed in St. John's Gospel. But it is St. Augustine who has seen it best.

Christ promises the Holy Ghost to the disciples who have followed Him (John, chaps. 14ff.). He promises His peace

(John 14:27ff.), incorporation in Himself as the branches are part of the vine (John 15:1ff.), to free them from their condition of slavery—which as St. Augustine informed us, is the usual condition of the Old Testament and of the world (John 15:9ff.). And he reminds them of all this because the world will consider them as outcasts and will excommunicate them with respect to all that is human; it will persecute and slay them. They believed in Jesus; they have known that the Father sent Him. The world is poles apart from this; it hated Him, and it hated the Father (John 15:8ff.). Because of their antimundane attitude, He promised His own the Holy Ghost. He also promised the Holy Ghost to the world, but in the capacity of accuser, as judge of its unbelief, its injustice, its blindness (John 16:5–11). The sadness [caused by] the bodily absence of Jesus and by persecution will turn to joy for those whom He has chosen to follow Him. St. Augustine comments that what He promises is the whole Blessed Trinity, because in this spiritual presence the three Divine Persons are not separated.[18]

We have stated that glory is the patrimony of the New Testament, even as the earth and the fullness thereof were the legacy of the Old Dispensation. Now we can understand better what all this means in St. Augustine as an exponent of evangelical thought. The inheritance of believers is not only glory as some distant reality at an indefinite time; glory is also the inheritance of a reality already present, which we hold as pledge of future glory. This guarantee is not only a promise, but a reality. It is a mysterious, hidden reality that we feel to be true by reason of the intimate experience of faith, which we know to be true by God's word.

The sum-total of the mysteries which we have here indicated, which we possess as co-heirs with Christ in His act of reparation when He redeemed the world, constitute a new era in human affairs. Man's life and man himself have been deified.

From that moment forward mankind will find its highest value and development in union with God. On the other hand, to trust human values, independent of the redemption, means to insist on remaining small, to reject God.

Man, who is born again into this divine life that places him in immediate contact with the triune God, in a special relationship with Christ the Redeemer, not only does not diminish his characteristically human qualities, but enhances them to the maximum of their potential. And it can be affirmed that the maximum of personal values coincides with the maximum indicated in the ascent toward perfection. Spiritual gifts—*bona fide* treasures, as St. Augustine proved to us—come to strengthen man's natural qualities, to draw them out of their narrow personal limitations. This same spiritual outpouring of gifts confers upon us a series of qualities which we did not have before we received them, among them, the living assurance of "direction" by virtue of which we know where we are going and, more or less, our present position. Faith gives our life an "interior" depth (truly a fundamental difference not only from animal creation, but also from worldly persons), a depth which in the non-believer scarcely goes beyond a certain nostalgia. It provides an understanding of the "exterior" which nothing can obscure, which we can regard as a true and immediate reward for having submitted our mind to the faith.

This mysterious inner life, together with Christ's teaching and our personal contact with Christ our Head (who is the true marvel of human valuation), give to our life a serenity and firmness which worldings themselves admire, though often this admiration is expressed in slanders and insults. Superficially this is paradoxical. Man is truly man only when he is united with the divine. Fundamentally this is a mystery. But even at the threshold of this mystery, before love alone prevails, we can find an explanation for this paradox. In reality, what God has taken from man in the transformation He has wrought in him is not his truly human qualities, but the false tendencies of human inclinations and traits, man's bestial qualities. In exchange, He has given Himself to man.

22

The Christian's Separation from This World

IN VIEW OF THE SPLENDOR with which God desired to enrich the Christian's soul and the intimacy to which He calls it, the whole world is necessarily unworthy of satisfying the Christian's love and filling his life. Based on the aforementioned truths of our union with Christ and our living fellowship with the entire Blessed Trinity, it is logical that the Christian should give to things here below the limited love and attention required to use them, leaving the rest of man's nature occupied in loving and living this love. The first-fruits of life are love, and from this mysterious inner life the Christian's thoughts and actions will derive their justification, if they are to be profitable in the order of salvation and sanctification.

In the following lines let us attempt to complete the thought of St. Augustine relative to man's separation from the world, paying particular heed to the individual who already is a Christian. We shall presuppose faith as the personal separation of the non-Christian or man in general from the world, although we shall not always be able to exclude faith from our statements. Instead of insisting on the human phase, as effort and cooperation in God's work (something which evidently exists), we shall insist on that which is the work of God. In the last analysis it is more Augustinian to insist on the divine activity than on the human.

Since man's elevation to the supernatural life is the focal point of his separation from the world, and since this includes his union with Christ and close association with the Blessed Trinity, evidently man needs that life and certain virtues which will put him in immediate vital contact with the Trinity. Moreover, since in that order of things and relations man is absolutely powerless, all these things must be gifts of God. These gifts are called grace, faith, hope and charity. Further, since this separation from the world is a way of life opposed to the world, which is pride, the foundation of everything is humility. Finally, inasmuch as the inheritance of the elect is God Himself, here on earth in His mystical presence, impelled by the dissatisfaction of love and the eager expectancy of faith, which desires presence and not absence, and there in glory by the full satisfaction of beholding Him face to face, it is logical that God should test His own by withholding those gifts which the world looks for, in order that they may learn to repose their hope, their happiness and their love in Him and not lose the notion of pilgrimage. The entire circle of material goods, honors and all that has worldly value enters into the economy of the New Testament. It is the logical consequence of the truth that no man can serve two masters and also of the opposition between the two Testaments and their respective economies. Therefore the Christian will have to respond to this torturing test, applied by God Himself, who desires us to be attached to nothing, with patience and complete submission to the will of God who, if He does not always respond when we pray amid the pressures of human needs, will always respond appropriately with interior or everlasting rewards. This is the synthesis of what follows. Now let us look at the details.

CHARITY

In their own manner, worldlings also have charity. They proclaim to each other how much it pains them to be separated, how much they enjoy each other's company and conversation, how they miss each other, how glad they are to meet again. This whole love is infernal. The Christian's charity joins us immediately with God and unites us with men in a supernatural brotherhood. Our love for one another is charity. Do you not know that it is our charity which makes us one with Christ? Charity cries out to Christ from within us; charity cries out for us from Christ Himself.[1] This is a love which is loftier than all natural loves, as that of a husband for his wife or a father for his children. . . . It is a love which makes a new people and a new spouse for the Son of God. . . . It does not resemble in any way the affections which are corrupt . . . nor is it the love men have for one another because they are human beings. Rather, they love one another because they are God's children, children of the Most High, in order to be brothers of the Only-begotten, and they love with the same love with which He loves us. It is a love which must carry them to the goal that will fully satisfy all their desires. And this goal will have no end. Yet no one reaches it who does not first die to the world, not with the complete death of separation of soul and body, but by dying to material things, whereby we raise up our hearts even while we still live in the flesh. It is this death of which St. Paul writes: "For you are dead, and your life is hid with Christ in God" (Col. 3:3). But this love is our very dying to the world, our life with God. This love makes us die to the world, though still living in the body. Moreover, this love is our very death to the world and our life in God. If the soul's separation from the body is called death, will not the separation of your love from the world also be death? Love is as strong as death. What is stronger than that which vanquishes death? [2]

The whole theology of charity is in these lines. Later theologians will explain the radical difference between charity and the love of concupiscence. They will explain its intrinsic unifying and communicative power, its penetrating power as regards God, its purgative power with respect to the world and ourselves, its fundamental significance for life and, therefore, its status as a regulating principle for the remaining obligations of the Christian. But in these lines there is summarized, deliberately and not accidentally, this whole magnificent panorama of charity.

Nor was the Saint satisfied with a panoramic view. Instead, he speaks constantly of charity, even to the point of devoting to it almost his entire commentary on the beautiful Epistle by St. John. In these continual references and explanations concerning charity he expounds the various aspects which are here synthesized. From their reading of St. Augustine, all the commentators select charity as the primary foundation of the Saint's spirituality.[3] This is logical. And if we overlook this, St. Augustine appears to us as too intellectual, for example, when we cite only some of his isolated statements. It is love alone, and the rule of love, which dominate life as a whole, from its first manifestations to the final heartbeat.

God promises not to defraud love. This would be the most discouraging of all deceptions. "Do not defraud your love, O believer! Believe that you will come to behold Me. You love and you do not see. Yet is it not this very love which brings you sight? Love! Persevere in loving; and I, who purified your heart, will not defraud that heart. Why did I cleanse it, except that you might see your God?" [4]

God will not cheat man in the next life, nor has He cheated him in this. No saint has ever felt that he was cheated. Familiarity with God in this world has always been a reflection and pledge of that which will follow in eternity. Therefore St. Augustine reproaches the soul and says to it: "Up to now you have been too long occupied and weighted down with a variety of desires, sick, distracted, divided by many affections, ever restless, nowhere secure. Withdraw into yourself, no matter what is delighting you externally; seek here within, Him who is your Maker," for He is more beauteous and desirable than all that fills heaven and earth.[5]

As a function of this intimacy, the love of God, progressing and penetrating, separates man from the world. This is the dynamic office of love, which, as St. Augustine observes, cannot be inactive. Love forever seeks greater intimacy and penetration, in whichever of the two directions it may turn, toward God or toward the world. And the intensity of love to one direction makes man incapable of intense love in the other direction. "Even as impure love inflames the soul, impels it to seek and desire what is earthly, so sacred love elevates man through his eagerness for everlasting treasures, and through love of that which fails not nor dies. It influences him, inflames him, lifts him from the depths of hell to heaven. Love possesses its own power, and it cannot remain static in the soul of him who loves. It must necessarily move him. Do you want to know what kind of love you have? Look where it leads you. Therefore, we do not say that you should love nothing, but we say that you should not love the world, so that in its place you may love Him who made the world. If the soul moves along burdened with earthly love, its wings are tied and it cannot fly. But cleansed of its earthly affections, of worldly preoccupations, it flies swiftly, its two wings stretched out (the two commandments of love, love of God and love of neighbor). And where shall it rise in its flight except to God, since it rises in love?" [6]

Let us note an important idea. Non-Christian existentialists wish to break, even with common sense, because this faculty is placed as a restriction on man and his potentialities. For this same reason they repudiate Catholic dogma and morals, believing that one cannot speak of a humanism which sets up obstacles through dogmas and ethics. We have seen that faith confers a sense of freedom, and now we shall see that love also has this quality. The Saint has told us this, but it is fitting to note it here. Love is an emancipation from the external environment and from ourselves. When flesh and spirit struggle within us, the stronger will prevail. If we see that flesh is going to win, let us humble ourselves, and through prayer and intercession let us call upon God's mercy, for He does not despise the contrite heart. Then, with the new assistance of charity, He will free us from danger. Because the Holy Ghost is the captain of our freedom.[7]

This charity, which in its inner dimension is intimacy, becomes a purification in its anti-worldly consequences. Charity is like a fire which consumes our weeds and underbrush, the wilderness of our sins and bad habits, allowing God to build His temple within us. . . . Who can resist death? One can resist fire, waves, iron; one can resist princes and powers. But death comes, and who can withstand? Nothing is as strong as death. Therefore love has been likened to death; and since love slays that which we were in order that we may become what we were not, it causes a kind of death within us. This death was experienced by him who said: "But God forbid that I should glory, save in the cross of our Lord Jesus Christ, by whom the world is crucified to me and I to the world" (Gal. 6:14). Moreover, those to whom he addressed these words had experienced the same death; "You are dead, and your life is hidden with Christ in God" (Col. 3:3).[8]

Persisting in his argument that we are pilgrims, St. Augustine explains the function of charity in the wilderness of this life. We are, he says, just as much pilgrims in this world as were the Israelites in the desert. . . . They were slow in reaching their fatherland, not because they were abandoned but because they were being tested. So also with us; we have been promised ineffable pleasures and delights, and therefore we are tested in temporal trials and temptations which instruct us in many things. But if you do not wish to die of thirst along the desert path, then drink of love. This is the fountain which God desired to give us, that we might neither faint nor fail along the way. And we shall drink far more deeply when we reach our fatherland.[9] Charity is the hymn of Christians along their journey; this is the fire which ever burns within them. The rest of the Christian's activities undergo interruptions, but charity never. There is a time for fasting, a time for almsgiving and works of mercy, a time to visit the sick, to reconcile discords, etc. All these activities have their times and seasons. But it is always time for love. Let love never be halted or interrupted, and let works of charity appear according to the times and season.[10]

HOPE

Prudence of the spirit (which is a distinctive quality of the New Testament) encounters its radical opposition in prudence of the flesh (the prudence of this world), because the former does not place its hope in this world's goods.[11] It is not that Christian prudence does not have hope, but it places it in something higher. Or, if you will, we can say that what formerly was an "external" aid is now an "internal" support. St. Augustine carefully notes this quality of the *interiority* of hope in his own conversion. When he observed that his interior was illuminated, that he no longer desired external things in which it seemed to him that he himself was multiplied, he noted that God had established him in hope.[12] His life then possessed an inward support which was far more secure. Hope does not signify the assurance of being able to eat or of having the things that are more or less essential to life. Hope is the inward assurance of life based on God's promise and on His omnipotence in fulfilling it. Yet so far as we are concerned, this is not an assurance exempt from fear, since we are evil. This vital sense of confidence in God makes our life serene amid trials and in the long hours of waiting.

It is a reply which God gives to the world. He willed to answer one by one the secularizing, worldly tendencies, and this is one response which preserves the same direction, but changes the target, raising it to supernatural status. He placed the darkness of mysteries and a hidden hope in the hearts of believers, where He Himself hides, without abandoning them. In this encompassing gloom we walk by faith, not by sight, until there comes that which we do not see but hope for, that which we await with patience.[13] Yes, "a hidden hope dwells secretly in the heart of believers, where God Himself hides." The entire life of a Christian must seem pure absurdity to one who does not understand where our hope resides. And the Christian who does not have recourse to hope will not know how to surmount torments and trials without or within. Our hope, as I already have stated once, is not the expectation of repeated failure which postpones until later what we cannot here achieve. Our hope is a theological virtue that joins us immediately to God. What we hope for is not what we lack here, but it is God Himself. What we lack here, what we suffer here, succeeds only in sharpening our desire and purifying our soul the better to possess it.

The Saint says: "We shall be like to Him, for we shall see Him as He is" (I John 3:2). Let the tongue continue to praise as much as it can, let the heart supply what is wanting! . . . All that we can say is less than the reality. But let us turn to our own inner self, there where we are being shown things we cannot express; and since we cannot as yet live these realities, let us busy ourselves in desiring them. You do not as yet see what you desire; yet by desiring it you make yourself more capable of being filled when what you desire shall come to pass. It is as if you wished to fill something—a bag, a wineskin. If you see that the amount which you have to enclose is great, then you first open the receptacle to its full capacity, since you see the large amount that you have to pour in, and the narrowness of the container. So also God; by postponing, He expands our desire; through desire He enlarges our soul; by enlarging our soul He makes it capable of holding more. Let us desire, brothers, because we must be filled. . . . This is our life, exercising ourselves in desiring. And the more this holy desire exercises us, the more we curtail our desire of loving this world. We have already stated this: First empty what is to be filled! If it is to be filled with goodness, then cast out the wickedness within. Supposing God wishes to fill you with honey; if you are filled with bitterness and gall, where will you put the honey? First you must empty out what the vessel contains; you must cleanse the receptacle itself; cleanse it, even though this requires great effort, scouring it so that it will be clean and suitable. Let us curse whatever it may be, whether gold or wine. All that we hope for, and cannot express, all that we wish to say, is God. And when we say God, what have we said? Have we stated in a single syllable all that we hope for?

Whatever we might be able to add is less. Let us extend ourselves toward Him, so that when He comes He will satisfy us. "We shall be like to Him, for we shall see Him as He is" (I John 3:2).[14] This is the internal ramification of our hope and the ultimate reason why we abstain from worldly things. Let no one say that we believe all things of this world to be wicked; what we say is that we intend to find full satisfaction in God alone.

For our long period of waiting, during which it seems that God tarries the longest, we have here within us our own dialogue and promise: "We know that the Christian's resurrection already has been accomplished in our Head, and that it will be wrought in the members. The Head of the Church is Christ; the members of Christ are the Church. What happened first to the Head will continue in the body. This is our hope. Therefore we believe. For this reason we persevere and endure in the midst of so much wickedness in this world, for we are comforted by hope, even before that hope achieves its fullness.[15] It is like the mooring of a ship; through hope we already have our life anchored in the port. Navigation continues, and we may even run into storms, but we know how we should maneuver, for we already have a safe port.[16]

HUMILITY

We have stated that Christ's humility made the foundations of the earth tremble. He made it tremble in a twofold manner, as St. Augustine explains. The first was by way of amazement. Those who loved the world could not understand why Christ should thus love and give preference to humility, poverty and death, which according to them are the greatest misfortunes. The other was that many were moved to despise the vanity they loved previously and to follow His example.[17] The example of

Christ will always be a scandal for this world. He chose lowly paths, and then He declared that He was a king, that He was God!

Christ continued His offensive against the world even to the last resistance; He defeated the world in society as a whole and in each individual. To overcome the world He chose the foolish and the lowly. St. Augustine observes that although Christ spoke such lofty words in praise of Nathaniel, He did not choose Him as an apostle, perhaps because the latter was so skilled in the law. Christ preferred common people, fishermen. Desiring to crush the stiff neck of the proud, He did not look to the orator, but rather to the fisherman; yet through the fisherman He won the emperor. Cyprian was a great orator, but first of all Christ chose Peter, the fisherman, through whom not only the orator but also the emperor came to believe. No aristocrat, no scholar was chosen first, because "God hath chosen the weak things of the world to put to shame the strong" (I Cor. 1:27).[18] Manifestly, humility is the salient trait in the "City of God," even as pride is the mark of the "City of Man." [19] Humility is the unifying force; and therefore it could not be wanting in the "City of God." And the lowliness of Christ possesses this unifying power in a special manner.[20]

In man, too, He has defeated every presumptuous impulse. He subdued the mind through faith; He crushed self-confidence through temptation. This is what our Master and Teacher wished to show us in permitting the fall of Peter, who trusted in himself.[21] And in another passage: "The oven trieth the potter's wares, and tribulation trieth men." The potter's wares must go into the oven. But the potter is not sure [of their quality] when they go in; only when they come out. However, God is sure, because He knows which ones are His own, and which ones will break in the oven. Those which do not break are the ones which do not have bubbles of pride. It is humility which preserves us in every temptation.[22] This means that all life is subject to God, because all depends on His grace.

As the devil is head and chief of the proud, so Christ humbled Himself in order to be the Head and Chief of men. This is the contrast and counterpoint which St. Augustine continually sets up, commenting on the Word made flesh.[23] Predicated on this incorporation in Christ, humility proceeds to cure us of our residual pride and of any new growth.[24] This is a subject which St. Augustine will frequently repeat, for humility is the root of all other virtues and gifts of God.

Our hope and our knowledge of ourselves establish us in the way of humility. We know that what we hope for is very great, but we also know that it is a low road [which leads to our destination].[25] Being persuaded of this, we prefer to be Christ's insignificant beasts of burden, which He shall ride and direct through life's paths.[26]

LIFE'S TRIALS

We are not speaking of God redeeming man in order to remove him from the world, but of God separating the Christian from the world. In every ascetical treatise this has two aspects. We can consider one as punishment, to eradicate what still remains of the world, and the other as a testing and purification, in order that the soul may rise higher on the ladder of perfection. Both represent a process of *desecularization*, but there is a shift of emphasis, since in the second phase God is moved by a special love for the soul when He thus acts.

TESTS WHICH GOD SENDS IN ORDER TO DETACH US FROM THE WORLD

St. Augustine has given us an extensive account of the first of these methods, particularly in his *Confessions*, where he himself is purged of his worldliness. He narrates how he followed the world's broad highways, eagerly desirous of its honors, its riches, or marriage; and God ridiculed him. Amid all these desires he suffered keen torments; nor did God permit him to find joy in them. How wretched was his soul! "And Thou, Lord, didst turn the knife in the most sensitive area of my wound, so that leaving all else I might turn to Thee, who art above all." [27] This he stated frequently, applying it to all who are sick with worldliness. "There are many proud individuals who, though Christians, put their trust in the world. They adore Christ, but they do not find full satisfaction in Him. They feel contented, they are filled with pride in themselves. They adore Christ, they venerate Christ, they ask Christ for favors. But they will not be filled with His wisdom and His righteousness. Why? Because they are not poor and lowly of heart." [28] The soul experiences a dissatisfaction with *things*, because these cannot fill it completely; and this is common to all men. Nor is there any greater discontent for Christians, since God has greater love for them and does not allow them to find elsewhere the delight which they expected. Nevertheless, profiting by this outward distraction and diversion of soul, things wound man still more deeply,[29] and as the Saint stated earlier, God thrusts the knife into the most sensitive area of the wound.

These are the Christians who complain that God does not hear their prayers. But God is deaf to our temporal demands, since He wants us to raise up our hearts to things eternal.[30] We should not, however, confuse matters, for then we lose hope and faith. God has promised His help to those that pray, but nowhere has He pledged Himself to take care of our vineyard or to guard our sheep. He has promised His help, and He gives it, with respect to life everlasting, as well as the consolations of heart and joys of conscience. This is precisely the sore-spot of the worldly.[31] It is not that God denies bread and water to His own, but He grants or denies to them those benefits in view of their salvation. God our Father knows full well that we need these things, nor will He deny us what we require. He knows also that in their own way material things are like little stars in life, in this world's night. But what He does not desire is that we transform these stars into footmen's running lights, confusing lights which collide with everything, for our life is illumined within by Christ. When He comes to the soul, kindles faith within it, endows it with patience, teaches it not to become unduly exalted in prosperity nor inordinately despondent in adversity, then the Christian begins to feel indifference in his use of the world. He does not grow proud when things go his way, nor does he despair if things turn against him; but in all things he blesses God.[32]

The self-seeking Christian has historical antecedents, as St. Augustine well knew. Explaining Christ's words to the Jews, "You seek Me, not because you saw signs and wonders, but because you were filled with My bread," the Saint says: "How many there are who seek Jesus because He favors them in temporal affairs! This person has some business, and seeks the intervention and assistance of the clergy; another individual feels himself oppressed by someone more powerful, and looks for refuge in the Church; still another wishes to have more influence with someone who has little; all of them with ostentation. Daily we find the churches filled with just such people. Scarcely anyone seeks Jesus for His own sake." [33]

The Saint explains God's providence in the division of temporal goods as follows: God gives temporal goods to the good and the evil. If He gave them only to the good, then the wicked might think that the good adore God only for the sake of the benefits they receive from Him. If He granted them only to the wicked, then weak Christians would be afraid to turn to Him, lest they suffer deprivation. . . . God must care for these weak persons; He must cultivate and prune them like tender trees. If He conferred benefits only on the good, then all would be converted in order to possess these things.[34]

In this same passage the Saint observes how God is accustomed to take away worldly possessions from the good so that they may learn rightly to appraise them, that they may not think they are deprived of everything before they have sampled it. The Saint brings the subject into focus from a general standpoint and reminds us that God takes away advantages from the good, but He also takes them away from the wicked. It is interesting to observe the different manner of dispossession: "If God took away things only from the wicked, they could think that in this alone He was punishing them. If He grants gifts to the good, He gives them as a relief for travelers. If He also grants gifts to the wicked, He reminds them that they should desire other gifts which He is not conferring upon them. He takes possessions from the good to test their strength, that those who perhaps did not know may now know whether they are able to say: 'The Lord gave; the Lord hath taken away. Blessed be the name of the Lord' (Job 1:21). God takes away what He gave; but He who gave all good things does not remove Himself. The soul which is not bound down by ties of earthly things shines with the splendor of virtues, flies on wings of love and soars impetuously through the free air. . . . To achieve this, He takes away what He gave. But someone feels weak and asks: When shall I be as brave as holy Job? You admire the strength of the giant tree, because you are still small; yet these great trees which you marvel at, beneath whose shade you find rest, one day were merely small shoots. With this in mind, are you afraid that He will deprive you of your possessions?

"Note that sometimes He takes them away from the wicked. Why, then, do you postpone your conversion? What you fear to lose if you are good, perchance you will also lose if you are bad. The difference is this: if you lose these things when you are good, your Comforter still abides with you, even He who took them away. The treasure chest is empty of gold, but the heart is filled with faith. You are poor without, but rich within. You bear within you certain riches which you will not lose, even if you should emerge naked from a shipwreck. . . . But the situation of the wicked is much worse; their house is empty, and their conscience is emptier still. When a wicked man fails, he no longer possesses externally what he formerly had, nor has he any refuge within where he may find repose. He leaves the scene of his failure; he no longer dares to appear before men. Nor can he turn inward, for there he has nothing.

"He has not imitated the ant; he did not store away his grain while it was still summer. What do I mean when I say summer? While his life was tranquil, while he was prosperous in this world, when he was rested, when everyone thought him happy, then was his August. He might have imitated the ant had he listened to God's words; then he would have gathered in grain and stored it within himself. Afterwards, had the temptation of misfortune come upon him, the paralyzing winter of his discontent, the tempest of fear, the icy blast of sorrow, whether in the form of injury or threats against his health or in mourning or disgrace or humiliation—to sum it up, his winter—then, like the ant, he would have recourse to what he stored up in the summer.

"Consider one of God's 'ants.' Daily he arises and goes to church; he prays, listens to readings, sings hymns, reflects on what he has heard, meditates, collects the grain which he gathered at the harvest. . . . All see him go to church, return from church, listen to sermons, listen to readings, open the book and read it. All see this, when he does it. The little ant, which has such a busy time going back and forth, carries the kernels before the same men who sift. But one day winter comes (and whom does it not visit?). Injury and loss occur; all are sorry for him, and consider him unfortunate, because they do not know that *within himself* he has nourishment. They say: 'Poor fellow, what a terrible misfortune has hit him!' Why do they say this? Because they are measuring others by their own standards and strength, and therefore they deceive themselves. They wish to measure with their own norms that which they do not know. . . . Do you believe that the person who suffers this misfortune has done something to deserve it? . . . . You do not know what you are saying; you are indeed your own enemy, because you have not stored up for yourself such things as he collected. Now the ant consumes what it gathered with such effort in the summer. You could see the ant while it was storing its provisions; now it consumes the grain, but you cannot see it." [35]

Here is the whole marvelous secret of Christian tranquillity amid suffering and misfortunes, all beautifully expressed, expounded with appropriate analogies of the seedlings and tiny tree, of God's eager "ant." Who does not tremble at the mere announcement of a hail storm of severe punishments? And we see here how these come upon a person, even on those who have always been "ants" of God, and fill their life with coldness and bitterness, perhaps to the point of destroying it. Here it seems as if God has abandoned the soul. It is impossible to combine more misfortunes and visit them simultaneously upon one single individual. We all are struck with consternation at seeing him suffer so greatly. . . . But when the storm has passed and the atmosphere has cleared, that pale, suffering figure acquires the stature of a giant, a mysterious depth, a beauty, a mastery, a dominion, a magnetism which comes to him from above the human.

The whole of rebellious "humanism," with all its polish, prestige and power, has not yet brought forth a life as brave and serene as this. It is a kind of transfiguration; love transfigures, even as sorrow also transfigures. Sorrow, because sorrow is a manifestation of love; love, because it is an expression of this "within," which St. Augustine describes to us as a house where God dwells, the sound of intimate conversations, the joy of secret songs. Outside, as long as God may so ordain, winter holds sway.

But no matter how much we may say about this inner mystery, a true power of resistance and a source of peace amid life's storms, it is certain that the tests which God imposes are a scandal for many Christians. Seeing that the good suffer trials (they themselves are the good but when others suffer it does not bother them) and the wicked triumph and prosper, they believe that God has no care for the things of this earth. In their consciences they already know that God is punishing them for some fault of theirs, but then they say: "Others are worse, and nothing happens to them." Consider, says St. Augustine, whether these are not evil persons who, wishing to justify themselves, attribute injustice to God.[36] If they do not attain something better, and if they notice that God does not relieve the poverty in which they live, while shameless sinners abound in everything, they also become shameless sinners, in order to acquire for themselves what God's providence has not conferred upon them. The Saint notes that this is the case of the fish, which is so happy when he has swallowed the bait, because the angler's hook has not as yet pulled him out of the water. . . . "If you wish to cross this ocean of temptations, do not avoid the Cross of Christ. Christ suffered as an example for you. . . . Do not become vexed by what happens to you in a short period of time, but rather measure these few days with the measuring rod of eternity, for all that is to happen has not yet come to pass." [37]

Whether your reaction is one of scandal or of patience, it is fitting to recall that all trials are controlled by God in the most minute details. The Saint often refers to Job's situation. In order to harm him, the devil had to obtain God's permission, because he has no such power except God grant it to him. Job himself, when he submits to the will of Him who is testing him, does not say, "The Lord gave to me and the devil hath taken away from me," but rather: "The Lord gave and the Lord hath taken away" [38] (Job 1:21).

God derives good from everything. We have the supreme example of this in Christ, who, "knowing that the Father has placed all things in His hands, even Judas, patiently employed His enemies for the benefit of His friends." [39] God knows perfectly what He is doing, because He knows perfectly what He wishes to confer upon us. He is like the father who has a son and heir. With advice or with the rod he teaches him what he should do, that he should not squander his inheritance after the father's death. God does the same, but with this difference, that we shall have our inheritance, not *after* Him but *with* Him, for all eternity. . . . "Be not solicitous, then, for the health of your body; instead you should be concerned to keep a sound heart (Matt. 6:25–30). There are many who lie in sick-beds, and persevere in their innocence, but would be wicked if they enjoyed good health. Are there not many who would be better off in sickness? Would not some illness be better for the criminal who chokes another with his own hands? Would not a fever be better for a man who now is able to get up at night to break into his neighbor's house? . . . The Lord knows what is good for us. Let us strive to keep our hearts pure; and if we are tempted and tried, let us resort to prayer.

"St. Paul besought the Lord to remove a goad or sting in his flesh, and God did not remove it (II Cor. 12:7–10). Was he troubled, did he grow sad and begin to protest, claiming that he was abandoned? The Physician's voice answered him: 'My grace is sufficient for thee, for virtue is made perfect in infirmity.' How do you know that God does not wish to heal you? Or in what aspect of life it is most advantageous for you to be punished? How do you know whether that which He amputates is gangrenous? Does not the physician know what he is doing, how deep he should make the incision? Will the patient's cries stay the physician's hand? The former cries out, but the surgeon continues the operation. Is he cruel because he does not listen to the sick man's cries? Or is he not rather merciful in seeking to cure the sick man?" [40]

TRIALS WHICH GOD SENDS IN ORDER TO PERFECT US

God has His plan for saving man, and according to this He adapts His tests. Because of this salvific will, the just man is more severely tested in this world. We observed it before. Just as in the economy of the Old Testament, temporal goods had the function of reward, so in the New Testament, God Himself is the reward. For this reason He purifies all the elect by means of trials and purifications which they receive especially in this life. St. Augustine touches on this thought continually: "In this life every just man, whoever he be, is destined to undergo sufferings and to bear with them." [41] And he formulates a general law in these terms: God punishes each son whom He receives. And the Saint observes that He did not dispense His own Son from this law.[42] This is a universal law from which only those are exempted of whose amendment God is distrustful. "Sometimes sinners are not punished, or very lightly punished in this life, because He sees no hope of their correction. Yet it is necessary that He strike and chasten those whom He is preparing for everlasting life." [43] In making this statement, Augustine exhausts his similes. He desired his faithful to have a clear understanding of the Christian's sufferings, and not to think, as bad Christians do, that suffering is only in proportion to their sins. There may be some chastisements which are like this, but there are also tests and trials from God which are exactly in proportion to the degree of purification which God wishes to effect in the soul. "The first concern," he says, "is that you should be dissatisfied with yourself, in order that you may change for the better. And precisely because you have changed, you should endure the trials of this world, and persevere in their midst even to the end." [44]

It is logical, completely logical, that it should happen this way, though men may not wish to understand it. In order to convince them, St. Augustine returns to the fundamentals of our religion. Our religion is a religion of grace. "Do you love God in order that He may give you this world's goods? Indeed, you belong to grace. If God gave you His grace, gave it to you freely, then love Him freely. Do not love God for what He can give you, but in order that God Himself may be your reward." [45] In this respect also God is man's center, and naught besides God avails in the present economy. We already have stated its value and function. This new foundation of the Christian religion eradicates every type of materialism. The following of Christ has no earthly promises of reward in terms of earthly goods. There is the model, Christ Himself, and one who departs from this norm is not a Christian.

Yet the Saint exhorts us. Christ chose a difficult way for Himself. We too must renounce all the easy roads, and as a reward He will give us everlasting happiness. If we compare what we give—a few bad days—with what He gives us—an eternity of happiness—we see that we are giving nothing. If it were a case of strict justice, rather than going to everlasting bliss, we would deserve the punishment of eternal wretchedness. But as everlasting damnation would never end, so too we never would attain to a happy eternity. It is necessary, therefore, that our trials be limited in time, so that when they have terminated we may enter into everlasting joy. This occurs not only because God wills that our trials should be temporary, but also because He wants us to merit everlasting happiness. Finally, man's days are few, and hence his suffering will not endure for long. But let us suppose that an individual spends every day of his life in toil, in suffering, in sorrow, in torment, in prison, in sickness, with hunger and thirst, day after day, hour after hour, until he reaches old age; in the last analysis, man's days are few and for past sufferings he comes into possession of an everlasting kingdom, becomes equal to the angels, enters into Christ's inheritance, becoming co-heir with Christ.

Veteran soldiers spend their lives amid wounds; they begin as young men and end as old men. In order to have some quiet, restful days in their old age, when the years begin to undermine what the wars have spared, how much they endure, what long marches, what endurance of heat and cold, what wounds and dangers they risk! These experiences did not frighten them; they awaited only the quiet days they would spend in their old age, though they do not know whether they will live to see them.

St. Augustine said all this with respect to Christ's way. If you are indeed a Christian—and he is a Christian who does not despise Christ's way—then follow closely in Christ's path, through His sufferings, and you will not depart from the road He traveled. Perhaps this will seem hard to you, but it is the only sure way. Other roads may have pleasures, but they are full of robbers.[46] Moreover, he tells those who want God to give them earthly goods, who turn away from Him if He does not give them, that in this life we are as God's workers, and every worker must first of all toil, and later receive his daily wages. How, then, will we dare to demand recompense before we have done the work? [47]

Unless we understand this thoroughly, it can lead us to a certain feeling of rebellion, because we will think that God, being all-powerful, can choose other less difficult ways, for example, to have us work hard in the dissemination of His teaching or in organizing His doctrine. To be sure, these activities are not excluded from God's kingdom, but in order to achieve what we are striving for, the way He has chosen is better. God has forcefully demonstrated that He loves us, submitting to sorrow, sacrifice, and even death for our sake. This is convincing proof, and no longer may anyone doubt that God loves us. Because He loves us He has chosen us, has made salvation easier for us. One way in which He facilitates salvation is to deprive us of this world's goods, so that we will desire those that are eternal.

Therefore, with respect to God, love is the explanation. To this love we should respond with our own love. Here also the surest proof of our love is suffering, whether in the form of bearing persecution, enduring privation, tribulation, or God's absence. Deception resides in all else—in our believing that we are apostolic heroes, when in reality we are looking for some distraction from our inner boredom. It is a deception when we think we are determined defenders of Christ, like Peter, before the arrival of the maid-servant who was to denounce him. St. Augustine notes this trait in the trials which God permits. If it is a question of tempting man in order to deceive and mislead him, to effect his damnation, these temptations are not from God. God's trials are intended to determine whether we love God, not because God does not know this, but because we do not know. And this test reveals us to ourselves. Such is the situation of Job, and that of Peter.[48] There is no sadism on the part of God, but only mercy and love—love which He has for us, and mercy which more readily enables us to renounce things that of our own strength we would with difficulty renounce. And on our part, love, above all else. Suffering without love can only be the sinister practice of the melancholy and the morbid, of Moslem fakirs. Suffering for its own sake, without love, is worthless.

To summarize, the trials of the Christian have so much importance in our life, viewed from the standpoint of salvation, that salvation cannot be conceived of in any other terms: "If you believe you can live without tribulation, you have not yet begun to be a Christian. Have you forgotten the Apostle's statement: 'All who desire to live piously will suffer temptations'? If you do not endure any persecution for the sake of Christ, you have not begun to live in Christ. When you begin to live for Christ, you are approaching the wine-press; prepare your soul for tests and trials. But do not become dried up, lest the wine-press squeeze nothing out of you." [49]

We can suffer without wishing to, but love is required so that when we go to the wine-press our sufferings will produce fruit. God will not let us lack trials and tests, since He knows we need them. We have heard how, in the face of a certain Christian's satisfaction that the persecutions had ceased on the emperor's conversion, St. Augustine asked, "But has the devil, then, been converted?" [50]

Christ cautioned His own that He was sending them as lambs among wolves. It matters little that the roar of the ocean from time to time is muted. And even if it should cease entirely, God would not lack means to test us, to improve us, to profit us, for when all is tranquil, "the treasures of the deep" will abide. And we know not what is in "the treasures of the deep," from which our Father can draw forth something to punish us.[51]

God has many ways to try us. St. Augustine presents several of them. In one, which includes every possible condition of the predestined, he informs us that we can distinguish four categories: 1) the temptation of error, and hunger for the word. This is a series of tests which ensue before men are converted. When they are still neglectful of God and entangled in the world, God proceeds to arouse them from their slumber. They realize the meaning of these symptoms which so hurt and wounded Christ: the flood-tide of error and the hunger for truth. This terminates in conversion. 2) The convert begins to fight against his sins and his evil inclinations; "he finds himself hobbled by concupiscence, and he cannot walk." He feels as if there were a wall in front of him which impeded his way, he sees all doors closed, nor can he find even one through which to escape and live right. Now he knows that he must live right; something he formerly did not know. But when he attempts it, he cannot succeed. Then he cries out to the Lord. The second difficulty, therefore, consists in behavior and conduct. 3) When God has granted them the mercy of living as they prayed to live, of overcoming temptations, then He tests them with spiritual lassitude and languor, especially in view of the waiting to which they are subjected in this life. This sometimes reaches the point where they do not wish to read or pray. First hunger, then satiety; precisely the opposite of their first trial. Nor is this a trivial temptation; and we should be alert lest it distort our way and destroy us. Yet, since the Lord delivered us from the two previous temptations, let us pray that He will also deliver us from this one. 4) It may come about that God will promote to places of authority in the Church those who have passed these three tests. The storms raging against the Church will trouble those who rule it. The greater the honors bestowed upon us, the greater our danger. These hazards may assume the form of solicitude on the part of one who is responsible for the souls of others, or they may be blows which the enemy directs especially at the individual who holds the tiller in his hands.[52]

In various parts of his works St. Augustine then explains, more or less, these tests and trials, adding details. We have quoted some of these already, in discussing the world's persecutions and the lack of understanding which the worldly manifest with respect to our very real trials and sufferings. Here we can add others, for example, the sufferings of the just man occur either because he is not yet in his true homeland (and only God understands such persons), or because he bears his own sorrows or those that others inflict upon him.[53] Some of the tests to which our life is subjected are like fire, others like water. Those which resemble fire are the ones which deprive us of happiness; those that are like water confer happiness upon us. The former burn us; the latter corrode and corrupt us.[54] In a noteworthy observation the Saint points out that the entire human race, as Adam's descendents, is being scourged. But while the wicked harden themselves even more, the elect, like children, "experience a feeling of sadness." They know full well who is scourging them, and therefore they cry out to heaven.[55]

Amid all these trials we should pray, both in those in which our test is the long boredom of a lengthy period of waiting, as well as in others where our agony is perhaps not so pure. During the interior trials there are groans emitted from the heart, which only God hears and understands.[56] During those trials they would prefer to possess God by means of sufferings rather than have their trials cease.[57] No matter how much we cry out, until we reach the degree of purity which God has ordained, our sufferings will not end. God, says the Saint, is like a mother who bathes her little children; even if they scream and kick, the mother continues bathing them, so that they will be clean and healthy.[58] So also it is not Christian conduct to have recourse to the mighty of this world, trusting in them and not in God, for they, and in fact everyone, lack the strength to help us.[59]

The pattern which God follows in hearing the prayer of the anguished is simple: in their hour of trial God hears the prayer of those to whom He has granted the gift of "being poor," that is, of divesting themselves of the love of this world, and He will grant them to experience a secret satisfaction.[60]

God moves in the midst of life's evils, helping.[61] And he whom God helps is confident.[62] What happens is that God gives us His assistance, and not always in the way we expected.[63] This procedure of modifying the way we had thought He would help us is really disturbing, if we do not reflect a moment. The change can be so radical that our prayer can be heard and help granted in the form of tribulation.[64]

In whatever way His help is granted or postponed, we must know that in curing evils, God looks to healing the soul rather than the body.[65] This is the basic distinction which St. Augustine makes in order to affirm two things which seem contradictory: God always hears us *ad aeternitatem* (with a view to our eternal salvation) and God does not always hear us *ad voluntatem* (according to our own will). In this statement he admits that prayer is always heard in relation to the goods or trials of this world.[66] Sometimes it is not that God refuses, but simply delays His gift, so that we will better appreciate it, because He knows the profitable hour for bestowing the gift.[67]

However, in connection with this entire question we should remember our union with Christ, from which suffering and prayer have their greatness and true meaning. It is not necessary for us to repeat what we have already stated; we need only add that the efficacy of prayer is in direct proportion to our union with Christ. It may come about that worldly desires and desires which proceed from our union with Christ may enter our prayer. We may think that both are fitting. But may God refuse to grant what is not for our own good! Rather, let us ask Him for what is proper and appropriate for us; and then He will give it to us. Yet, if He does not bestow it upon us, this is an indication that what we are asking is not a consequence of our union with Christ and that the effect of His words does not abide with us. In this instance it is a case of our concupiscence expressing itself. Let us take as our model His own words in the *Our Father*; let us not depart from the letter or spirit of this prayer, and then He will give us what we ask for.[68]

As a consequence of this principle of our union with Christ, that prayer which is not founded on faith and that prayer which militates against our eternal salvation are alien to Christ;[69] in other words, prayer which does not have its roots in Christ (and faith is our root in Christ) and prayer that is opposed to our salvation (which is the purpose of our incorporation in Christ). Manifestly we need someone to direct us and to teach us how to pray; otherwise our prayer might ask for that which we do not know to be suitable for us. Christ already provided for this by His example and by teaching us the *Our Father*. The prayer from the Cross also contains a lesson in this respect.[70] But it is the Holy Ghost who groans within us and makes intercession for us when He causes us to cry out in love.[71]

To summarize, since we are convinced of the great gift which God has conferred on us through His election and that we are destined to possess Him as our heritage, we should at every moment observe the attitude and conduct of pilgrims. We are journeying through this world, and all the possessions we have amassed here are merely rations for our march. The rest and repose which we derive from material things are only a brief restoration of strength at an inn, so that we can continue our progress.[72] We are weary travelers, for within us our very flesh makes war against us[73] (because it has an exasperated desire for resurrection), and outside of us the world tortures us with scandals and hatreds. We are thirsty travelers whose thirst cannot be slaked at any little fountain along the way, because we thirst for God.[74] Further, since we know the sublime good which awaits us, of which we already possess an assurance and pledge in our hearts, we try to bless God and love Him when He prunes us and cauterizes us.[75] We are mariners on a treacherous sea, but Christ, who walked on the waves, treading surely on their liquid inconstancy, travels with us.[76]

23

Synthesis and Conclusion

ST. AUGUSTINE IS PARTIAL to syntheses, extensive syntheses which provide clarity and scope, which reveal to the mind of the faithful the whole life of God as well as the life of men. Often the Saint repeats two words to summarize the entire mystery of our faith: *create* and *re-create.* This appears in many passages, for St. Augustine was tireless in speaking and tireless in repeating. To find synthesis for this present work, we shall begin by employing one that St. Augustine prepared in his old age.

1) All creatures that enter into existence and depart from it in such magnificent order come from God. "Thou hast wrought all things in wisdom." These last words serve St. Augustine as points of departure for a stroke of genius: Therefore Thou hast wrought all things in Christ. He that was despised, spat upon, crowned with thorns; He that was crucified; in Him Thou hast done all things. . . . "And the whole earth is filled with Thy creation." The whole earth is filled with Christ's creation. . . . What has He wrought except by means of His Son?

St. Augustine finds the best support for this conclusion in

St. Paul himself: "But we preach Christ Crucified, unto the Jews a stumbling block, and unto the Greeks foolishness; but unto them which are called, both Jews and Greeks, Christ the power of God, and the wisdom of God" (I Cor. 1:23–24).

2) The work of creation was restored and perfected by the work of Redemption. What the Saint expresses as "re-create" has a substantive equivalent which comprehends all: the Church. This is the "new creature" which God has also wrought through Christ, new with the fresh luxuriousness of a freshly sown field, where the green verdure of the grain arises from the wheat kernel that died. In only one place on the earth's surface was He crucified; the grain fell on only one small spot, and there it died. But how great is the yield which it brought forth! There are not many, but there is only one new creature here produced, made up of all who believe in Christ, who have stripped themselves of the old man and put on the new.[1]

Such is the synthesis of God's work. Let us now consider the sum total of man's accomplishments.

In the scale of creatures, man's position is at the summit. There is a perfect gradation from the lowest to the highest, which is found in man. What places man at the very zenith of things created is God's image, which he bears stamped upon his soul. Although the whole array of lower beings cannot know God, man can know Him and *has the obligation to know Him.* This knowledge of God has been conferred on human nature; ignorance is not the fault of nature, but of negligence. God does not demand such knowledge of the donkey or the mule, because this is not one of their traits. But what is natural for the donkey and the mule is a crime in man. And this is the offense men commit against God: first, that they do not wish to know Him; therefore they do not wish to recognize Him. The Saint puts this complaint into God's mouth, and says: I do not demand that those that I do not make in My image should participate in My wisdom (knowledge of God, says St. Augustine); but where I made such an image, there I demand it, and I require that the faculty which I conferred should function properly. I demand that men render unto God what is His, if they render unto Caesar what is Caesar's. I mean that they should return to Caesar his image, and give back to God His image, lifting up their minds, not to themselves, but to their Maker, to that light whence they came forth, to that spiritual fire which can set them aflame, for they have withdrawn from this light and they abide in darkness; and if they turn from this fire, they will grow cold.[2]

Previous pages have considered man's story in his state of darkness and coldness as a first step, and in his criminal status of resembling the donkey and the mule in his second state. The sequence of thought runs this way: for St. Augustine the beginning of all our evil and wretchedness is found in original sin; and original sin was the beginning and foundation of the world.

The world, in its simplest, most general sense, means "separation from God." Man separated himself from God, a separation which occurred through pride, through arrogant vainglory. This is not a warlike separation, but a separation dictated by personal independence, an attitude which sought to arrogate to self an attribute which belongs to God alone: to be completely independent and to be a norm and standard unto oneself. This implies an inordinate self-love, a contempt for God.

Slipping downward into the chasm of this rebellious humanism, by virtue of God's punishment, men first fell upon themselves, and they suffocated in that sad and narrow enclosure, and life lost its breadth and scope. Afterwards they slipped farther down into the abyss of bestiality; and man stamped the image of beasts on his own life.

Such is the story of the world, of the "City of Man" in its first stage. But the devil has been present from the beginning, in order further to degrade man's state. Satan hid his presence, to make man believe that he was being left as ruler of the city which Cain founded. Yet it was assuredly the devil who was king. And he undertook to do evil against God and against man. What had begun as selfishness and self-love, degenerated into hatred of God; what was born as "humanism," became bestiality.

In order that these roads might be more infernal, he arranged things so that there would be no return route. He hardened man's heart, which, despite the many evils that came to man because of his apostasy, remained cold and stubborn. Therefore, when God decided to show man that he had done wrong and was lost, some men insisted that they were satisfied with what they had done. And thus, in self-satisfaction, they again rejected God. This is the second state of the world.

God's work in the Redemption is so wondrous that all man's words and the profundity of human thought cannot succeed in penetrating His greatness and majesty. St. Augustine acknowledges this in the synthesis which we now are considering, and he adds: He who gave us our being also gave us the capability of goodness. Did He not go out to seek those fugitives from justice who went their own way? Did He not come down to them? Was not the Word made flesh and did it not dwell among us? Did He not light the torch of His body as He hung from the Cross, and set out in search of the lost drachma? He sought and found it, while all the neighbors rejoiced, that is, every rational creature which, because it is such, bears some resemblance to God. The coin was found amid rejoicing in the neighborhood. Man's soul also was found amid the angels' rejoicing.[3]

Evidently, then, God permits man to search, to flee from

God and go his own way. God affirmed that man had sinned, and that He came to save him. But if man, even though bruised by all manner of misfortune and shamefully degraded, was content with his fate, then actually he was implying that he did not recognize the existence of such sin. Consequently, he did not accept the Redeemer.

The antagonism which presently exists between God and the world thus has a new quality: lack of faith. This incredulity may take the form of simple inhibition, blindness due to pride, or even hatred of Christ. It may be hatred for Christ directly or against the "new creature" which has appeared in the world through Christ's action. Yet, if in this new era of the world the chief sin no longer is original sin but incredulity, then the basic elements of original sin still remain: pride and the devil.

St. Augustine has given us a profound explanation and extensive deductions from the antagonism between God and the world. This was a conflict which existed obscurely in the Old Testament, but came to the surface in the Synoptic Gospels, and in St. John's Gospel it acquires an awe-inspiring majesty and dramatic force. When we reflect that Jesus refused to pray for the world just before He went to die for men (John 17:9), we can perceive that the world must be something diabolically opposed to Jesus. Actually this is not only an opposition of attitude but of origin and destiny. Jesus is goodness, and the world is wickedness. Jesus is God; the world is of the devil. Jesus is grace and salvation, but the world is sin, perversion, damnation. The world's response to the Redeemer has been that of rejection and hate. God's answer to the world was to send the Holy Ghost as accuser to testify to the world's sin and to God's righteousness, that the world may be condemned at this tribunal.

But St. Augustine has just told us how Jesus found the

coin which He was looking for. The Redemption was not a failure, for many received Christ and believed. Thus was born a "new creature" which regained the spiritual dimension of life and was adopted by God in a special sonship to a new intimacy and the inheritance of His only-begotten Son.

However this was not a human movement which sought Christ, but a reality, a divine adventure in search of man. Christ, Son of the Eternal Father and the infinite expression of the nature of the Father, was sent to communicate this divine nature to men by means of grace. For that reason men have been raised up to a mysterious union with Christ and with God.

Further, a splendid retinue of gifts and graces comes to the soul in order to divest it completely from the world. But these gifts and graces do not always bear holiday attire, according to the world's standards.

Our conclusion, after reading what St. Augustine has told us about the world and God's action to save it, is that we human beings have been sharply divided into two absolute categories: those who belong to the world and the predestined. The world is all that is separated from God, everlastingly separated from Him; all the damned belong to the world. All wickedness, all the forces of evil, belong to the world. Whatever is not of Redemption is of the world. Whatever is not supernatural is the world.

This division into two and only two categories, is it of the Gospel or did St. Augustine originate it? And if it is Augustinian, is it of the Christian Augustine or the Manichean Augustine who still is living in the Christian Augustine? Father Vega wrote these words: "Perhaps without his realizing it, by reason of its superficial, suggestive reality, Manichean dualism impressed on Augustine's soul a concept of life as a conflict; nor is it entirely presumptuous to find a far-off echo of this even in *The City of God*. And further on he notes: "We allude to the antagonism and conflict of the two 'cities' as perhaps a reflection or revival of that other conflict between light and darkness, those who abide in light and those that dwell in the shadows. We say 'perhaps,' because this concept may have been of Christian, more specifically, of Pauline origin." [4]

The two ideas which the editor of the Spanish edition of St. Augustine's works expresses seem to be wanting in accuracy. We have studied exhaustively "the conflict concept of life," and have seen that the Saint considers this to be God's punishment for the sin of "living according to our human nature." This cannot be Manichean, since it has been the repeated experience of those who have fallen "into themselves" and have expressed their experiences. I believe his doubt concerning the antagonism between the two "cities" disappears when we meditate upon St. John's Gospel. This antagonism is not Manichean, nor even limited to St. Paul, but rather evangelical, and more specifically, St. John's Gospel, though it appeared earlier in the Synoptic Gospels and has strong confirmation in St. Paul.

It is perhaps more correct to say that St. Augustine's mind, intensely influenced by Manicheism, was especially prepared to discern the dualism between Christ and the world. Actually St. Augustine was the theologian who most clearly detected this and investigated it most fully. Yet this antagonistic dualism does not proceed from an Augustinian concept, nor is it mere Augustinian symbolism formulated in *The City of God.* It was in revelation; and St. Augustine has captured it in a magnificent manner.

The subject is quite logical, in view of the irreducible separation between the elect and the damned, and allocating those two categories, the former to the Church and the latter to the world, the resulting antagonism is not at all Manichean nor did it originate with St. Paul. It is a concept which permeates Christ's entire message. From the first verses of St. John's Gospel there is an absolute antagonism between Christ and the world. This runs through the entire Gospel, as well as through the first Epistle of St. John. In my opinion this antithesis may be clearly described in two ways: in a series of textual quotations and in a series of events. This sequence of events is often supported by a series of texts which give us their meaning. But in examining both texts and acts we come to the conclusion that *everything* is comprehended within the dilemma of this division, that there is no third position for "neutrals." There is a series of texts which we have examined, along with their comments by the Saint. We can harmonize these texts with John 1:5 as well as 1:10–11, and with the sermon at the Last Supper in chapters 13–17, without excluding other passages such as the parables of the good shepherd, the vine and the branches, etc. The antagonism expressed by these events culminates in the Passion, and in all the circumstances which led up to it. We will cite two passages that illustrate this.

In John 8:12, Jesus proclaims Himself as the light of the world. The remainder of this chapter is devoted to proving this claim of Jesus. It is a dispute with the world, in the person of the Pharisees. Jesus clarifies His assertion and uses the occasion to define the world: they are darkness, ignorance, human pride. They are of the world, from below, and they are guilty of the grave worldly sin of incredulity. The sentence is pronounced on this basis: You shall die in your sins. The following chapter marks the beginning of the practical application of what has been argued in the previous one. Jesus puts His claim into practice, performing a miracle which also has symbolical significance: He cures a blind man. The attitude and words of the Pharisees, in their conversations with the blind man who was cured, as well as with his parents, are rich in their reference to the world. Finally, seeing that the cured blind man persists in his defense of Jesus, they cast him from the Temple. It is a serious situation, which calls forth all St. Augustine's exegetical powers. This man does not belong to Christ by the mere fact of his being cured. In healing him, Christ did not use His customary expression, "Thy sins are forgiven thee." Neither did he belong to the synagogue, from which they had just expelled him. Is there, then, some intermediate zone? Within a few days Jesus meets him on the highway. He knows they have cast him out of the synagogue and He asks the man if he believes in the Son of God. And predicated upon an act of faith, Jesus explains the meaning of these deeds: I have come into the world that the blind may see, and that those who see may become blind (John 9:1–39).

Judas, on the other hand, is the world, and as St. Augustine has told us, in his day he was the outstanding representative of the world. He was with Jesus, and left Him. Was there an intermediate zone? No. In St. John's Gospel the darksome and diabolical scope of his dominion is expressed: "And after the piece of bread, Satan entered into him. . . . He went immediately out; and it was night" (John 13:27, 30). Evidently the Gospel makes the same affirmation as St. Augustine. Hence there was clearly no intermediate zone. "He that is not with Me is against Me."

We must thoroughly probe this serious result, otherwise we will not understand the Gospel or history which is its commentary. Men are polarized with reference to the dual alternatives of destiny, and there are only these two: Adam and Christ; the world and the Church. Despite many attempts, no other has arisen which can rally men beneath a third standard independent of the two foregoing. It is useless to inaugurate apostasy with a claim of independence; no such independence exists. Either we are under the sign and destiny of Adam, or under the banner and destiny of Christ. We belong either to the world or to the Church.

History confirms that all movements which initially considered themselves independent always bore within themselves the seed of wickedness which presently burst forth in grave evil, perhaps even as degeneration (though possibly quite contrary to the intention of those who planned it), for the simple reason that these movements were never indifferent, since there is no third realm which is independent or neutral.

This radical mark of division not only separates men into two classes with respect to their destiny, but the very actions of each individual are classified in one of these two categories. It is desirable to take cognizance of these precedents for St. Augustine's thought, in order better to organize and arrange his thinking relative to the possibility or existence of indifferent acts, and perhaps better to understand St. Thomas.

It is all the more necessary in order to understand the Gospel. Postulating a division of the entire human race into two groups, as well as an identical division of all human acts into two classes, will help to clarify not a few misunderstandings. Among those who acknowledge the existence of sin, the thought is generally accepted that all sinfulness is alien to Christ and the Redemption. But they have not understood why an area where the human element as such triumphs, where the natural element remains as a region independent of the supernatural, is evil. Such persons have not comprehended all the scope and dominion of both the Church and the world. They have not understood that the Church is supernatural, with a unity characterizing this supernature. They have failed to grasp that the world is nature and a unity satisfied with this nature. They have not recognized and appreciated the hostility between the world and Christ; therefore they do not understand Christ's words: "He that is not with Me is against Me."

When we know the dividing line between the two "cities," we comprehend the theology of history as we study evil. All evil, all wickedness is united in a terrible fellowship called the world. All wickedness, too, by virtue of complicated and subtle calculations, becomes diabolical, anti-Christian.

In a vital sense men are classified as evil or good; they are necessarily fitted into one of these societies. But if the mere thought of a living society abiding in wickedness can produce nausea, then the society living in the supernatural is our greatest happiness. Concentrated in this unity which is called Christ, we include the scope of the Incarnation. The Incarnation is the chief festival which God celebrates with human nature; but its roots lie in the everlasting decrees of God, who has predestined the elect in His love for His only-begotten Son. With the second Person of the Blessed Trinity placed at the very summit of creation by the hypostatic union, God has polarized all the redeemed in one vast unity, of which He is the active center of attraction as well as the transforming shoot engrafted on our fallen human nature.

Not only did the Incarnation bring forth the mysterious Person of Christ (Man-God), but also the mysterious person of the Church, the whole Christ. He has joined a human nature to the divine Person of the Word, and has also joined the whole of redeemed human nature to Christ, as well as the continuation of the Incarnation in each individual. Sanctification of our human nature as an immediate result and its glorification as an ultimate consequence—both as effects combined with the sanctification of the human nature which was assumed by the Word and in that glorification which the Father conferred upon Him —these illustrate the profound solidarity of all the members of Christ with their Head, together with the unity of life and destiny of that person whom we call the whole Christ, the mystical Christ.

St. Paul derives two significant, productive conclusions from this fundamental truth. He not only shows the active part of Christ in this entire vital whole, in teaching us the doctrine of Christ as Head of the mystical body, but he also demonstrates the second vital function in Him, which pertains to man. Man's life should be lived according to the life of Christ. Human sorrow and suffering are the prolongation and fulfillment of Christ's sacrifice. Our baptism is a dying with Christ. Our resurrection completes that of Christ. And in the same manner, our personal striving that Christ may transfuse and assimilate unto Himself what still remains within us that is unabsorbed and uncontrolled—whether outside us or within us, but especially within—this completion or filling up what is still wanting in the Incarnation is an action which God has left to our free will.

It is this vital oneness of the whole Christ which endows human nature with its true greatness, its basic freedom, not because that nature is human, but because it has been redeemed. And after this majestic unification, in which the whole man, all man's ideas and all his affections are transfigured by Christ, it is ridiculous to speak of purely human greatness and liberties. Moreover, it is madness to claim any kind of independence for our scanty human eminence after the Incarnation has raised human nature to the very pinnacle of divinity.

An objection may be made to the whole Augustinian concept of the world, by saying that it is a vast and beguiling notion but that this is not the idea contained in the deposit of Revelation, because the Church teaches otherwise. Thus, the Council of Trent (Sess. VI, cap. 13; Denz. 806) and all catechisms speak, not of one enemy, but of three: the world, the flesh and the devil. Therefore the concept of world which St. Augustine thought he found in the Gospel is not that of the Gospel or of St. Paul, but his own.

We reply by stating that neither the Council of Trent nor the catechisms are opposed to St. Augustine, but that they have divided the hostile world into three hostile powers or enemies, conforming in this division to their instigating causes and their status as agents. But as regards other causes, especially the formal cause, our enemy is one: the world.

Nevertheless, it is appropriate to note the two meanings which the world has, that of Revelation, contained in both Old Testament and New Testament sources, and that of the catechisms (with the latter appearing almost exclusively in modern ascetical works). The former is the world in its full sense; the latter is a division of the former, and hence contains only part of the meaning which Revelation has given it.

If we note only this limited meaning of the world, the Gospel cannot be understood. And I actually believe that because dogmatic theologians have departed from it, they have not found in this world a concept which is useful for dogmatic theology. If we restore to the word "world" its full Gospel meaning, so admirably discerned by St. Augustine, we shall find a concept that we need in order to penetrate more deeply the treatises on original sin, Christ, the sacraments, and grace. This St. Augustine has done; and in his works there originates a good part of our best theology.

Footnotes

AUTHOR'S PREFACE

[1] Cf. *Confessions,* IV, 7; Romano Guardini, "*Solo quien conoce a Dios conoce al hombre,*" *Cuadernos Hispanoamericanos,* LI, pp. 323ff.

[2] Cf. *De Doctrina Christiana,* III, cap. 31, n. 44.

1. MAN AS A PROBLEM

[1] *Enarrat. in Ps.,* 36, serm. 2, 13; P.L. 371.

[2] *Enarrat. in Ps.,* 101:11; P.L. 1302.

[3] *Confessions,* III, 7.

[4] *In Evang. Joan.,* tract. 23, 6; P.L. 1585.

[5] St. Augustine sometimes speaks of man's independence with respect to the stars, to caution his people not to believe in cosmic slavery.

[6] *Enarrat. in Ps.,* 101:11; P.L. 1302.

[7] Consistent with this principle, St. Augustine finds the most convincing evidence of God in man, and on this he constructs his psychological proof of the Trinity.

[8] *Confessions,* III, 8, 15.

[9] *Ibid.,* III, 6, 10.

[10] *De Civ. Dei,* XIII, 14; P.L. 386.

[11] *Enarrat. in Ps.,* 35:12; P.L. 1350; *De Civ. Dei,* XIII, 23; P.L. 397–398.

2. THE PROBLEM OF EVIL

[1] *De Genesi contra Manichaeos,* Lib. II, 16, N. 24; P.L. 209. Cf. *De Civ. Dei,* XIV, 17; P.L. 425.

[2] *Enarrat. in Ps.,* 48:9; P.L. 848.

[3] *De Civ. Dei,* XIII, 13; P.L. 386.

[4] *De Civ. Dei,* XIV, 12; P.L. 420.

[5] *De Civ. Dei,* XII, 3; P.L. 351.

[6] *De Civ. Dei,* XIV, 13.

[7] *De Spiritu et Littera,* cap. 28, n. 48.

[8] *Enarrat. in Ps.,* 66:4; P.L. 806.

[9] *Confessions,* III, 6, 10.

[10] *Enarrat. in Ps.,* 101:5; P.L. 1297.

[11] *Enarrat. in Ps.,* 34:2[a], 14; P.L. 279.

[12] *De Trin.,* XII, 11, N. 16; cf. also *De Civ. Dei,* XIII, 21; P.L. 395.

[13] *In Evang. Joan.,* tract. 15, 19; P.L. 1516–1517; *Enarrat. in Ps.,* 26:2[a], 3; P.L. 200.

[14] *In Evang. Joan.,* tract. 52, 11; P.L. 1773; *De Civ. Dei,* XIII, 3; P.L. 379; XIII, 14; P.L. 386–387; XIII, 23; P.L. 395–398.

3. EGOISM AND THE WORLD

[1] *In Evang. Joan.,* tract. 25, 17; P.L. 1605.

[2] *Ibid.,* tract. 16; P.L. 1604.

[3] *Ibid.,* tract. 25, 17f.; P.L. 1605.

[4] *Loc. cit.,* 15; P.L. 1603.

[5] *Enarrat. in Ps.,* 18:2[a], 15; P.L. 163.

[6] *Enarrat in Ps.,* 70:2[a], 6; P.L. 895–896; *De Trin.,* 12, 11, N. 16.

[7] Heinrich Kerber, in a letter to Max Scheller.

[8] *Enarrat. in Ps.,* 41:8; P.L. 469.

[9] *Enarrat. in Ps.,* 118, serm. 16, 1; P.L. 1545.

[10] *In Evang. Joan.,* tract. 25, 16m; P.L. 1604.

[11] *In Evang. Joan.,* tract. 38, 5–6; P.L. 1677–1678.

4. THE HUMAN DIMENSION OF LIFE

[1] *De Civ. Dei,* XIV, 11f.; P.L. 420.

[2] *De Civ. Dei,* XIV, 3; P.L. 406.

[3] *Ibid.,* XIV, 12; P.L. 420.

[4] *De Gen. contra Manichaeos*, II, 9, 12; P.L. 203.
[5] *Ibid.*, II, 27, 25; P.L. 209.
[6] *De Civ. Dei*, XII, 1, 1; P.L. 349.
[7] *Ibid.*, XV, 1, 2; P.L. 437.
[8] *Loc. cit.*
[9] *De Civ. Dei*, XIV, 4, 2; P.L. 407.
[10] *Ibid.*, XIV, 13; P.L. 420–422.
[11] *De Civ. Dei*, XII, 6; P.L. 353.
[12] *Ibid.*, XII, 9; P.L. 356–357.
[13] *Summa theol.*, Ia IIae, q. 82, a. 2.
[14] *De Gen. contra Manichaeos*, II, 15, 22; P.L. 207–208.
[15] *De Civ. Dei*, XIV, 13; P.L. 420–422.
[16] *Summa theol.*, IIa IIae, q. 163, a. 2.
[17] *De Gen. contra Manichaeos*, II, 15, 22; P.L. 207–208.
[18] *De natura boni*, cap. 35; *Contra Gent.*, III, 109, caps. 34, 36.
[19] *De Civ. Dei*, XIV, 15, 1; P.L. 423.
[20] *Summa theol.*, IIa, IIae, q. 163. a. 2; *Contra Gent.*, III, 109.
[21] *Summa theol.*, Ia, q. 63, a. 3.
[22] Concerning the two basic assertions relative to pride and naturalism, cf. *De Civ. Dei*, XIV, 3; P.L. 406. For naturalism with respect to Adam, cf. *De Civ. Dei*, XII, 6; P.L. 353–355; XIV, 11; P.L. 419; *De Vera Relig.*, cap. XIII, *et alibi*.
[23] *De Civ. Dei*, XIV, 13, 1; P.L. 421.
[24] *Loc. cit.*
[25] *De Civ. Dei*, XIII, 21; P.L. 395.
[26] *Ibid.*, XIV, 15, 1; P.L. 423.
[27] *Ibid.*, XI, 16, 24; P.L. 208–209.
[28] *De Gen. contra Manichaeos*, II, 16, 24f.; P.L. 209.
[29] *De Civ. Dei*, XIII, 21; P.L. 395.
[30] *Ibid.*, XIV, 4, 1; P.L. 407.
[31] *Ibid.*, XIV, 28; P.L. 436.
[32] *Ibid.*, XV, 1; P.L. 437.
[33] *In Evang. Joan.*, tract. 7, 2; P.L. 1438; *Enarrat. in Ps.*, 122:3; P.L. 1631.
[34] *In Evang. Joan.*, tract. 28; 5; P.L. 1624; and 8; P.L. 1626.
[35] *In Evang. Joan.*, tract. 52, 11; P.L. 1773.

5. CONSTITUTION OF THE CITY OF MAN

[1] In various passages the Saint presents the notion of the identity existing between Rome and the "City of Man": *De Civ. Dei*, XIV, 18; P.L. 426; *Enarrat. in Ps.*, 26:18; P.L. 208.

[2] *De Trin.*, XII, 11, N. 16.
[3] *De Civ. Dei*, XIV, 13, 1; P.L. 421.
[4] *Ibid.*, II, 19; P.L. 64–65.
[5] *Ibid.*, II, 20; P.L. 65–66.
[6] Cf. *Enarrat. in Ps.*, 26:18; P.L. 208.

6. DEFINITION OF THE WORLD

[1] We can summarize the various meanings of the term "world" as follows: 1) *Cosmos or mundus:* a) in profane literature it means production, fabrication, order in general, order among men or an adornment, especially of women; b) in a philosophical sense it means order of the world, relations of the world with God, the contents of the world; c) in the vernacular it means earth or humanity; d) in Judaism it means heaven (Deut. 4:19; Gen. 2:1), adornment (Judg. 1:14; II Mach. 2:2); heaven and earth (Gen. 1:1; Wisd. 9:9); earth (Septuagint); Moulton believes that the pejorative sense of world is of Jewish origin; e) in the New Testament it is never used in the sense of order and it is used in the sense of adornment only in I Pet. 3:3, but it is used to signify the universe, the fullness of creation, fallen humanity, or refuge (John 21:25).

2) *Saeculum* or *aion:* a) non-biblical usage: life, generation, time of life, duration or time, eternity; b) in biblical usage: long period of time or eternity (John 9:32; 4:14; Luke 1:55); the eternity of God (Rom. 16:26); time of the world (Matt. 24:3; 28:20); the world (Cor. 1:20; 7:33); the present age and the age to come; personification of the *aion*. Moulton observes that in Sanskrit *ayus* is the equivalent of the concept of life, and especially of a long life. He says that outside the New Testament both in classical and vulgar Greek it always has the meaning of perpetual and generally is applied to the emperor (James H. Moulton and G. Milligan, *The Vocabulary of the Greek Testament* [London, 1929]).

[2] *Passim, e.g., In Evang. Joan.*, tract. 2, 11; P.L. 1393.
[3] *Enarrat. in Ps.*, 48, part. 2, 2; P.L. 556.
[4] *In Epistolam Joannis ad Parthos*, tract. 2, 8–14; P.L. 1993–1997.
[5] *Enarrat. in Ps.*, 141:14; P.L. 1841–1842.
[6] *In Evang. Joan.*, tract. 79, 2; P.L. 1838.
[7] *Ibid.*, tract. 38, 5–6; P.L. 1677–1678.
[8] Cf. John 1:5; 10:8ff.; 15:18ff.
[9] *De Civ. Dei*, XIV, 1; P.L. 349.
[10] *Enarrat. in Ps.*, 147:41; P.L. 1917.
[11] *Obras de San Juan de la Cruz*, ed. P. Silverio de Santa Teresa, IV, pp. 218–220 (Burgos, 1931).
[12] *In Evang. Joan.*, tract. 87, 2; P.L. 1853.

[13] *Loc. cit.*

[14] Cf. de Lubac, *El drama del humanismo ateo* (Madrid, 1949), p. 60, n. 112.

[15] *De Trin.*, XII, 12, n. 17.

7. PATHLESS AND IN ANXIETY

[1] Cf. Bartmann, *Manuale di Teologia Dogmatica* (Alba, 1950), I, 416–417 (note to the Italian edition); G. K. Chesterton, *El Hombre eterno*, pp. 227 et seq. (Editorial Poblet).

[2] *In Evang. Joan.*, tract. 22, 3; P.L. 1575.

[3] *Enarrat. in Ps.*, 62:12, 13; P.L. 755.

[4] *In Evang. Joan.*, tract. 22, 6, 8; P.L. 1577–1578.

[5] Cf. *Enarrat. in Ps.*, 63:8–9; P.L. 752–753.

[6] *Enarrat. in Ps.*, 114:3; P.L. 1487.

[7] *Quarundam Props. in Epist. ad Rom.* 53; P.L. 2074–2076.

[8] Cf. *In Ps.*, 77:4.

[9] The anguish of realizing that we are pilgrims, and that we possess no certainty of what we hope for; cf. *Enarrat. in Ps.*, 41:10–11; P.L. 1471–1472.

[10] *Enarrat. in Ps.*, 62:6–7; P.L. 751–752; note 7 above.

[11] Concerning the isolation and solitude which the righteous experience: *In Ps.*, 25, enarrat. 2ª, N. 5; P.L. 191.

[12] *Enarrat. in Ps.*, 91:1; P.L. 1171.

[13] Cf. *Enarrat. in Ps.*, 62:2, vv. 8–9; P.L. 749, 752–753; *In Evang. Joan.* 5, 1; P.L. 1414; *id.*, 6, 2; P.L. 1425.

[14] Cf. chaps. 3, 12, 20.

[15] Cf. *In Ps.* 118, serm. 8, 1; P.L. 1519.

8. LIKE BEASTS

[1] *Enarrat. in Ps.*, 70, serm. 2, 6; P.L. 896.

[2] *De Gen. contra Manichaeos*, VIII, 12, 26; P.L. 383.

[3] *De Civ. Dei*, XIII, 21; P.L. 395.

[4] *De Trin.*, XII, 11, 16.

[5] *Conf.*, VII, 11; P.L. 742.

[6] *Enarrat. in Ps.*, 100:4; P.L. 1286.

[7] *Conf.*, VIII, 7, 16; P.L. 756.

[8] *Conf.*, IV, 16, 30; P.L. 705.

[9] *Ibid.*, II, 6, 14; P.L. 681.

[10] *Ibid.*, VII, 16, 22; P.L. 744.

[11] *Ibid.*, II, 6, 13–14; P.L. 680–681.
[12] *In Ps.* 70, *serm.* 2, 6; P.L. 896.
[13] *Conf.*, II, 1; P.L. 896.
[14] *Ibid.*, IX, 4, 10; P.L. 768.
[15] Portalié, *D.T.C.*, "*Augustin* (*Saint*)," cols. 2328–2329.
[16] Cf. *Conf.*, I, 6, 7.
[17] *Enarrat. in Ps.*, 102:8; P.L. 1322.
[18] *Exposit. in Ep. ad Gal.*, 36; P.L. 2131.
[19] *Enarrat. in Ps.*, 71:6; P.L. 917–918.
[20] Cf. Augustine's commentary in *Expositio quarundam propos.*, 49; P.L. 2073.
[21] *Enarrat. in Ps.*, 73:3; P.L. 932.
[22] Ideas concerning the goodness of things and their "sacramental value" are fully developed in Salvador Cuesta, S.J., *El equilibrio pasional en la doctrina de los estóicos y en la de San Agustín*, 240 (Madrid, 1945). I have followed his plan and have amplified his claims and quotations.
[23] *Enarrat. in Ps.*, 72:33; P.L. 928.
[24] *Enarrat. in Ps.*, 72:33; P.L. 928.
[25] *In Epist. Joannis ad Parthos*, tract. 10, 5–6; P.L. 2057–2058.
[26] *Enarrat. in Ps.*, 48:8; P.L. 548–549.
[27] Encycl. *Divini Redemptoris*, *A.A.S.* (1937), pp. 65–66, 69.
[28] *Conf.*, IV, 8, 13; P.L. 699.
[29] *Ibid.*, IV, 12; P.L. 700–701 (entire chapter).
[30] *Ibid.*, IV, 14, 22–23; P.L. 702.
[31] *Ibid.*, IX, 4, 10; P.L. 768. "Nec volebam multiplicari terrenis bonis."
[32] Note how purgative asceticism consists precisely in this. Cf. St. John of the Cross, *Ascent of Mount Carmel*, III, 16.
[33] *Enarrat. in Ps.*, 75:3; P.L. 1083.
[34] *Enarrat. in Ps.*, 124:1; P.L. 1648–1649.
[35] *Enarrat. in Ps.*, 131:7; P.L. 1719.
[36] *Enarrat. in Ps.*, 137:8; P.L. 1778.
[37] *Enarrat. in Ps.*, 72:12; P.L. 920.
[38] *Enarrat. in Ps.*, 75:11; P.L. 964–965.
[39] *Enarrat. in Ps.*, 21:31; P.L. 170.
[40] *Expost. Quardumdam Props.*, 49; P.L. 2073.
[41] *Enarrat. in Ps.*, 118, serm. 12, 2; P.L. 1532–1533.
[42] *Enarrat. in Ps.*, 118, serm. 2, 1; P.L. 1531–1532; 40:3; P.L. 456.
[43] *Enarrat. in Ps.*, 26, enarrat. 2, 16; P.L. 207.
[44] *Enarrat. in Ps.*, 29, enarrat. 2, 9; P.L. 222.
[45] *Enarrat. in Ps.*, 136:13; P.L. 1768–1769; 120:3; P.L. 1606–1607.
[46] *Enarrat. in Ps.*, 101:1; P.L. 1293–1294.
[47] *Enarrat. in Ps.*, 48:3; P.L. 515.
[48] *Enarrat. in Ps.*, 137:7; P.L. 1777.

[49] *Ibid.*, 53:5; P.L. 624.
[50] *Enarrat. in Ps.*, 104:4; P.L. 1404.
[51] *Ibid.*, 52:5; P.L. 616.
[52] *Ibid.*, 75:9; P.L. 963.
[53] *Ibid.*, 121:11; P.L. 1628.
[54] *Ibid.*, 68, p. 2, 18; P.L. 864–865.
[55] *Ibid.*, 83:3; P.L. 1057.
[56] *Enarrat. in Ps.*, 62:14; P.L. 755–756.
[57] *In Evang. Joan.*, tract. 40, 10; P.L. 755–756.
[58] *Enarrat. in Ps.*, 32, enarrat. 2, serm. 2, 25–26; P.L. 298.
[59] *Enarrat. in Ps.*, 79:14; P.L. 1028.
[60] *Enarrat. in Ps.*, 26:16; P.L. 207; 75:11; P.L. 1089–1090.
[61] *Enarrat. in Ps.*, 48:62; P.L. 560.
[62] *Enarrat. in Ps.*, 43:16; P.L. 488–489.
[63] *Enarrat. in Ps.*, 121:12; P.L. 1628–1629.
[64] *In Evang. Joan.*, tract. 13, 5; P.L. 1495.
[65] *Enarrat. in Ps.*, 39:8; P.L. 439.
[66] *Enarrat. in Ps.*, 91:1; P.L. 1171.
[67] *Enarrat. in Ps.*, 48:17; P.L. 555.
[68] *Enarrat. in Ps.*, 48:9; P.L. 549–550.
[69] *Enarrat. in Ps.*, 111:4; P.L. 1469.
[70] *In Evang. Joan.*, tract. 15, 32; P.L. 1522.
[71] *Enarrat. in Ps.*, 25:2; P.L. 647; 120:8; P.L. 1611–1612.
[72] *Enarrat. in Ps.*, 33, serm. 2, 14 *et seq.*; P.L. 315–316.
[73] *Enarrat. in Ps.*, 26:10, 18; P.L. 198, 208.
[74] *Enarrat. in Ps.*, 48, parts 2, 3; P.L. 556–557.
[75] Cf. concerning wisdom, *Contra Academicos*; the conditions for happiness, *De Trinitate,* XIII, caps. 5–6, nn. 8–9; that happiness consists in the possession of God, *De Vita Beata*; cf. Boyer, *L'idée de la verité dans la philosophie de Saint Augustin* (Paris, 1925) Angel C. Vega, *Introducción a la filosofía de San Agustín,* 122 (Madrid, 1943); Muñoz Vega, *op. cit.*, p. 7.
[76] *Retract.*, I, 14, 2; P.L. 606; *ibid.*, I, 4, 3; P.L. 590.
[77] *Enarrat. in Ps.*, 36, serm. 3, 14; P.L. 392.
[78] *In Evang. Joan.*, 28:7; P.L. 1625.
[79] *Enarrat. in Ps.*, 118, serm. 1; P.L. 1502.
[80] *In Evang. Joan.*, tract. 86, 1; P.L. 1950–1951.
[81] *Enarrat. in Ps.*, 125:6; P.L. 1561.
[82] *Ibid.*, 51:1; P.L. 600.
[83] Cf. *In Evang. Joan.*, tract. 20, 2; P.L. 1556.
[84] *Enarrat. in Ps.*, 50:4; P.L. 587.
[85] *Ibid.*, 26; enarrat. 2, 7; P.L. 200.
[86] *Ibid.*, 64:8; P.L. 779.

87 *Enarrat. in Ps.*, 68:1; P.L. 840.
88 *Enarrat. in Ps.*, 55:16; P.L. 657–658.
89 *Enarrat. in Ps.*, 33, serm. 2, 17; P.L. 317–318.
90 *Enarrat. in Ps.*, 70:9; P.L. 881.
91 *Enarrat. in Ps.*, 36:3; P.L. 357–358.
92 *Enarrat. in Ps.*, 136:9; P.L. 1766–1767.
93 *Enarrat. in Ps.*, 123:9; P.L. 1645.
94 *Enarrat. in Ps.*, 136:5; P.L. 1764.
95 *Ibid.*, 113:7; P.L. 1479.
96 *Ibid.*, 36:10; P.L. 361.
97 *Enarrat. in Ps.*, 105:13; P.L. 1411.
98 *In Evang. Joan.*, tract. 15, 16; P.L. 1513.
99 *Enarrat. in Ps.*, 123:9; P.L. 1645.
100 *Ibid.*, 51:18; P.L. 612.
101 *In Evang. Joan.*, tract. 26, 17; P.L. 1605.
102 *Enarrat. in Ps.*, 91:14; P.L. 1180.
103 *Ibid.*, 48, part 2, 8; P.L. 561–562.
104 *Ibid.*, 38:2; P.L. 413.
105 *Ibid.*, 74:1; P.L. 946.
106 *Enarrat. in Ps.*, 131:8; P.L. 1719.
107 *Enarrat. in Ps.*, 123:11–12; P.L. 1647.
108 *Ibid.*, 93:16; P.L. 1204–1205.
109 *Ibid.*, 96:19; P.L. 1251–1252.
110 *Enarrat. in Ps.*, 36, serm. 3, 14; P.L. 392.
111 *In Evang. Joan.*, 28:7; P.L. 1625.
112 *In Evang. Joan.*, tract. 26, 4–5; P.L. 1608–1609.
113 *In Evang. Joan.*, tract. 7, 1–2; P.L. 1438.
114 *Enarrat. in Ps.*, 74:1–2; P.L. 946–947.
115 *Enarrat. in Ps.*, 32, enarrat. 2, serm. 2, 17–18; P.L. 294–295.
116 *Enarrat. in Ps.*, 36:9; P.L. 360–361.
117 *In Evang. Joan.*, tract. 23, 5–6; P.L. 1584–1585.
118 *In quarundam propositionum ex Epist. ad Rom.*, 49; P.L. 2073.
119 Cf. Part II, chap. 7.

9. A CHARACTERIZATION OF THE WORLD

1 *Enarrat. in Ps.*, 52:2–3; P.L. 613–614.
2 *Enarrat. in Ps.*, 36:2; P.L. 356–357.
3 *Conf.*, III, 1, 1.
4 *Enarrat. in Ps.*, 68:9; P.L. 848.
5 *Enarrat. in Ps.*, 36, serm. 3, 14; P.L. 392.
6 *In Evang. Joan.*, 45:2–3; P.L. 1720.

[7] *Ibid.*, 30:7; P.L. 635–636.
[8] *Enarrat. in Ps.*, 51:14; P.L. 609–610.
[9] *Enarrat. in Ps.*, 32, enarrat. 2, serm. 2, 15–16; P.L. 293–294.
[10] *Enarrat. in Ps.*, 64:9; P.L. 780–781.
[11] *Ibid.*, 39; P.L. 440.
[12] *Enarrat. in Ps.*, 31, enarrat. a. 5; P.L. 1260.
[13] *In Epist. Joannis ad Parthos*, tract. 7, 3; P.L. 2030–2031.
[14] *Enarrat. in Ps.*, 33, serm. 2, 10; P.L. 314.
[15] *Ibid.*, 72:15; P.L. 122.
[16] *Ibid.*, 50; P.L. 588.
[17] *Ibid.*, 47:9; P.L. 539.
[18] *Enarrat. in Ps.*, 51:7–8; P.L. 604–605.
[19] *Ibid.*, 57:1, 3; P.L. 673, 675.
[20] *Ibid.*, 51:10; P.L. 606.
[21] *Ibid.*, 51:12; P.L. 607.

11. AND THEY RECEIVED HIM NOT

[1] *Enarrat. in Ps.*, 81:5–6; P.L. 1049–1050.
[2] *Ibid.*, 88:11–12; P.L. 1126–1127.
[3] *Ibid.*, 81:6; P.L. 1050; *In Evang. Joan.*, tract. 53:13; P.L. 1780.
[4] *Enarrat. in Ps.*, 139:7–8; P.L. 1807.
[5] *Ibid.*, 88:11–12; P.L. 1126–1127.
[6] *Conf.*, VI, 6, 9.
[7] *Enarrat. in Ps.*, 118, 12:2; P.L. 1532.
[8] *In Evang. Joan.*, tract. 52, 53.
[9] *Enarrat. in Ps.*, 58:6–7; P.L. 695–696.
[10] *Passim, In Evang. Joan.*, tract. 53:8; P.L. 1777 *et seq.*
[11] *Enarrat. in Ps.*, 70:18; P.L. 887–888.
[12] *Enarrat. in Ps.*, 93:8; P.L. 1198.
[13] *In Epist. Joannis ad Parthos*, 5:9; P.L. 2017.
[14] *Exposit. in Ep. ad Gal.*, 59; P.L. 2145; *Tract. in Epist. Joannis ad Parthos*, 6:2–3; P.L. 2020–2021.
[15] *Conf.*, VI, 6, 9.
[16] *In Evang. Joan.*, 6:10; P.L. 1429–1430; *Enarrat. in Ps.*, 111:4; P.L. 1469; *ibid.*, 1:1; P.L. 67.
[17] *In Evang. Joan.*, 1:19; P.L. 1388.
[18] *Ibid.*, 3:5; P.L. 1398.
[19] *Ibid.*, 79:2; P.L. 1838.
[20] *In Evang. Joan.*, 5:1; P.L. 1414.
[21] *Enarrat. in Ps.*, 106; P.L. 1421–1426.
[22] *Conf.*, III, 6, 11.

[23] *Conf.*, VII, 7, 11.
[24] *In Evang. Joan.*, 4:4; P.L. 1407.
[25] *Ibid.*, 89:1; P.L. 1856–1857.
[26] *Loc. cit.*; P.L. 1857.
[27] *In Evang. Joan.*, 44:17; P.L. 1719.
[28] *Ibid.*, 29:8; P.L. 1631.
[29] *In Evang. Joan.*, 3:4–5; P.L. 1397–1398.
[30] *Ibid.*, 12:12–14; P.L. 1490–1492.
[31] *Ibid.*, 12:14; P.L. 1492.
[32] *In Evang. Joan.*, 89:1; P.L. 1856–1857.
[33] *Loc. cit.*; P.L. 1857–1858.
[34] *Ibid.*, 95:2–4; P.L. 1871–1873; cf. *Enarrat. in Ps.*, 77:14 P.L. 993.
[35] *In Evang. Joan.*, 29:8; P.L. 1631.

12. THE HOUR OF DARKNESS

[1] *In Evang. Joan.*, tract. 93:4; P.L. 1867.
[2] *Ibid.*, tract. 38:2; P.L. 1676.
[3] *Ibid.*, tract. 119:4; P.L. 1952.
[4] *Ibid.*, tract. 38:2; P.L. 1676.
[5] *Ibid.*, tract. 93:4; P.L. 1867.
[6] *Ibid.*, tract. 28:8; P.L. 1625.
[7] John 15:24–25.
[8] *In Evang. Joan.*, tract. 91:1–4; P.L. 1860–1862.
[9] *Ibid.*, tract. 90:1, 3; P.L. 1858–1860.
[10] *Enarrat. in Ps.*, 128:4; P.L. 1690.
[11] *In Evang. Joan.*, tract. 88:2–4; P.L. 1854–1855.
[12] *Enarrat. in Ps.*, 64:11; P.L. 782.
[13] *Enarrat. in Ps.*, 92:7; P.L. 1187–1188.
[14] *In Epist. Joannis ad Parthos*, tract. 4:4; P.L. 2007–2008.
[15] *Enarrat. in Ps.*, 64:11; P.L. 782.
[16] *Enarrat. in Ps.*, 136:9; P.L. 1766–1767.
[17] *Enarrat. in Ps.*, 53:7; P.L. 625.
[18] *Enarrat. in Ps.*, 93:28; P.L. 1215; 30:2, 5; P.L. 250–251.
[19] *Enarrat. in Ps.*, 136:9; P.L. 1766–1767.
[20] *Enarrat. in Ps.*, 75:11; P.L. 964–965.
[21] *Enarrat. in Ps.*, 122:9; P.L. 1636–1637.
[22] *Enarrat. in Ps.*, 122:8; P.L. 1636.
[23] *Ibid.*, P.L. 1637–1638.
[24] *In Epist. Joannis ad Parthos*, tract. 4:4; P.L. 2007.
[25] *Enarrat. in Ps.*, 147:8; P.L. 1919.

[26] *Enarrat. in Ps.*, 52:2–3; P.L. 613–614.
[27] *Enarrat. in Ps.*, 136:9; P.L. 1766–1767.
[28] *De Civ. Dei*, II, 20; P.L. 65.
[29] *Enarrat. in Ps.*, 139:4; P.L. 1805–1806.
[30] *Enarrat. in Ps.*, 119:3; P.L. 1599.
[31] *Enarrat. in Ps.*, 119:3; P.L. 1599–1604.
[32] *Enarrat. in Ps.*, 90:1, 4; P.L. 1151–1152.
[33] *In Evang. Joan.*, tract. 5:5; P.L. 1416.
[34] *Enarrat. in Ps.*, 64:13; P.L. 782–783.
[35] *Enarrat. in Ps.*, 69:2; P.L. 866–867.
[36] *In Evang. Joan.*, tract. 11:12; P.L. 1482.
[37] *Enarrat. in Ps.*, 141:8; P.L. 1836.
[38] *Enarrat. in Ps.*, 142:4; P.L. 1847.
[39] *Enarrat. in Ps.*, 30:2, 11; P.L. 245.
[40] *Enarrat. in Ps.*, 68:9; P.L. 847.
[41] *Enarrat. in Ps.*, 68:9; P.L. 848.
[42] *Enarrat. in Ps.*, 142:7; P.L. 1849.
[43] *Enarrat. in Ps.*, 141:11; P.L. 1840.
[44] *Enarrat. in Ps.*, 141:7; P.L. 1837.
[45] *In Evang. Joan.*, tract. 88:2; P.L. 1855.
[46] *Ibid.*, tract. 21, 7–8; P.L. 1568.
[47] *Loc. cit.*
[48] *Enarrat. in Ps.*, 64:5; P.L. 776.
[49] *Enarrat. in Ps.*, 43:5; P.L. 479.
[50] *Enarrat. in Ps.*, 65:18; P.L. 798.
[51] *Enarrat. in Ps.*, 64:4; P.L. 775–776.
[52] *Enarrat. in Ps.*, 85; P.L. 1081 ss.
[53] Cf. *Enarrat. in Ps.*, 74:10; P.L. 1075–1076.
[54] *In Evang. Joan.*, tract. 28:11; P.L. 1628.
[55] *Enarrat. in Ps.*, 85; P.L. 1081.
[56] *Ibid.*; P.L. 1082.
[57] *Ibid.*; P.L. 1085.

[58] Our anxiety is something more than suffering evils, since this is common to the good and to the bad (*Enarrat. in Ps.*, 122:2; P.L. 1631); for Christians, sufferings are a blessing and help along our pilgrim's way (*Enarrat. in Ps.*, 62:10; P.L. 753–754); in the matter of God's absences cf. *Enarrat. in Ps.*, 142:12–15; P.L. 1852–1853; with respect to hunger and thirst, Chapter VII, first part of this work.

[59] *Enarrat. in Ps.*, 48:11; P.L. 551.
[60] *In Evang. Joan.*, 27:11; P.L. 1621.
[61] *Enarrat. in Ps.*, 57:16; P.L. 685–686.
[62] *Enarrat. in Ps.*, 138:21; P.L. 1797–1798.

[63] *Enarrat. in Ps.*, 34:5; P.L. 325.
[64] *Enarrat. in Ps.*, 45:7; P.L. 518 *et seq.*
[65] *Enarrat. in Ps.*, 54:10; P.L. 635–636.
[66] *Enarrat. in Ps.*, 34:8–9; P.L. 338.
[67] *In Evang. Joan.*, tract. 25:5–6; P.L. 1598–1599; *Enarrat. in Ps.*, 101:4; P.L. 1307.

13. THE FATHER OF THIS WORLD

[1] *Enarrat. in Ps.*, 58; P.L. 709.
[2] *Enarrat. in Ps.*, 34; P.L. 325; 76:7; P.L. 975.
[3] *In Evang. Joan.*, tract. 53; P.L. 1777–1778.
[4] *In Evang. Joan.*, tract. 41:7; P.L. 1696; tract. 79, 2; P.L. 1838.
[5] *In Evang. Joan.*, tract. 42, P.L. 1703–1705; *In Epist. Joannis ad Parthos*, tract. 4:10–11; P.L. 2011, etc.
[6] *Enarrat. in Ps.*, 26; P.L. 208–209.
[7] *Enarrat. in Ps.*, 139:7–8; P.L. 1807.
[8] *Enarrat. in Ps.*, 82:3; P.L. 1052.
[9] *Enarrat. in Ps.*, 108:18; P.L. 1438.
[10] *Enarrat. in Ps.*, 77:28; P.L. 1001–1002.
[11] *Enarrat. in Ps.*, 61:6; P.L. 733.
[12] *Enarrat. in Ps.*, 103; P.L. 1386.
[13] *Enarrat. in Ps.*, 77:28; P.L. 1002.
[14] *Enarrat. in Ps.*, 48:2; P.L. 556–557.
[15] *In Evang. Joan.*, tract. 52:9; P.L. 1772.
[16] *Ibid.*, tract. 27:8; P.L. 1619.
[17] *Enarrat. in Ps.*, 40:4; P.L. 456; 48:2–3, P.L. 556–557.
[18] *In Epist. ad Gal.*, 32; P.L. 2128–2129.
[19] *Enarrat. in Ps.*, 55:19; P.L. 659–661.
[20] *Enarrat. in Ps.*, 143:4–5; P.L. 1858–1859.
[21] *Enarrat. in Ps.*, 90:2, 4; P.L. 1150–1152.
[22] *Enarrat. in Ps.*, 93:20–21; P.L. 1208–1209.
[23] *In Evang. Joan.*, tract. 5:12; P.L. 1420.
[24] *Enarrat. in Ps.*, 93:19; P.L. 1207.
[25] *In Evang. Joan.*, tract. 52:11; P.L. 1773.
[26] *Enarrat. in Ps.*, 51:13; P.L. 722–723.
[27] *Enarrat. in Ps.*, 129:7–8; P.L. 1806.
[28] *Enarrat. in Ps.*, 141:3–4; P.L. 1834–1835.
[29] *Enarrat. in Ps.*, 90:1; P.L. 1150; Ps. 55:9; P.L. 652–654.
[30] *Enarrat. in Ps.*, 55:4; P.L. 549.
[31] *In Epist. Joannis ad Parthos*, tract. 2; P.L. 1996.

14. WHAT GOD THINKS OF THE WORLD

[1] *In Evang. Joan.*, tract. 38:4; P.L. 1676–1677.

[2] *Enarrat. in Ps.*, 113:6; P.L. 1478–1479.

[3] *In Evang. Joan.*, tract. 12:4; P.L. 1486.

[4] *Ibid.*, tract. 18:7; P.L. 1540.

[5] *Enarrat. in Ps.*, 99:17; P.L. 1279.

[6] *Ibid.*, 35:12; P.L. 350.

[7] *Enarrat. in Ps.*, 91:10; P.L. 1178; and at greater length in *Epist. Joannis ad Parthos*, tract. 9:11; P.L. 2048–2053.

[8] *Enarrat. in Ps.*, 30:7; P.L. 227.

[9] *In Evang. Joan.*, tract. 107:1; P.L. 1912.

[10] *In Epist. Joannis ad Parthos*, tract. 3:10; P.L. 2003.

[11] *In Joan.*, tract. 95:1–4; P.L. 1870–1871; *Enarrat. in Ps.*, 109:8; P.L. 1451–1452.

[12] We shall also state later that the worldly are not accustomed to look forward to the future which awaits them. This does not refute what we say here, since the pattern of temptations is not constant or balanced.

[13] *Enarrat. in Ps.*, 57:17–18; P.L. 686–688.

[14] According to the preliminary statistics of the National Health Survey, *Sickness and Medical Care Series Bulletin*, No. 6, U.S. Public Health Service, Washington, D.C., 1938, there were 132,500,000 work days lost during the preceding year (1937) because of nervous and mental ailments. This was much more than time lost because of any other ailment, and double the total of all the others, except rheumatic and heart diseases.

[15] *Enarrat. in Ps.*, 57:19; P.L. 688–689.

[16] *Ibid.*, 57:20; P.L. 689–690.

[17] *Loc. cit.*

[18] *Enarrat. in Ps.*, 17:8; P.L. 149.

[19] *Enarrat. in Ps.*, 81:7; P.L. 1050.

[20] *In Evang. Joan.*, tract. 38:6; P.L. 1677–1678.

[21] *Quarundam Prop. ex Epist. ad Rom.*, 52; P.L. 2073–2074.

[22] *In Epist. Joannis ad Parthos*, tract. 9:6; P.L. 2049.

[23] *Enarrat. in Ps.*, 118, serm. 10:1; P.L. 1525.

[24] *In Evang. Joan.*, tract. 22, 3; P.L. 1575; *Enarrat. in Ps.*, 62:12–13; P.L. 755; *In Evang. Joan.*, tract. 22:6–8; P.L. 1778.

[25] *Enarrat. in Ps.*, 90:20f.; P.L. 690.

[26] *Enarrat. in Ps.*, 90:11; P.L. 1158.

[27] *Enarrat. in Ps.*, 145:19; P.L. 1897.

[28] *Enarrat. in Ps.*, 53:9; P.L. 623.

[29] *Enarrat. in Ps.*, 51:12; P.L. 607.

[30] *Enarrat. in Ps.*, 48, part 2:11; P.L. 564.

[31] *In Evang. Joan.*, tract. 75:2; P.L. 1829; *ibid.*, tract. 95:4; P.L. 1872–1873.

15. TWO VICTORIES OVER THE HUMAN ELEMENT

[1] *Conf.*, V, 2, 2; VIII, 7, 16.
[2] *In Epist. Joannis ad Parthos*, tract. 5:9; P.L. 2017.

16. THE WORLD'S FRONTIERS

[1] *Enarrat. in Ps.*, 67:41; P.L. 838.
[2] *In Evang. Joan.*, tract. 49, 15; P.L. 1753–1754.
[3] *In Epist. Joannis ad Parthos*, tract. 4, 1; P.L. 2005.
[4] *In Evang. Joan.*, tract. 89, 1; P.L. 1856–1857.
[5] *In Evang. Joan.*, tract. 26, 5; P.L. 1608–1609.
[6] *Enarrat. in Ps.*, 31:3–4; P.L. 259–260.
[7] *In Enarrat. in Ps.*, 31; P.L. 258.
[8] Cf. *Enchiridion*, caps. 8, 30.
[9] *Conf.*, VIII, 12, 29–30.
[10] *Conc. Trid.*, Sess. VI, 5–8; Denz. 797–800.
[11] *In Epist. Joannis ad Parthos;* tract. 10, 1–2; P.L. 2054–2055.
[12] *Loc. cit.;* P.L. 2054.
[13] *De utilitate credendi*, caps. 15, 33.
[14] *In Evang. Joan.*, tract. 22, 6 & 8; P.L. 1577 & 1578.
[15] *Conf.*, IX, 1, 1.
[16] *In Evang. Joan.*, tract. 26, 13; P.L. 1612–1613.
[17] Cf. de Lubac, *op. cit.*, 72.
[18] *Quarundam Prop. ex Epist. ad Rom.*, 53; P.L. 2075–2076.
[19] *Enarrat. in Ps.*, 62:2, 8–9; P.L. 749, 752–753.
[20] *In Evang. Joan.*, tract. 26, 2; P.L. 1607.
[21] *In Evang. Joan.*, tract. 26, 4–5; P.L. 1608–1609.
[22] *Loc. cit.;* P.L. 1608.
[23] Cf. *In Evang. Joan.*, tract. 41, 8–13; P.L. 1696–1700; *ibid.*, tract. 42, 1; P.L. 1700.

17. CHRISTIANITY AS EMANCIPATION

[1] Cf. de Lubac, *op. cit.*, pp. 20–21.
[2] *Expost. in Epist. ad Gal.*, 43; P.L. 2136–2137.
[3] *In Evang. Joan.*, tract. 42, 1; P.L. 1700.

[4] *Expost. in Epist. ad Gal.*, 43; P.L. 2136–2137; *Enarrat. in Ps.*, 30:8–9; P.L. 227; *Enarrat. in Ps.*, 67:13; P.L. 820.

[5] *Enarrat. in Ps.*, 99:7; P.L. 1275.

[6] *In Epist. Joan. ad Parthos*, 7:2; P.L. 2030.

[7] *Enarrat. in Ps.*, 30:9; P.L. 227.

[8] *In Evang. Joan.*, tract. 41:8–10; P.L. 1696–1697.

[9] *Enarrat. in Ps.*, 93:19; P.L. 1206–1207.

[10] *Enarrat. in Ps.*, 48:2; P.L. 544.

[11] *De Civ. Dei*, XIV, 27; P.L. 436.

[12] *In Evang. Joan.*, tract. 26, 2; P.L. 1607.

[13] *Loc. cit.*; *Expost. in Epist. Joannis ad Parthos*, 7:2; P.L. 2030; *Enarrat. in Ps.*, 26; P.L. 208.

18. THE PRINCE OF FREEDOM

[1] *In Evang. Joan.*, tract. 92, 2; P.L. 1865.

[2] Scheeben, *op. cit.*, pp. 465–466.

[3] Cf. Scheeben, *op. cit.*, pp. 268 *et seq.*

[4] *Enarrat in Ps.*, 119:2; P.L. 1598.

[5] *In Evang. Joan.*, tract. 23, 13; P.L. 1591.

[6] *Ibid.*, tract. 23, 5–6, 17 *passim*; P.L. 1584–1585, 1592.

[7] *Ibid.*, tract. 38, 4–6; P.L. 1676–1677.

[8] *Ibid.*, tract. 79–2; P.L. 1838.

[9] *Ibid.*, tract. 37, 1; P.L. 1670.

[10] *Ibid.*, tract. 77, 3; P.L. 1834.

[11] *In Evang. Joan.*, 15:2; P.L. 1939.

[12] *Ibid.*, tract. 103, 3; P.L. 1901.

[13] *Enarrat. in Ps.*, 102:7; P.L. 1321.

[14] *In Evang. Joan.*, tract. 52, 11.

[15] *Ibid.*, tract. 17, 13; P.L. 1534.

[16] *Enarrat. in Ps.*, 59:3; P.L. 716.

[17] *In Evang. Joan.*, tract. 98, 3; P.L. 1882.

[18] *Enarrat. in Ps.*, 81:6; P.L. 1050; cf. *In Evang. Joan.*, tract. 53, 13; P.L. 1780.

[19] Nietzsche, cited by de Lubac, *op. cit.*, p. 137.

[20] *Conf.*, VII, 17–18, 23–24.

[21] *Enarrat. in Ps.*, 81:5–6; P.L. 1049–1050.

[22] *Ibid.*, 88:11–12; P.L. 1126–1127.

[23] *Ibid.*, 53:3–4; P.L. 620–623.

[24] *In Evang. Joan.*, tract. 116, 1; P.L. 1941.

[25] *Ibid.*, tract. 2, 2, 4; P.L. 1389–1391; cf. *Enarrat. in Ps.*, 103; P.L. 1380–1381.

[26] *In Evang. Joan.*, tract. 35, 8–9; P.L. 1661.
[27] *Ibid.*, tract. 15, 19; P.L. 1517.
[28] *Ibid.*, tract. 54, 4; P.L. 1782.
[29] *Ibid.*, tract. 35, 1; P.L. 1657.
[30] *Op. cit.*; P.L. 1658.
[31] *Op. cit.*; P.L. 1659.
[32] *Ibid.*; tract. 34, 6; P.L. 1654.
[33] *Ibid.*; tract. 26, 10; P.L. 1610.

19. I HAVE CHOSEN YOU

[1] *Retract.*, I, 3, 2; P.L. 588–589.
[2] *In Evang. Joan.*, tract. 12, 13; P.L. 1491.
[3] *Conf.*, VIII, 5, 12.
[4] *Enarrat. in Ps.*, 6:7; P.L. 93–94.
[5] *Ibid.*, 113:3; P.L. 1477.
[6] *In Evang. Joan.*, tract. 106, 5; P.L. 1910–1911.
[7] *Ibid.*, tract. 111, 4; P.L. 1928–1929.
[8] *Ibid.*, tract. 106, 1–4; P.L. 1908–1910.
[9] *Ibid.*, tract. 27, 7; P.L. 1618; tract 92, 1; P.L. 1862.
[10] *In Evang. Joan.*, tract. 106, 5; P.L. 1910.
[11] *Ibid.*, tract. 108, 1; P.L. 1915.
[12] *Loc. cit.*; cf. also n. 3; P.L. 1916.
[13] *Ibid.*, tract. 108, 5; P.L. 1916.
[14] *In Evang. Joan.*, tract. 28, 9; P.L. 1626–1627.
[15] *De quantitate animae*, cap. 33.
[16] *In Evang. Joan.*, tract. 28, 7; P.L. 1625.
[17] *Enarrat. in Ps.*, 141:18–19; P.L. 1843–1844.
[18] *Ibid.*, 77:21; P.L. 996.
[19] *In Evang. Joan.*, tract. 26, 10; P.L. 1610.
[20] *In Evang. Joan.*, tract. 110, 4; P.L. 1922–1923.
[21] *Ibid.*, tract. 32, 9; P.L. 1646–1647.
[22] *Ibid.*, tract. 110, 3; P.L. 1921.
[23] *In Evang. Joan.*, tract. 111, 1; P.L. 1925–1926.
[24] *Ibid.*, tract. 55, 1; P.L. 785.

20. FOR THEY ARE I

[1] *In Epist. Joannis ad Parthos*, tract. 2. 2; P.L. 1990.
[2] *Enarrat. in Ps.*, 23:2; P.L. 183.
[3] *Ibid.*, 28:10; P.L. 214.

[4] *In Evang. Joan.*, tract. 25, 2; P.L. 1597.
[5] *Ibid.*, tract. 39, 5; P.L. 1684.
[6] *In Epist. Joannis ad Parthos*, tract. 5, 7; P.L. 2016.
[7] *Enarrat. in Ps.*, 123:5; P.L. 1642.
[8] *In Evang. Joan.*, tract. 108, 5; P.L. 1916.
[9] *In Evang. Joan.*, tract. 21, 7; P.L. 1568.
[10] *Enarrat. in Ps.*, 75:5; P.L. 1085.
[11] *Ibid.*, 101:3; P.L. 1296.
[12] *In Evang. Joan.*, tract. 110, 5–7; P.L. 1923–1925.
[13] *Ibid.*, tract. 111, 4, 6; P.L. 1928–1929.
[14] *Enarrat. in Ps.*, 74:4; P.L. 949.
[15] *Ibid.*, 88, 5; P.L. 1122.
[16] *Enarrat. in Ps.*, 88, serm. 2, 5; P.L. 1133.

21. THE MYSTERY WITHIN

[1] *In Evang. Joan.*, tract. 106, 4; P.L. 1909–1910.
[2] *Ibid.*, tract. 21, 3; P.L. 1565.
[3] *Enarrat. in Ps.*, 9:31; P.L. 129.
[4] *In Evang. Joan.*, tract. 110, 5; P.L. 1923.
[5] *Ibid.*; P.L. 1925.
[6] *In Evang. Joan.*, tract. 111, 6; P.L. 1929.
[7] *Ibid.*, tract. 107, 2; P.L. 1912.
[8] *In Evang. Joan.*, tract. 107, 6; P.L. 1914.
[9] *Ibid.*, tract. 111, 2; P.L. 1926.
[10] *Ibid.*; P.L. 1925.
[11] *In Evang. Joan.*, tract. 111, 2; P.L. 1926.
[12] *Ibid.*, tract. 111, 3; P.L. 1928.
[13] *Ibid.*, tract. 110, 4; P.L. 1922.
[14] *Ibid.*, tract. 111, 3; P.L. 1928.
[15] *In Epist. Joannis ad Parthos*, react. 1, 3; P.L. 1980
[16] *Enarrat. in Ps.*, 122:4; P.L. 1632.
[17] *In Evang. Joan.*, tract. 76; P.L. 1831.
[18] *In Evang. Joan.*, tract. 94, 5; P.L. 1869–1870.

22. THE CHRISTIAN'S SEPARATION FROM THIS WORLD

[1] *Enarrat. in Ps.*, 140:2–3; P.L. 1816–1817.
[2] *In Evang. Joan.*, tract. 65, 1; P.L. 1808–1809.

[3] Cf. Pourrat, *Christian Spirituality*, I, pp. 231ff.; *Dictionnaire de Spiritualité*, Boyer, "Augustin (*Saint*): *La Charité*," I, pp. 1105–1106.

[4] *In Evang. Joan.*, tract. 21, 15; P.L. 1573.

[5] *Enarrat. in Ps.*, 145:5; P.L. 1573.

[6] *Ibid.*, 121:1; P.L. 1618.

[7] *Expost. in Epist. ad Gal.*, 54; P.L. 2142–2143 *ad sensum; ibid.*, 43; P.L. 2136–2137; *Enarrat. in Ps.*, 99:7; P.L. 1275.

[8] *Enarrat. in Ps.*, 119:5; P.L. 1600–1601; *ibid.*, 121:12; P.L. 1628; 96:7; P.L. 1242; 47:13; P.L. 541; 81:7; P.L. 1050–1051, etc.

[9] *In Epist. Joannis ad Parthos*, tract. 7:1; P.L. 2029.

[10] *Ibid.*, tract. 8, 3; P.L. 2037.

[11] *Expost. quarundam prop. ex Epist. ad Rom.*, prop. 49; P.L. 2073.

[12] *Conf.*, IX, 4, 10–11.

[13] *Enarrat. in Ps.*, 17:12; P.L. 149.

[14] *In Epist. Joannis ad Parthos*, tract. 4, 6; P.L. 2008–2009.

[15] *Enarrat. in Ps.*, 65:1; P.L. 786.

[16] *Ibid.*, 64:3; P.L. 774–775.

[17] *Ibid.*, 81:5–6; P.L. 1049–1050.

[18] *In Evang. Joan.*, tract. 7:17; P.L. 1446.

[19] *De Civ. Dei*, XIV, 13; P.L. 421.

[20] *In Evang. Joan.*, tract. 6, 10; P.L. 1430.

[21] *Ibid.*, tract. 66, 2; P.L. 1811.

[22] *Enarrat. in Ps.*, 120:14; P.L. 1617.

[23] *In Evang. Joan.*, tract. 25, 16 & 18; P.L. 1604–1606.

[24] *Ibid.*, tract. 7, 18–19; P.L. 1446–1447.

[25] *Ibid.*, tract. 28, 5; P.L. 1624.

[26] *In Epist. Joannis ad Parthos*, tract. 7, 2; P.L. 2030.

[27] *Conf.* VI, 6, 9.

[28] *Enarrat. in Ps.*, 131:24; P.L. 1726.

[29] *Conf.*, IV, 8, 13.

[30] *Enarrat. in Ps.*, 43:2; P.L. 483.

[31] *Ibid.*, 53:8; P.L. 625.

[32] *Ibid.*, 138:16; P.L. 1794.

[33] *In Evang. Joan.*, 25:10; P.L. 1600.

[34] *Enarrat. in Ps.*, 66:3; P.L. 803–804.

[35] *Ibid.*, 66:3; P.L. 803–804.

[36] *Enarrat. in Ps.*, 74:8; P.L. 951; *ibid.*, 70:14; P.L. 883–884.

[37] *Ibid.*, 9:7–8; P.L. 1175–1176.

[38] *Enarrat. in Ps.*, 77:28; P.L. 1001.

[39] *In Evang. Joan.*, tract. 55, 5; P.L. 1756.

[40] *Ibid.*, tract. 7, 12; P.L. 1443–1444.

[41] *Enarrat. in Ps.*, 93:18; P.L. 1206.

[42] *Ibid.*, 36, serm. 3, 9; P.L. 389.

[43] *Ibid.*, 37:23; P.L. 409.

[44] *Ibid.*, 51:5; P.L. 717; *Expost. in Epist. ad Rom., inchoata* 10; P.L. 2095.

[45] *In Evang. Joan.*, tract. 3:21; P.L. 1405.

[46] *Enarrat. in Ps.*, 36, serm. 2, 16; P.L. 372–373.

[47] *Ibid.*, 35:13; P.L. 351.

[48] *In Evang. Joan.*, tract. 43, 5–6; P.L. 1707–1708; *Enarrat. in Ps.*, 58:9; P.L. 687.

[49] *Enarrat. in Ps.*, 55:2; P.L. 647.

[50] *Ibid.*, 93:19; P.L. 1207.

[51] *Enarrat. in Ps.*, 32, serm. 2, 8–11; P.L. 289–291.

[52] *Enarrat. in Ps.*, 106:4–12; P.L. 1421–1426.

[53] *Ibid.*, 37:13–16; P.L. 403–406.

[54] *Ibid.*, 65:17; P.L. 797.

[55] *Ibid.*, 122:6; P.L. 1634–1635.

[56] *Ibid.*, 37:13–14; P.L. 1403–1404.

[57] *Enarrat. in Ps.*, 76:3; P.L. 972.

[58] *Ibid.*, 33, serm. 2, 20; P.L. 319.

[59] *Ibid.*, 45:2; P.L. 515.

[60] *Ibid.*, 9:10; P.L. 121; 21:25; P.L. 169; 21:30; P.L. 170; 21:27; P.L. 170.

[61] *Ibid.*, 59:8; P.L. 719.

[62] *Ibid.*, 36, serm. 3, 11; P.L. 390.

[63] *Ibid.*, 90:11; P.L. 1169.

[64] *Expost. quarundam prop. ex Epist. ad Rom.*, 54; P.L. 2076.

[65] *In Evang. Joan.*, 17:1; P.L. 1527.

[66] *Enarrat. in Ps.*, 21:4–5; P.L. 173; *ibid.*, 144:23; P.L. 1883.

[67] *In Evang. Joan.*, tract. 102, 1; P.L. 1896; *Enarrat. in Ps.*, 144:19; P.L. 1881.

[68] *In Evang. Joan.*, tract. 80, 4; P.L. 1842.

[69] *Quaestiones evang.*, Lib. I, 28; P.L. 1328; *In Evang. Joan.*, tract. 73, 1–4; P.L. 1824–1826; *ibid.*, tract. 102, 1–2; P.L. 1896–1897.

[70] *In Epist. Joannis ad Parthos*, tract. 1, 9; P.L. 1985.

[71] *Expost. quarundam prop. ex Epist. ad Rom.*, 54; P.L. 2076. That the sufferings of life are the result of our lack of faith in the unity of the mystical body: *Enarrat. in Ps.*, 37:16; P.L. 406; that our prayer must be joined with Christ: *Enarrat. in Ps.*, 108:9; P.L. 1436; Christ's presence in our prayer: *Enarrat. in Ps.*, 75:1; P.L. 1081–1082.

[72] *In Evang. Joan.*, tract. 40, 10.

[73] *Enarrat. in Ps.*, 114:3–4; P.L. 1487; *Expost. quarundam prop.*, 53; P.L. 2074–2075.

[74] *Enarrat. in Ps.*, 62:5; P.L. 750–751.
[75] *Ibid.*, 144:4; P.L. 1871.
[76] *In Evang. Joan.*, tract. 25, 5–7; P.L. 1598–1600.

23. SYNTHESIS AND CONCLUSION

[1] *Enarrat. in Ps.*, 103, serm. 3, 25–26; P.L. 1377.
[2] *Ibid.*, 103, serm. 2; P.L. 1378–1379.
[3] *Ibid.*, 103, serm. 4, 2; P.L. 1379.
[4] A. Vega, Prologue to the B.A.C. edition of the *Confessions*, II, pp. 263–264.